GANGS OF NEW YORK

MAKING THE MOVIE

GANGS OF NEW YORK

MAKING THE MOVIE

Introduction *by* **LUC SANTE**

Interviews with **MARTIN SCORSESE, LEONARDO DiCAPRIO, DANIEL DAY-LEWIS, CAMERON DIAZ**

Photographs by **MARIO TURSI** *and* **BRIGITTE LACOMBE**

headline

Copyright © 2002 Miramax Books

Photo/Illustration Credits:
p5: Bettman/Corbis
pp 10-11, 12: Museum of the City of New York
p21: Photos courtesy of Photofest
p154: New York Historical Society

First published in the USA in 2003 by Miramax Books

First published in Great Britain in 2003
by HEADLINE BOOK PUBLISHING

10 9 8 7 6 5 4 3 2 1

ISBN 0 7553 1210 4

Printed and bound in France by Pollina - n° L88052

Every effort has been made to fulfil requirements with
regard to reproducing copyright material. The author
and publisher will be glad to rectify any omissions at
the earliest opportunity.

HEADLINE BOOK PUBLISHING LTD
A division of Hodder Headline
338 Euston Road
London NW1 3BH

www.headline.co.uk
www.hodderheadline.com

CONTENTS

INTRODUCTION:
LUC SANTE
12

DIRECTOR:
MARTIN SCORSESE
19

SCREENWRITERS & RESEARCHER:
SCREENWRITERS: JAY COCKS, STEVE ZALLIAN,
KENNETH LONERGAN, HOSSEIN AMINI
24

RESEARCHER: MARIANNE BOWER
35

SETS & DECORATION:
PRODUCTION DESIGNER: DANTE FERRETTI
40

SET DECORATOR: FRANCESCA LO SCHIAVO
47

THE CAST:
CASTING DIRECTOR: ELLEN LEWIS
50

THE ACTORS:
LEONARDO DiCAPRIO, DANIEL DAY-LEWIS,
CAMERON DIAZ, LIAM NEESON,
JIM BROADBENT, HENRY THOMAS,
JOHN C. REILLY, BRENDAN GLEESON,
GARY LEWIS
54

DIALECT COACH:
TIM MONICH
98

COSTUME DESIGNER
SANDY POWELL
104

WARDROBE SUPERVISOR: PAOLO SCALABRINO
111

HAIR & MAKEUP ARTISTS
HAIR: ALDO SIGNORETTI
117

MAKEUP: MANLIO ROCCHETTI, SIAN GRIGG
119

CINEMATOGRAPHER:
MICHAEL BALLHAUS
126

PRODUCTION:
EXECUTIVE PRODUCER: MICHAEL HAUSMAN
1ST ASSISTANT DIRECTOR: JOE REIDY
132

ACTION DIRECTORS:
ACTION UNIT DIRECTOR: VIC ARMSTRONG
STUNT COORDINATOR: GEORGE AGUILAR
144

EDITOR:
THELMA SCHOONMAKER
154

SCREENPLAY
160

CAST & CREW
254

BEHIND THE SCENES:
PHOTOS BY BRIGITTE LACOMBE
256

LOOKING BACK:
HIGHLIGHTS BY HARVEY WEINSTEIN
282

BIOGRAPHIES & ACKNOWLEDGMENTS:
286

GANGS OF NEW YORK takes place in the early 1860s, in a slum district of Manhattan called the Five Points. It was the poorest part of the city and by the time of the Civil War had been that way for more than a half century. A pond had once covered much of the site; on its banks had stood foul-smelling tanneries. Even after the pond was drained and the tanneries closed down in the early nineteenth century the stigma remained—only the poor would live there.

The neighborhood got its name from an intersection of three streets (today's Worth, Baxter, and Mosco streets), in the middle of which was a small triangular plaza called Paradise Square. Looming over the neighborhood was the Old Brewery, a five-story brick building built in 1792 that brewed beer until 1837; after that the building became the city's first tenement, an immense squat in which uncounted numbers lived and died in misery.

(12)

The population of the Five Points was predominantly Irish, with significant minorities of African Americans and Germans, including German Jews. We get little more than teasing glimpses of the black population from contemporary chroniclers, although we do know that there were many black musicians

and that the Five Points was the birthplace of tap dancing. The respectable population of the city was horrified by the sexual aura of the place—the ad hoc living arrangements, the open prostitution—perhaps even more by the suggestion of race mixing. Residents' fortunes were varied—recent archaeological evidence has shown that many inhabitants were at least lower middle class—but the neighborhood was enduringly associated with extremes of poverty and vice. Many people of all origins were only erratically employed; houses were badly built; sanitation was poor to nonexistent; pigs wandered freely in the streets. The impressions of Charles Dickens, who visited the Five Points in 1841, are typical of the appalled reactions of visitors, including those from other parts of the city:

Let us go on again, and plunge into the Five Points....This is the place; these narrow ways diverging to the right and left, and reeking everywhere with dirt and filth....Debauchery has made the very houses prematurely old. See how the rotten beams are tumbling down, and how the patched and broken windows seem to scowl dimly, like eyes that have been hurt in drunken frays. Many of these pigs live here. Do they ever wonder

ABOVE: *The Five Points*

why their masters walk upright instead of going on all-fours, and why they talk instead of grunting?....Here, too, are lanes and alleys paved with mud knee-deep; underground chambers where they dance and game...ruined houses, open to the street, whence through wide gaps in the walls other ruins loom upon the eye, as though the world of vice and misery had nothing else to show; hideous tenements which take their names from robbery and murder; all that is loathsome, drooping and decayed is here.

The Sixth Ward, which contained the Five Points, was also known as the Whiskey Ward. On every corner there was a "grocery," and in each grocery was a back room dispensing strong drink. Eventually the groceries moved to the middles of the blocks, leaving the corners to the saloons. From the back rooms and the saloons came gangs. There had always been gangs in New York, although some were relatively benign youth clubs; but the Five Points produced the first armed gangs. They were Irish: the Kerryonians, the Chichesters, the Roach Guards, the Plug Uglies, the Shirt Tails. The Dead Rabbits are alleged to have been born of a dispute among the Roach Guards—to make his point, one of the break-away faction flung a rabbit carcass into the middle of the room (at the time a "rabbit" was a tough guy and "dead" was an intensifier signifying "best" or "baddest"). Some of these gangs lasted as long as thirty years, drawing energy from the unending war they fought against the gangs of the Bowery, which were composed of toughs who were native-born, largely Anglo-Saxon, and resolutely anti-immigrant. In these battles the two sets of gangs drew support from their more peaceful compatriots—the Irish gangs, for example,

would consistently float a rumor that the Nativist gangs planned to burn down the old St. Patrick's Cathedral on Mott Street. One battle between the Dead Rabbits and the Bowery Boys in 1857 saw at least eight dead and over a hundred wounded, and was quelled only by the appearance of three National Guard regiments.

Both sets of gangs were useful to the deeply corrupt political machines of the day. The Irish gangs worked for the political machine Tammany Hall, the Bowery gangs for the anti-immigrant parties, most prominently the Nativists, who were called Know-Nothings because they claimed ignorance on every question posed to them. Tammany may have begun during the Revolution as an anti-British secret society, and may have been anti-immigrant for its first few decades as an arm of the Democratic Party, but practical considerations overrode ideology, and it began soliciting the Irish vote, quietly at first and openly by the 1840s, its voting bloc burgeoned by the waves of arriving Irish immigrants. The gangs served the political parties as enforcers, poll watchers, poll fixers, and repeat voters. That corruption ran deeper than tribal loyalty can be gauged by the fact that a number of figures switched sides during their careers, some of them more than once.

Running along the same lines as the gangs and the political clubs were the volunteer fire companies, which were composed of the same aggressive young men and were equally prone to violence. Houses really did burn down while rival companies fought each other for the right to extinguish the blaze. All of these organizations were the functional equivalents of fraternities for young men from poor families; the connections they made eventually led them, assuming they survived, to careers in politics or saloon keeping. Young women, on the other hand, really had only one avenue for their ambitions: prostitution.

In the early 1860s Fernando Wood was enjoying his third term as mayor of New York. He had started as a reformer, but it had taken him less than a year not only to slide into corruption, but to become a dictator. The apex of his ambition came just before the Civil War, when he proposed seceding from the Union and establishing the nation of Tri-Insula, composed of Manhattan, Staten Island, and Long Island. In the mid-1850s his behavior had so alarmed the New York State legislature that it created the Metropolitan Police Force to enforce the law in defiance of Wood's Municipal Police, whose members were required to pay regular bribes directly to Wood's office—its commissioner had acquired his position for $50,000. For much of 1857 the two police forces competed, fought, released each other's prisoners, and added considerably to the anarchy of the streets. That year, which saw both the Police Riots and the Dead Rabbit Riots, profoundly destabilized the city; banks failed, factories closed, and the poor were made even poorer. Few New Yorkers were reassured by the presence of cops, even afterward—slum dwellers seldom saw them at all, because protection had to be paid for and they couldn't afford it. When the Tammany chief William Marcy "Boss" Tweed became the unelected ruler of the city in 1870, he regained municipal control of the police and brought corruption to stratospheric heights unequaled since.

The Civil War was not popular in New York, especially in the slums. Demagogues had for years been swaying crowds in favor of slavery on the grounds that the issue obscured their own fight against wage slavery. In the summer of 1863, it was reported that Robert E. Lee was leading an enormous Confederate army north toward Pennsylvania, whereupon the city's troops were mobilized, leaving the place guarded only by a skeleton force. Meanwhile, a draft ordered by President Lincoln the previous April was set to be carried out in July. The draft was especially unpopular, since those eligible could engage a substitute for three hundred dollars, a substantial sum then, and an option not available to the poor.

On Monday, July 13, a crowd whose numbers were estimated at between five thousand and fifteen thousand walked from downtown to Central Park, where a rally was held, and then down to the draft office at Broadway and 29th Street. Led by the "Black Joke" Volunteer Fire Company Number 33, whose members had just learned that their draft deferments had been suspended, the mob rushed the building, destroyed its contents, and set it on fire. More than three days of rioting ensued. The mob lynched black people, burned the Colored Orphan Asylum, attacked the homes of prominent Republicans (including that of Horace Greeley, publisher of the New York *Tribune*), raided armories, sacked and incinerated the homes of the rich. It was speculated that if it had not been for a torrential rainstorm on Tuesday night, which put out most fires, the whole city might have burned to the ground.

There were said to have been between fifty thousand and seventy thousand rioters; as many as two thousand died, along with at least a hundred African-American citizens, three cops, and some fifty guardsmen, while

ABOVE: Robbers' Roost *(Jacob Riis, 1870s)*

many thousands were wounded, including every policeman in the city. More than a hundred buildings were destroyed by fire; property losses were staggering. Boss Tweed was instrumental in restoring the peace—he was at once prowar and pro-Irish, and thus could straddle the lines. The mob's energy was dissipated and it never arose again. The Draft Riots themselves became a skeleton in the city's closet, uncommemorated and increasingly forgotten as the generations passed.

By the late nineteenth century the term "Five Points" had itself fallen out of usage, although the neighborhood continued much as before. In 1890 the great reformer Jacob Riis published his groundbreaking exposé *How the Other Half Lives*, the principal subject of which was the oversized slum block called Mulberry Bend, the southwest angle of which was one of the five points. Most of its constituent houses dated back a half century or more; the misery had continued unabated. Riis's urgings led to the slum's demolition. A park now covers the site, while the rest of the Five Points lies beneath a federal courthouse.

(15)

THE DIRECTOR

WHEN I WAS GROWING UP in New York's Little Italy, our church was St. Patrick's Old Cathedral. St. Patrick's was on Mott Street, and it had the first Catholic graveyard in New York City. I shot a scene in that graveyard and other scenes nearby for *Mean Streets*.

I remember hearing stories about the neighborhood and the church when I was a boy. It was local history, but the stories were passed down as legends. One story was about a group of people (mostly Irish immigrants who belonged to St. Patrick's) having a showdown in front of the church with a gang of Protestant American-born men, who felt they were the only true Americans. The Irish, because of their large numbers and their Catholic religion, posed a serious threat to the native domination over the lower Manhattan neighborhood. On this occasion the immigrants banded together, gathering up all the weapons they could find, and defended their church against the attacking mob. This took place in 1844.

The stories haunted me over the years. I was fascinated with this period in New York history because it was also a critical moment in American history. At the height of the Irish immigration, as many as fifteen thousand people poured into New York in one week. There was no work and very little in the way of housing for them. The country had to make room for them—physically, financially, and morally. This was a crucial time in which the principles of American democracy were put to the test.

In 1970 quite by accident I first came across a book by Herbert J. Asbury, *The Gangs of New York*, which chronicled the history of New York street gangs from the early eighteenth century up to 1928, when he wrote the book. I knew almost immediately that I wanted to make a film about the world described in Asbury's book. Soon after, my friend Jay Cocks started working on a script.

In the mid-nineteenth century, New York was in the process of developing its identity as a city. Corruption was rampant in political circles, there were rival police forces and privately owned competitive fire companies. In short, life in New York was tribal. The old families of New York, the upper-class later depicted in my film *The Age of Innocence*, were a tribe, and they lived above the fray—literally, as the residential center of New York was moving northward. On the lower rungs of the economic ladder, a series of gangs were constantly fighting for their piece of turf. These gangs—with such fantastic names as the Plug Uglies, the Dead Rabbits, the Roach Guards, the Shirt Tails, the Bowery Boys—had gained actual political power because of the large numbers of votes they controlled. They

(19)

ABOVE: *Martin Scorsese and Daniel Day-Lewis*
OPPOSITE: *St. Thomas Church, modeled on the St. Patrick's Old Cathedral*

were a force to be reckoned with by Tammany Hall, the powerful political machine, and eventually by City Hall.

The poor lived in unimaginable squalor crowded into a small area known as the Five Points. Every day they had to fight for their economic and physical survival. And when the pressure from the Civil War and the Conscription Act of 1863 affected New York, the powder keg was lit. For three hundred dollars, you could buy your way out of the draft, which meant the poor had to go to war. They had no recourse but to revolt, and the city nearly burned to the ground. After four days of burning, looting, and lynching in the heat of August and with uncounted numbers dead, the Draft Riots (which had turned into a race riot) were finally quelled. It took the army to put down the battle on the streets.

Writing the script for the movie was quite a task, in part because the writers had to deal with one of the most horrifying (and least discussed) events in American history, and convey all of the different historical factors that had created this powder keg. And we knew that we had to do so on an epic scale, like that of the films we'd known and loved as kids. Against this complex background we composed a personal story that revolved around the classic theme of revenge. We based some of our characters on real-life people and created others. We also took dramatic license by moving a few dates and places.

It took twenty-five years to bring *Gangs of New York* to the screen. We took out an ad in the Hollywood trades to announce the film in 1977, but the project stalled. By 1980 the time when directors were given large sums of money to make personal movies had ended. Over the years, I kept trying to make the picture, but the cost was always an impediment. We couldn't shoot it in New York, because the New York of the 1860s no longer existed and the sets of an entire neighborhood would have to be built.

Finally, in the late 1990s everything came together. Harvey Weinstein at Miramax agreed to do the picture, with Graham King at Initial picking up the foreign rights. Leonardo DiCaprio, Cameron Diaz, and Daniel Day-Lewis were cast in the main roles along with a brilliant group of supporting actors. Dante Ferretti designed and built the sets in Rome, Sandy Powell created the costumes. And in September 2000, I passed through the gates of Cinecittà Studios, walked into the old New York that Dante and his brilliant crew of Italian craftsmen had re-created, and with cinematographer Michael Ballhaus began shooting the movie I had imagined all these years, about the city I love and how it re-created itself. This film is my impression of that extraordinary time.

(20)

ABOVE: *Ad placed in* Variety *in 1977 announcing the movie*

MOVIE LIST

Some of the films watched during the preparation and shooting of *Gangs of New York* for general inspiration, editing (the Russian films especially), period detail, historic incidents, and revenge stories

Arsenal (1928, Alexander Dovzhenko)
The Big Country (1958, William Wyler)
The Big Heat (1953, Fritz Lang)
The Big Trail (1930, Raoul Walsh)
Billy The Kid (1930, King Vidor)
***The Bowery* (1933, Raoul Walsh)**
Children of Paradise (1945, Marcel Carne)
Chimes at Midnight (1966, Orson Welles)
Chinatown Nights (1929, William Wellman)
Corridors of Blood (1962, Robert Day)
Deserter (1933, Vladimir Pudovkin)
The Docks of New York (1928, Josef von Sternberg)
The Doctor and the Devils (1985, Freddie Francis)
Earth (1930, Alexander Dovzhenko)
Fellini Satyricon (1970, Federico Fellini)
The Flesh and the Fiends (1953, Robert Siodmak)
Gentleman Jim (1942, Raoul Walsh)
Heaven's Gate (1980, Michael Cimino)
Hellgate (1952, Charles Marquis Warren)
I Shot Jesse James (1948, Samuel Fuller)
It's a Dog's Life (1955, Herman Hoffman)
Law and Order (1932, Edward L. Cahn)
Little Big Horn (1951, Charles Marquis Warren)
October (1928, Sergei Eisenstein)
***Oliver Twist* (1948, David Lean)**
Once Upon a Time in the West (1968, Sergio Leone)
Park Row (1952, Samuel Fuller)
Pat Garrett and Billy the Kid (1973, Sam Peckinpah)
The Penalty (1920, Wallace Worsley)
Potemkin (1925, Sergei Eisenstein)
Regeneration (1915, Raoul Walsh)
Ride Lonesome (1959, Budd Boetticher)
Sanjuro (1962, Akira Kurosawa)

***The Shanghai Gesture* (1941, Josef von Sternberg)**
The Tall Target (1951, Anthony Mann)
The Threepenny Opera (1931, G.W. Pabst)
Underworld U.S.A. (1961, Samuel Fuller)
Wait Till the Sun Shines Nellie (1952, Henry King)
The Wild Bunch (1969, Sam Peckinpah)
Winchester '73 (1950, Anthony Mann)

SCREENWRITERS & RESEARCHER

We took a bunch of names and the ambience from it.

QUESTIONER: How did you come to write the script for *Gangs of New York*?

JAY COCKS: Marty and I, who were already close friends, discovered independently of each other Herbert Asbury's *The Gangs of New York* over what I believe was a Christmas–New Year's week. Marty saw it at somebody's house, and I found it in a bookstore. It was just synchronicity. The producer Alberto Grimaldi optioned it for us. I moved to Los Angeles in 1977 and started working on a first draft of the screenplay that I completed in 1978.

Q: How did you begin your research?

JC: It seemed like I had done a lot of research, but there was a lot more done since we started, those decades ago. Luc Sante's book *Low Life*, for instance, has been written since. I'd say there were a couple dozen primary source volumes. *Lights and Shadows of New York* was one. The primary source, which we read only once, actually, was Herbert Asbury's book.

Q: You mentioned that you and Martin Scorsese both loved what you saw as the potential mythology of the period.

JC: Because it was virgin territory. Most people are unaware of this little period in New York's history. I always thought about this movie the way Marty once described it to me—a Western on Mars.

Q: Did you know much about the Irish immigration, or about the Draft Riots beforehand?

JC: I had read very little about the Draft Riots. I had read Cecil Woodham Smith's book *The Great Hunger*, which was about the Irish potato famine and the subsequent Irish immigration. I read it at the behest of Michael Powell. But I was pretty much unaware of the rest until I read Asbury's book, which is largely mythological. The early version of the script began with a Bruce Springsteen lyric. It began, "You can waste your summer praying in vain for a savior to rise from these streets." And the

(24)

ABOVE: *Daniel Day-Lewis (Bill the Butcher) wounded by an unknown assailant*

script ended with a quote from another Springsteen song called *Adam Raised a Cain*: "Lost but not forgotten from the dark heart of a dream." These formed the parentheses which I started to fill in.

And three gigantic characters took shape there. The first inkling I had of Amsterdam's character was his father's voice. I scribbled this thing down on a piece of paper: "The blood always stays on the blade." That line was the first thing that was ever written for *Gangs of New York*. The reason Amsterdam was created seemed also to create Bill the Butcher, and Jenny seemed to spring from Amsterdam's need for some sort of respite. There wasn't any respite in that neighborhood, so they had to create it together.

Q: You wrote the screenplay for *The Age of Innocence* for Martin Scorsese. How different was this experience and how did you work with him?

JC: I believe that we wrote the first draft of *The Age of Innocence* in seventeen days. The process technically was a lot different because we had a brilliant novel. On *Gangs of New York*, all we had was a lot of time, over twenty years. And a lot of persistent visions— dreams, notions, ideas that we started to work somehow into those parentheses.

Q: And you first imagined the story going on longer than it is now?

JC: Yes, Amsterdam was going to help build the Brooklyn Bridge. I still want to write that. But after I got up to page 200 of the first draft, and wrote "End of Part One," I thought, We're never going to be able to do that now. Maybe

someday. In a sense I always felt that Amsterdam had redeemed himself in his father's memory at the end of Part One, and then he was sort of free to go on having made—remade himself. He was free to go on and make the city.

Q: What was your reaction to seeing the sets in Rome?

JC: I think that when you see a dream made real you're always disoriented, and I think that after some momentary disorientation I felt immediately at home, because I felt that whatever had been in my head and in my heart had been externalized by Marty and Dante Ferretti. I felt like I belonged there in a way.

Q: Did you have any feelings about the twenty–year gestation period?

JC: I'm glad that it took all this time because there was a certain rawness to the material subsumed into something a little more pointed and subtle and poignant. The movie has many more facets, and some of those facets come from having lived another twenty-five years. It kept our eyes open. I will say that I don't think there's another filmmaker in the world who would have had the commitment and the stubbornness to see this through. That was all Marty. He never gave up. He never gives up.

Marty not only shapes but in a sense discovers the soul of the movie in the editing. Everything, the writing and even the shooting, leads up to that process of discovery that is only finalized in the editing. Some people get it on the page. Other people find it on the set. But Marty, he uses those two processes to lead him to the final result.

(25)

QUESTIONER: How and when did you come on *Gangs of New York*?

HOSSEIN AMINI: I worked on two drafts of *Gangs*, the first time in December-January 1999-2000 in New York, and the second time in July-August 2000 in Rome. Harvey Weinstein had shown some of my previous work to Martin Scorsese, and after a series of meetings, I was invited to New York to work with him on the screenplay. I spent four weeks there, and loved every moment of it, writing every day in a hotel room, then walking a few blocks to Marty's house or office to show him the pages. Unfortunately, I had a contractual obligation to start work on another script, and I had to leave.

The second draft I worked on was an unexpected bonus. The film was set to start shooting in September. One day I got a call from Miramax asking me if my wife and I would like to visit the set in Rome. Of course we jumped at the chance. There was no mention of work, and I thought it would be a great weekend holiday. But as soon as we checked into the hotel in Rome, I realized that wasn't going to be the case. I think I saw my wife for a couple of hours that whole weekend, and ended up staying in Rome for four more weeks.

Q: What area of the script did you focus on?

HA: The work I did on the screenplay was mainly character work, particularly on the Johnny-Amsterdam friendship, and the triangle between them and Jenny. I also did some work on the Amsterdam and Bill story, trying to bring out the father-son subtext in their scenes.

Q: How did you work with the director?

HA: We'd usually start by talking about other movies, a part of me consciously or unconsciously trying to delay the moment when I finally had to show him pages. Marty's probably the greatest film buff in the world, so we'd talk for at least an hour before we got down to work. Then the dreaded moment came when I handed over the pages. One of the great things about Marty with writers is that even if a scene is terrible, he'll start out by saying something nice about it, and preserving your dignity and confidence. The effect this has, is that later when he tells you to change the scene completely, you still feel confident and enthusiastic enough to have another go at it. So often directors take the wind out of you by sounding disappointed or critical of a first pass. That was never the case with Marty. He always made you feel as if you'd written something almost great. Then he'd get to work on the scene himself. One of the things that had always intimidated me about working on *Gangs* was the stylized period dialogue that Marty and Jay Cocks had created over the years. I didn't need to worry. Whatever dialogue I wrote, Marty would instantly translate into the language of that world, almost like a computer. He wouldn't write it, he'd act it out, word for word. I'd take notes and go and fix the scene the next day.

Q: Did you also work with the actors?

HA: Probably the toughest, but one of the most rewarding of the meetings with the actors was a two-day, twelve-hour-a day marathon with Leonardo DiCaprio on his character and dialogue. It wasn't always easy, but by the end of it I think some great ideas came out of these

ABOVE: *The Chinese Pagoda scene with its golden cages*

grueling sessions. Leo wouldn't let a single line go by, questioning the motive and intent of the character, analyzing and re-analyzing it. Just when you thought you'd got away with it, he'd come up with a new idea or solution. It was admittedly hard work, but it was invaluable to be challenged like that, and I think ultimately made for a much better script.

What was interesting to me, was that Marty was open and collaborative in these meetings. He was always respectful of other people's ideas. If he disagreed he'd argue it out and wouldn't take the shortcut of saying I know best. I think one of the things that makes him such a constantly innovative filmmaker is that he's as nervous and motivated and open to help and suggestions as someone making their very first film.

Q: What was your reaction to seeing the film for the first time?

HA: Everything I'd imagined in my head was bigger on screen and that rarely happens for a writer. When you work on a screenplay, you often have an unachievable, impossibly expensive idea of a scene in your imagination, so when you see the finished product it's invariably disappointing. Not this time. If I imagined one woman hanging down from a golden cage in the Chinese Pagoda, there were seven. The boxing boat sailing down the Hudson river was twice the size I expected it to be. The shot of Amsterdam walking through Satan's Circus was far more elaborate than anything written on the page. It's quite an experience to work with a director who can create something on a scale that you can't even imagine in your head. Emotionally too, I thought the film was extremely moving, mixing violence and humanity in a way that I hoped would work, but never thought would succeed so well.

STEVE ZALLIAN:

SCREENWRITER

QUESTIONER: Can you talk about your contribution to the film, and those elements in the story that you concentrated on?

STEVE ZALLIAN: As you know, *Gangs of New York* took many years to write, and many writers. It's difficult sometimes, even for those involved, to sort out precisely who did what. I know I was very interested in trying to develop and weave the personal-revenge drama into a larger historical story of the Irish in New York in the 1860s. To me, the struggle of the Irish (and other immigrants), the Civil War, the political corruption of Tammany Hall, and even the Five Points gang wars—all pointed to one question: Who does America belong to— whomever was here first, or all of us? That became the theme, as far as I was concerned, and the reason to make the film, and I worked to detail and drive the social and personal stories together.

Q: How much did you know about the era in which the film is set before you began writing?

SZ: Ironically, I had come across the Herbert Asbury book, *The Gangs of New York*, like Marty, many years ago. I was drawn to it in the late 1970s, in a public library in Los Angeles, by its title and evocative illustrations. It was a curiosity. It portrayed the gangs and the times in lurid and romanticized fashion, yet still seemed somehow authoritative. I read it and forgot about it. Some twenty years and a lot of writing of other things later, Marty called.

Prior to Marty's phone call, I did not have a great knowledge of the period. Only what I'd read in the *Gangs* book. Soon, though, I took a crash course, reading everything Marty and his researchers sent, including Stephen Crane's *Maggie, A Girl from the Streets*; Luc Sante's *Low Life*; *Incredible New York— High Life and Low Life*; *Chants Democratic*; *New York Gas Light*; *The Virtues of the Vicious*; *The Diary of Philip Hone*; *Gotham*—everything from ancient Celtic rites to the *National Police Gazette*, and everything ever written on the Draft Riots, which isn't much, by the way. Which makes you think, maybe it's a chapter of our history we'd rather forget.

Q: Can you describe your working process with Martin Scorsese?

SZ: I've had the pleasure of working with Marty a couple of times now. We talk a lot, but not so much that we're left with nothing to discover. I've learned a lot from him in terms of history, film history, and filmmaking. It may be his great stature as an artist that challenges you to do your best work, or his great enthusiasm. In any case, you want to keep up with him—and he runs fast.

OPPOSITE: *Jim Broadbent (Boss Tweed) rallying his constituents*

QUESTIONER: What were your major contributions to the screenplay?

KENNETH LONERGAN: I concentrated mostly on the characters and the dialogue. I made no major structural changes, but I tried to link several of the scenes together dramatically so that they would follow from one another. For instance there's a scene where Amsterdam meets Bill for the first time. And then there's a scene where Johnny and his gang are sent to loot a Portuguese ship. In that scene Amsterdam comes up with the idea of selling a dead body because they don't find anything else of value on the ship. So I tried to link the scenes together dramatically by having Bill say when he meets Amsterdam: "Don't come back here again unless you have some money." This put some dramatic pressure on Amsterdam to do well on this assignment, whereas before they were somewhat unrelated episodes.

Q: Amsterdam and Jenny connect on an intimate level in a tough world.

KL: That was one of the things I worked on the most. There was a scene where Amsterdam had met Jenny with Johnny, and then later he sees her get on a trolley to go uptown. Even though he knows Johnny likes her, he follows her because he's interested. And I changed that to have her steal his medal so that he has to follow her, and then that led into the scene where he tries to get the medal back, and they have this flirtatious scene together where she gets interested in him.

Q: Can you talk a little about specific areas that you worked on?

KL: I came on the movie when the shooting had begun. So what I tried to do was take the existing structure and make it as dramatic as possible, and make the scenes force the next scene whenever possible. Amsterdam's character had gone through a lot of permutations. At one point he was a cold-blooded killer who had come back to destroy Bill, and had gotten seduced by him. We tried

(30)

ABOVE: *Cameron Diaz (Jenny) and Leonardo DiCaprio (Amsterdam)*

to humanize Amsterdam and to make his mission a little more pointed.

He's basically there to kill the king, and he does not particularly want to get involved with Jenny, but he can't help it because he likes her, and the same thing with her. She's trying to save up money so she can get out of the Five Points, and she doesn't want to fall in love with him either.

They live in a very dangerous place, and falling in love is not really the greatest idea, but they do. And I thought it strengthened the whole conflict between Amsterdam and Jenny,

and Amsterdam and Bill when he finds out that she's been involved with Bill. I also added to the scene where Bill talks to Amsterdam and tells him that he's never had a son, and Amsterdam's sitting there in bed not knowing what to say.

Q: What adjustments did you make to the character of Bill the Butcher?

KL: Bill was quite developed when I came on. He was already a flamboyant and fascinating character. I tried to clarify his feelings toward

(31)

ABOVE: *Daniel Day-Lewis (Bill), Leonardo DiCaprio (Amsterdam),
and Jim Broadbent (Tweed) in a heated political argument*

Amsterdam; and I added the idea that Bill's world is collapsing, and that he knows it.

Q: You wrote Amsterdam's voice-over.

KL: We wanted to blend the historical material in with the personal story. Marty had always talked about Amsterdam's journey after he failed to assassinate Bill. He's left at the lowest point he's ever been, and he has to rethink everything. With Monk's help he unites the Irish, not as a gang of killers, but as a political force. He finds himself becoming a political leader. But when Bill goes back to the old ways and simply kills Monk, Amsterdam is forced back into a gang fight because there's no other way to resolve it.

At the same time, other forces are gathering. What is happening at the Five Points is a smaller version of what's happening all over the country: groups jockeying for power in this new land. Suddenly they're swept away by the winds of history.

Q: Did you do a lot of historic research before working on the script?

KL: I have an amateur interest in the Civil War, and I had read or at least skimmed the book *The Gangs of New York*. I didn't read so much as I listened to Marty talk about everything he was interested in and everything he was trying to get into the film. I did use a lot from a great book called *The Rogue's Lexicon*. We didn't want to use the period slang to the point where people couldn't understand what the characters were saying, but the language is so colorful. The actors loved that stuff, so we tried to get as much in as possible.

Q: Tell us more about your working process with Martin Scorsese.

KL: We would have discussions about the scenes, and how they related to the overall movie. We would talk about what the problems were with the scene. Then I would make changes and show it to him, and when we were both happy with it we would show it to the actors. Ultimately, it was fun because I never felt like it was my voice against the cacophony of others. When I came on to the movie, everybody there had been thinking about their characters and about the story for longer than I had, so I was just jumping in trying to make my contribution. This was a situation where there was an overall mind guiding everything, which was Marty, and all of us trying to make his vision.

Q: What did you discover about this period while working on the movie?

KL: First of all about the physical life of the Five Points, which was so masterfully re-created by Marty and Dante. It's a set that you walk through as if it's a whole town, and with all the extras on it—it was literally like going back in time. You're surrounded by fishmongers, prostitutes, horse and buggy drivers, and soldiers. Only if you turn in a certain direction do you see a camera crew.

Marty senses the period as being a cauldron of conflict and violence out of which New York and this country were created. It was a point of view I just hadn't had before. That was illuminating, and I don't think I'll ever look at that period in quite the same way. I feel that I have a visceral sense of the city at that time that I didn't have before.

MARIANNE BOWER:

RESEARCHER

QUESTIONER: Would you describe your role in the research process, and what kind of research you did for *Gangs of New York?*

MARIANNE BOWER: I came onto the film just as it was really getting into gear. For the many, many years prior, Marty had been collecting engravings and books of the time period to help the designers, writers, and actors. What I did was provide images and information to the art department for the set dressing, and some historical details for costuming, such as a police uniform. Marty would also ask me factual or interpretive questions.

An example is the omnibus that you'll see in the film. Someone from the art department had gone to look at an actual omnibus, and took its dimensions. But Marty had imagined a different omnibus that he really liked the look of, and wanted to make sure that its style was appropriate for the period. In that instance I had to call around to people who specialized in city transportation as well as omnibus history.

The next question about the omnibus was: What was written on it and where did it go? I went to the New York Public Library and found council manuals for each year. One manual listed all the peddlers who had licenses, including everyone who ran an omnibus line. So I took a period map of the city and diagramed each omnibus line. Marty wanted this omnibus to pass through an upscale neighborhood, and it had to start down close to the Five Points. The route chosen gave us the information that would be written on the side of the omnibus.

Q: What resources did you use to research the fire engines of the time?

MB: The Fire Museum in New York was invaluable. At a certain point the man-drawn fire trucks became horse drawn. We needed the date when that turnover occurred. Everyone had a different opinion. But the Fire Museum had the date that the volunteer unit became a professional unit. At that time the man-drawn vehicle went out and the horse-drawn ones came in.

Q: Do you remember what date that was?

MB: It was 1865. *Gangs* takes place before then, so the man-drawn fire engines were used in the film, and you'll also see that there are hand as well as steam operated pumps. Bill the Butcher arrives on a steam engine. It was a great source of machismo to draw the fire engine yourself, and competition was fierce between the fire companies.

Then I would be asked completely different kinds of questions. My worst and most frightening day occurred when I was in New York. While they were shooting in Rome, they were also still building sets. I was asked to get material about what Broadway shops looked like, because those sets were built last. At the same time I had to answer questions for the scenes being shot that day. I got a call at 4:30 P.M. New York time on a Friday from Joe Reidy, the assistant director. He said, "We have a couple questions for a scene we're shooting tomorrow morning." The first question was: If a

OPPOSITE: *Leonardo DiCaprio (Amsterdam) getting off a Manhattan omnibus*

person were beaten up in a certain way and stabbed in the gut and rendered unconscious, when he was woken up by a doctor, what would he be able to do? The second part of the question was: When he was treated by the doctor, what anesthetic would be used and how would it be administered? After a few minutes of panic I called a medical research library in Los Angeles, because of the time difference, but it was too interpretive a question for them to feel comfortable answering. So I called St. Vincent's Hospital here in New York and spoke to a doctor, who kindly called me back. We had a twenty-minute conversation about ways that a person would react to different degrees of injury.

Q: That would be the same today as then.

MB: That's right. But the anesthetic question, of course, was about that time period. I called several people at the Smithsonian, but they had all left their offices. By chance I had the home number of the ex-curator of a related field. Miraculously, he had the answer for me (we discussed ether, chloroform, and laudanum). I went on the Internet to just make sure the company that he had named (Squibb), who made a certain kind of anesthetic, was in production at the time of the movie. It was. In fact, it had just started to mass produce ether to provide it to the Union Army.

Q: What were the basic source materials that you used in addition to those that Marty had collected?

MB: Marty had collected a wide array of books, such as *Secrets of the Great City*, which was written in 1868. It describes riding in an omnibus and gives the whole protocol of getting on and putting money in the box. It also describes walking down Broadway and what kinds of people you would see. He also had books like *Volcano Under the City*, which gives a detailed account of the Draft Riots and was written close to the time period of the film. The books I tended to use included titles like *Workers in the Metropolis*, which lists statistics, for instance, about immigrants—where they came from, what they did, what neighborhoods they lived in.

My main resource was the New York Public Library. There, for instance, I found a book from 1855 that gave exact details about how to build a billiard table, so I photographed the images and e-mailed them to Dante Ferretti, and he re-created the table. I went to the New-York Historical Society for engravings, and to the Museum of the City of New York. I'd often call a historian or author to help me with a specific question. I called the Smithsonian quite often. Other places were incredibly helpful, like the Methodist Archives. I called them in a panic about what kinds of hymns would be sung and they sent me pages from old hymnals and sermons by the reverend who ran the mission in the Five Points. The American Music Research Center was a big help, but the list of helpful people goes on and on.

Q: Did the director give you any overall direction or advice?

MB: The first researcher, Deanna Avery, who had made these incredible research binders that the actors, art director, and designers all received—a book of three hundred engravings that showed all aspects of what would be depicted in the film. There were images of the Five Points, the people who lived there, the Draft Riots, fires—all the different cultural events in the film. I took my cue from that level of detail.

ABOVE: *The teeth of the actors (Henry Thomas as Johnny and Cameron Diaz as Jenny) were made up to reflect 19th-century dentistry*

One of the first questions I was asked was from Daniel Day-Lewis, who wanted to know whether or not he could have a false tooth. I called my dentist to find out who the best dental historian was and then called him. Then I bought a book that had images of dentistry from the time period. I wrote a long paper on dentistry from the 1840s up to the 1860s—what would happen if you had an abscess, what kind of false teeth they had then, what kind of material would it be made of for a poor person. I'm sure Daniel Day-Lewis just wanted to know if he could wear a false tooth!

Q: In the end did he wear one?

MB: Yes, I think he wore a couple of false teeth, and I know many of the other characters had dental peculiarities.

Q: What was your reaction when you saw the set for the first time?

MB: I was completely amazed. When I first walked around the Five Points neighborhood, it felt like a ghost town. It was so real, and so authentic to all those engravings and photographs I'd been working with. I went up to a rock outcropping and touched it. It was made of fiberglass. I really enjoyed looking at the Broadway sets because that was the area I had done intense research for, and in a couple instances Francesca Lo Schiavo re-created the storefronts just like the originals. I particularly remember the carpet shop because that was one of the places that we had a really nice period photograph of, and the carpets stood on their ends in the window. She had re-created that identically. It was incredible.

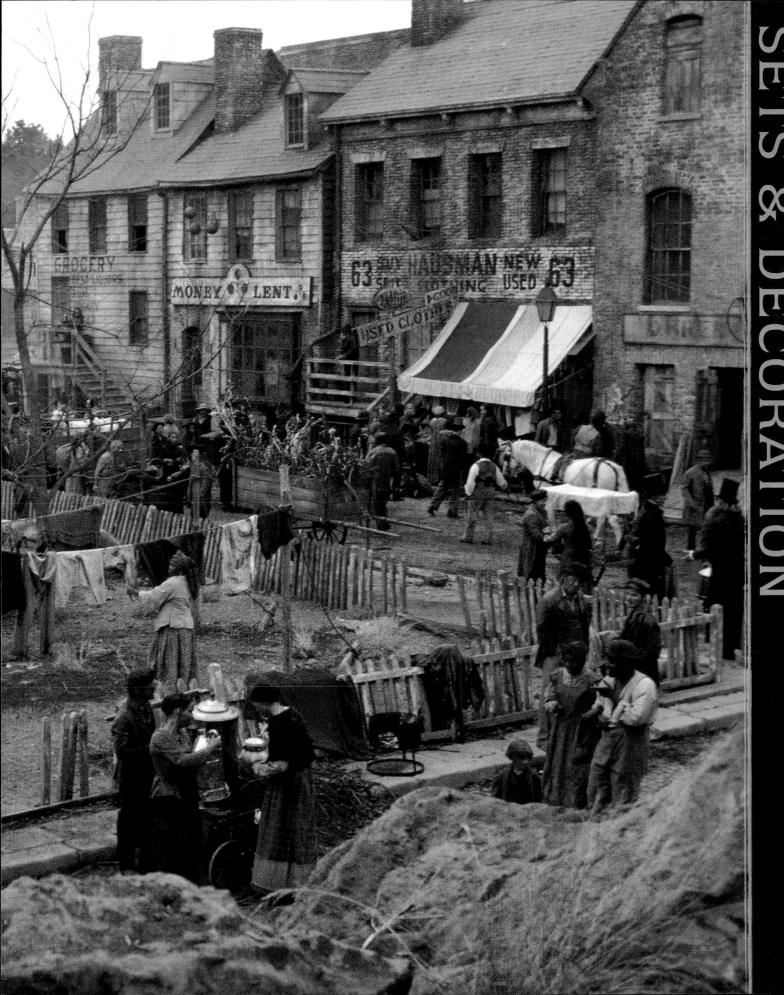

MARTIN SCORSESE (IN ROME): Let's walk through Paradise Square. There's the Old Brewery, Satan's Circus, Don Whiskerando's barbershop. The rock formations and houses are based on engravings and later photographs.

DANTE FERRETTI: Originally the Square was full of rocks, with houses built on top of them. Then the Square was flattened.

MS: The Old Brewery is based on engravings, as are the buildings next to it. Even the relationship of Paradise Square to the water is accurate.

DF: Do you remember when you first talked to me about the burned building? We were filming *The Age of Innocence* in Troy, New York.

MS: We saw a photograph at the mayor's office of a number of burned buildings with icicles hanging off of them, and I realized that it would be great for *Gangs of New York*, if the movie ever got made.

Now the Native Americans, a gang led by Daniel Day-Lewis, come out of the building with the icicles to Paradise Square in the opening scene of the movie.

DF: Here are the Five Points, the intersection of five streets.

MS: They kept changing the names of the streets in the 1840s, 1850s, 1860s. Mulberry Street was one of them, Baxter, Worth. It was well known that the Five Points were the worst, most dangerous street corners in America.

Dignitaries from around the world would come to visit the Five Points. Charles Dickens wrote about it in *American Notes* in 1851. Lincoln came in 1860 on his famous trip to New York when he spoke at Cooper Union. Even Daniel Boone came to visit the area. The Old Brewery was a true den of iniquity. However, by the 1860s, the Old Brewery had become a mission house.

It was a brewery in the late eighteenth century, which was abandoned in the late nineteenth century and became a place where poor people and new immigrants came and lived. It also became a hideout for criminals. Nearby was Murderers' Alley, and there were all sorts of special names for the little nooks and crannies inside the Old Brewery.

DF: The problem we had when we designed the Brewery was that there was no record of

ABOVE: *Burned building in Paradise Square*

what the interior looked like. Our technical advisor, Luc Sante, told us that vats were still in there. We were inspired by a picture of a brewery of the same period in France.

MS: I fantasized the building sliced like a cake to show all of the different rooms inside where people were eking out an existence. There were connecting catwalks and people living in underground tunnels.

DF: It's like an inferno or something from *Les Miserables*.

MS: There is a spiral staircase where the gangs would come up from the underground tunnels in the first part of the film, the 1846 section. They'd come up into the square to fight with rival gangs. We show how the people lived—barely existed—in these cubbyholes. Later in the movie, in 1860 when Amsterdam (Leonardo DiCaprio) comes back, the Brewery is a mission house. The interior looks pretty much the same, but it's used for different purposes.

DF: Yes. It's just a little cleaner.

(41)

TOP: *Old Brewery on right*

ABOVE: *The Five Points is the corner by the burned building at the rear where five streets meet*

TOP: *Storefronts and houses on a street leading to the harbor*

ABOVE: *The barbershop built on rocks*

ABOVE: *Dante Ferretti's sketch for the interior of the Chinese Pagoda*

MS: But not much cleaner. Reverend Raleigh throws a dance there.

Satan's Circus was the hangout of Daniel Day-Lewis's gang, the Native Americans. He surveyed his kingdom from here. They called themselves the Native Americans because their Protestant families had been in America for a while and some had fought in the Revolutionary War. They were opposed to the mass of Irish-Catholic immigrants who were coming in.

We also have a bar at Satan's Circus. This part of the city wasn't planned. Some of the buildings were placed on top of rock formations and tree trunks. Tree roots would come through the walls. The ceiling here is very low, and down below was a pit where people would bet on how many rats a dog could kill. A fox terrier, Towser, was the champion at the time.

There was a butchering area where the meat was hung on hooks. A lot went on in here. Satan's Circus is the name of a real place

(44)

that existed a few years later in the Five Points—but this is more our fantasy of what it might have looked like.

DF: This is the set for Sparrow's Chinese Pagoda. It, too, takes the name of a real place built a little later, in the 1870s.

MS: It is the set with which we took the most liberties. We were inspired by the set in Josef von Sternberg's *Shanghai Gesture*. Our place is run by Bill the Butcher and his gang. The Chinese worked for them, although in reality at this time there wasn't a large community of Chinese in New York. The main room is semicircular, facing a stage where there are occasional performances. Bill puts on a show there throwing knives one night. The customers bid on the girls in the cages: prostitutes and slave girls.

DF: There is even an opium den.

MS: This is where the Native Americans come to roust out some voters. It didn't matter that they were drugged. They'd wake them up and get them to vote for their candidates.

DF: And there are also some rooms upstairs where Bill hangs out sometimes—a brothel with gambling.

MS: We've created our own world in the spirit of old New York, an underworld not many people know about. It's important to know that the bars in the Five Points were called "groceries." We have a lot of signs around that say GROCERY. There they'd make a clear liquid that people would drink, similar to sailor's "grog."

These are not the Americans we learned about in history class, but anonymous members of the working class and infamous figures of the underworld. Politicians realized that the Five Points could provide them with a great deal of power.

It was a mixture of people from different countries, of different religions, different races—and everybody trying to live together. The politicians were very much involved with the control of this world. And in our film it's further complicated by the Civil War.

DF: Our next set is the street we built as Broadway. There is an omnibus based on a real one of the period. And we have a scene that takes place at P. T. Barnum's American Museum, based on the actual façade. The museum did burn at one point in that period. And Apollo Hall is right across the way here.

MS: A little farther and we have the Metamora Hose Company, one of the fire brigades. There wasn't a fire department in New York at the time. It was a series of privately run gangs of firemen. Up to that point the men would run on foot, pulling the fire engines. Sometimes the firemen would literally set fires.

DF: Here's the exterior of Delmonico's, the famous restaurant. It's also the exterior of Tammany Hall. We had to compress some of this. Across the street is the office of the *Tribune*, Horace Greeley's newspaper, based on the real building. In front is a bulletin board where papers were posted with headlines such as "Hundreds Wounded at Gettysburg." There is also a recruiting office, which is later burned in the film.

MS: Thirty thousand volunteers were wanted for the Civil War. Voters were gathered up at the Board of Elections, in some instances, in not the most legal way.

DF: We also have many shops, and these sets have interiors. From Tweed's office in Tammany Hall you can look out over Broadway. And there's a kitchen inside Tammany Hall. And we have the exterior of an upper-class mansion, the Schermerhorn house which gets attacked and looted during the Draft Riots. It wasn't really on Broadway.

MS: Neither was the Metropolitan Police Station. But our Broadway sort of represents the other side of life in New York, the middle- and upper-class side. Dante built everything, even the cobblestones.

(46)

FRANCESCA LO SCHIAVO:

SET DECORATOR

IT WAS A FANTASTIC ADVENTURE to re-create the New York of 1860. It was also a challenge because this movie is huge—I think I did a hundred sets.

Dante Ferretti and I work in two different phases. I have to take care of the decoration once the set is built. My job starts when Dante has finished his sketches. It's important to have good research before I start the job. Dante starts his construction while I'm doing research and drawing pieces of furniture and thinking about the little details. There were over a hundred craftsmen working for me on this movie, including painters, plasterers, blacksmiths, and upholsterers.

When I first read the script the number of sets seemed overwhelming. Aside from the Five Points area we had all of Broadway, with Tweed's office and the Schermerhorn mansion. Several sets had to be dressed for the interior of the mansion: a billiard room, a breakfast room, a dining room, a parlor, and a grand staircase. Then everything gets destroyed in the riots. The set has a very short life.

This movie shows how different people lived at that time, the problems they had, and how difficult it was to make a living.

It gives us an extraordinary look at a world that few people know about. I worked with my team for five months before the start of photography, and we continued throughout the shoot. We designed lampposts, shop windows, fire engines, posters, and a hearse. We had to have almost 90 percent of everything made, because only objects from the wealthy houses still exist.

(47)

ABOVE: *Hearse designed for the movie*

OPPOSITE: *Dante Ferretti and Francesca Lo Schiavo in the Chinese Pagoda*

QUESTIONER: How did this experience differ from all the other films you've done with Martin Scorsese?

ELLEN LEWIS: I feel that each of the movies we've worked on together has taken me to another world, and it's one of the joys of working with Marty. The films we've done have been so diverse: We've gone from *GoodFellas* to *The Age of Innocence*, from *Casino* to *Kundun*—and in each place, I'm building the cast of the world that he's creating.

Q: What research did you do for this film?

EL: We looked at old prints, lithographs, and references from movies for distinctive faces. In this era, facial features were more pronounced than they are today. Back then, everybody had very distinctive and large features.

Q: What films did he ask you to watch?

EL: There was one in particular, *The Bowery*, which was very helpful.

(50)

ABOVE: *Daniel Day-Lewis (Bill) giving Leonardo DiCaprio (Amsterdam) a tour of the Five Points*

Q: How did you start the casting of the film?

EL: In this case we felt that because the movie was going to be shooting in Italy and because it was about Irish immigrants, that we were better off primarily casting out of Europe. So I went to London, and from London I went to Dublin and Glasgow, and that's where we got the bulk of our actors. In England I put actors on tape for Marty to see. Then I met with him in Rome and showed him all the different people.

We knew that Jim Broadbent was going to do the movie, which was very exciting. Of course Marty was familiar with his work and I was anxious to get him a copy of a short, *A Sense of History,* that Jim had written and Mike Leigh directed. I knew Marty would love it. When I was in London seeing people, Eddie Marsan (Killoran, Tweed's side-kick) was somebody about whom I was very excited. He was an actor I didn't know prior to this, and I loved how his face looked. I felt that he was going to be a great foil for Jim Broadbent. When we were in Rome Brendan Gleeson (Monk McGinn) came to meet with Marty, who immediately liked him for the part. Later on, when we were getting quite close to shooting, we were discussing actors for the role of the corrupt cop, Happy Jack. I had met John C. Reilly several months earlier, and I knew he might seem young for the part, but Marty loved the idea of working with him. When I went to Glasgow, Gary Lewis (McGloin) came to see me and I put him on tape. I knew that Marty was going to be very excited by him, by his presence, and by his energy. He's a wonderful actor, and I thought that he would be a good combination with Daniel Day-Lewis.

Q: Who is in Leonardo DiCaprio's gang?

ABOVE: *Leonardo DiCaprio, Stephen Graham (Shang), and Larry Gilliard (Jimmy Spoils)*

EL: Stephen Graham, Neven Finnigan, and Larry Gilliard. Larry has a great old-fashioned face and he's a wonderful actor. Stephen Graham had been in the film *Diamonds*, which hadn't come out yet, and he came to see me like an energetic bulldog walking into my office. I thought Marty would really respond to him. Neven, who's an eccentric Irish fellow, seemed to be a good combination with the other Dead Rabbits and Henry Thomas (Johnny).

Q: How did you find the actors in Daniel Day-Lewis's gang?

EL: They're rough-and-tumble guys from various parts of Ireland and England. I met them through agents. When I went to Ireland and Scotland it was one wonderful actor, one wonderful face after another coming through the door. And I worked from morning until night videotaping people.

Q: How did you find Cara Seymour?

EL: I knew Cara from New York and the theater work she had done. I thought that she had a really interesting face, and there's a toughness and a street savvy to her that I thought Hell-Cat needed.

Q: There are cameo roles played by Alec McCowen (Reverand Raleigh) and David Hemmings (Mr. Schermerhorn).

EL: Marty had worked with Alec in *The Age of Innocence* and was excited to work with him again. David Hemmings was suggested to me by his agent, and when I spoke with Marty he said immediately, "Well, I have to work with him." He plays an aristocrat, Mr. Schermerhorn. Of all the actresses I met, I thought Lucy Davenport (Miss Schermerhorn) looked the most like him, with her blond hair and blue eyes. Barbara Bouchet (Mrs. Schermerhorn) lives in Rome. Marty knew her work and thought she'd be good. So the family unit was made.

Q: How did you cast Michael Byrne, who plays Horace Greeley?

ABOVE: *Michael Byrne (Horace Greeley), Barbara Bouchet and David Hemmings (Mr. & Mrs. Schermerhorn)*
OPPOSITE: *Cara Seymour (Hell-Cat Maggie)*

EL: When casting historical characters, if I don't have an exact match for somebody I try to find the essence of that person in an actor. Michael had his essence.

Q: You have a well-known British actor, John Sessions, playing Abraham Lincoln in a stage production of *Uncle Tom's Cabin* within the movie.

EL: He was so excited to have the opportunity to work with Marty, and that was true with the actors we found in London and Dublin and Glasgow.

Q: How did the size and scope of the film affect your job? I understand that there were a hundred and twenty speaking parts.

EL: It's a challenge, but we had a very large cast in *GoodFellas* and probably a hundred and ten people in *Casino*. So it's not something that we haven't faced before. It was a little harder to do the casting abroad, a little more difficult given the challenge of being in Italy working on a movie about Americans and Irish immigrants. We tracked down Irish priests and people at Army and Naval bases in Rome.

QUESTIONER: Can you talk a little bit about the character of Amsterdam?

LEONARDO DiCAPRIO: My character Amsterdam is a composite I based on information taken from the books *The Gangs of New York* and *Low Life*. Even more specifically, I was influenced by a handwritten account that was discovered by a team of researchers. This journal describes the life of a young man who spent his entire youth in a juvenile prison called a "house of reform." The journal conveys such extreme desperation that it becomes the perfect back-story for Amsterdam's obsession with revenge.

(54)

Q: How does Amsterdam change in the course of the drama?

LD: When Amsterdam arrives in the Five Points after spending fifteen years away in a house of reform, he learns to suppress his desire for revenge until the appropriate time. First he has to learn the rules and codes of this new and unfamiliar world. In order to rid himself of his father's ghost, Amsterdam learns the hard way the skills necessary to challenge Bill the Butcher on his own level.

Q: How did you prepare for the role?

LD: Physically, I began preparing for the role about eleven months before the actual start date. My regimen included weight training, knife-throwing, and various fighting methods from the period. Amsterdam has a few advantages over the hordes of low-life characters in the Five Points. Besides being physically tough, he has the determination that comes with his desire for revenge. Unlike the rest of the cast of characters, Amsterdam has been spared the neurological damage of drinking the "all sorts" (a barrel at Satan's Circus full of remnants of customers' drinks). He is a little quicker than most.

Q: Did Dante Ferretti's sets and Sandy Powell's costumes help you enter the world of *Gangs of New York*?

LD: The atmosphere of the sets and costumes were a great help in entering the period and the mindset of the character. It's an unusual period. Lower-class urban life in mid–nineteenth-century America is rarely, if ever,

ABOVE & OPPOSITE: *Leonardo DiCaprio (Amsterdam)*

depicted in the movies, and at Cinecittà the sets designed by Dante Ferretti were so big that it was like living in the actual city at that time. The alleys of the Five Points seemed alive, as if the Bowery characters could walk out of the walls. Sandy Powell's costumes were so believable that you wondered where in the Five Points the street people rested their heads each night.

Q: What was it like, working with Martin Scorsese?

LD: It was great to collaborate with a director who has been developing a project for twenty-five years. The passion for accuracy in every detail of the period and historical context resonates throughout Marty's work. I heard about the project when I was sixteen—the story of a young Irish immigrant in the 1800s who is placed in the center of the biggest urban riot in the New World. I was so determined to do this project with him that I actually changed agencies when I was seventeen in order to be in closer contact.

Q: How would you describe working on the film?

LD: My experience turned out to be the most rewarding of my films thus far. Despite our initial operatic Italian arguments about the story and Amsterdam's character, I have to say that I will truly never forget our first meetings on *Gangs of New York*. It was when I first learned that Marty has seen every movie ever made until the 1980s—I was working with a true visionary, someone who can masterfully assemble all the hidden mechanisms that make a movie operate with seamless reality and dramatic force.

(57)

LEFT: *Leonardo DiCaprio (Amsterdam), Stephen Graham (Shang) with the Dead Rabbits*

DANIEL DAY-LEWIS:

WILLIAM CUTTING, "BILL THE BUTCHER"

QUESTIONER: Tell us about your preparation for *Gangs of New York*.

DANIEL DAY-LEWIS: Like everybody who worked on the production, I started with the same basic reading material. For a film about this period there's not much archive footage or sound recording available. Everyone gleans what they can from the literature and then begins to invent for themselves whatever world they can, and you just hope that all these worlds will coincide at some point. It's very hard to describe the process where one arrives at one thing as opposed to something else. General discussion helps create the larger visible world, but in creating an internal reality each person is on their own.

Q: What research material did you use?

DDL: For all of us, Luc Sante's wonderful book, *Low Life*, was the bedrock. *The Gangs of New York* itself, though it's a little quaint and only in part covers the period of our story; Jacob Riis, his photographs particularly; Walt Whitman, whose identification with the feverish diversity of New York streets was total. And the *Police Gazette*, which I enjoyed. It's probably the mother and father of all tabloid journalism. There's something about the nature of the publication—you can almost smell the life on its pages. But the page only takes you so far, and everyone works away on their own little private places.

(58)

RIGHT: *Daniel Day-Lewis (Bill) reminiscing*

ABOVE: *Daniel Day-Lewis (Bill) as a "hooligan dandy"*
OPPOSITE: *Bill with his Native Americans*

Q: Didn't you work with a butcher? Was that helpful?

DDL: You never know what will help. I assume that everything is helpful. In the end what you don't need will fall away naturally, like dead skin. It's not a science. Whatever discipline is involved merely helps to contain the disorder—the mess within which you must grovel for some sense of the life you're borrowing. You follow the clues. The clues

lead into the mess but they don't lead you out of it—only instinct, imagination, and luck can do that. I suppose for my part, in an imaginative sense, all those doors that have Do Not Enter written on them in bold red letters—I just crash right through them without knocking. As a sense of the person emerges, it's the character himself who dictates the nature of the inquiry.

If the film works on the level that we hope it will, most of this will explain itself. But if it doesn't work, then nothing we can say is going to make it work.

Q: What was your reaction to Bill's costumes?

DDL: It goes without saying that Sandy Powell's work on the film (which I personally think is magnificent) apart from the significance it has for the film as an entire piece of work, makes a huge difference to us as individuals. Clothes become part of your life, part of the life that you're trying to re-create. Sandy and I had a chance to meet in Dublin before we started shooting. She spoke from her point of view, and I from mine, and then she showed me a collection of pictures, etchings, ideas plucked from here and there that were beginning to move her imagination. And then we went our separate ways, and when I came

back a month later, to my astonishment I found the rack of clothes she had created.

I hadn't imagined Bill being such a peacock, but the discovery was a really wonderful one, a hooligan dandy. It made me think a little differently. Dress it any way you like. The primitive is still visible. In fact, the more you disguise it, the more remarkable the stench, the greater the menace. That we should wear our new-found wealth so ostentatiously seemed fitting—an almost consciously obscene parody of the uptown swells. "Hey, you uptowners! We're from the slums but we're getting closer. Would you like me for a neighbor?" Yet the threat is a kind of joke, because whilst everybody else making money in the city thinks only to emulate their "betters," we, through a blend of fierce tribalism and working-class pride, are inextricably

bound to the streets we come from. From the moment I tried on the costumes, I was utterly delighted.

Q: The things Sandy Powell takes inspiration from, including even contemporary things, somehow work in context. Did the sets work in the same way for you?

DDL: Everything works for you that isn't working against you. To my mind, I can't imagine a world more entirely and perfectly re-created than the world Dante Ferretti gave us. My personal favorite was the Five Points—the area that I grew to love more than anything, particularly at nighttime. After we'd had a couple of storms, which had etched their own character into the streets, the cobblestones turned to muck. I just loved that place. I loved being in it. It was my home.

And after all the horror that Dickens might have felt on his visit to the Five Points, which he describes vividly in *American Notes*, for me it was just sheer love. I just loved being around that place and at Satan's Circus particularly. That was my home, and the place does so much of the work for you.

The difficulty when you build sets is that you have to invest them with life. To the naked eye those places might have a startling reality, but you have to fill them with life. When you work on location you use streets and houses. In the countryside—no matter where, the whisper of life is already there. It may conflict in some way with what you're trying to do,

but even that conflict can help you, a healthy counterpoint to one's expectations. Dante and his department provided us with, in every detail, the best possible beginning, which then had to be invested with the life of the movie, with the spirit of the place. When you see the Five Points thronging with people, animals, and the bustle of everyday life, that's beautiful.

Q: Was this collaboration with Martin Scorsese different from yours on *The Age of Innocence*?

DDL: In some ways yes, in some ways no. We had a wonderful foundation from *The Age of Innocence*. I trust him implicitly, and I enjoy being around him. I remember on *The Age of Innocence* how we were all amazed at our own good fortune to be able to spend that time with him. And of course that carries over, that remains. In terms of the difference, I suppose it was as different as the nature of the piece was different. I think we had a more formal relationship during *The Age of Innocence* because that's what the piece demanded. We laughed a lot on this set. I felt a great sense of complicity with him on both films.

Q: Bill is such a larger-than-life character and is so full of rage; how did you manage to live with him for so long?

DDL: That's hard to talk about. You might ask my family...

ABOVE: *Daniel Day-Lewis (Bill) giving Leonardo DiCaprio (Amsterdam) a butchering lesson*
OPPOSITE: *Entrance to Satan's Circus*

The moment you walk away from a set for the last time—no matter how vivid the experience—one's connection to it begins to melt, as with the memory of pleasure or of pain. But if I focus my mind on it, a wisp of smoke will still appear. Looking back I'd say that I relished Bill's companionship and he was never less than fascinating to me. The passage of time allows me this objectivity which I couldn't afford whilst still inside the experience.

It's true that rage is an indigestible emotion, but at least Bill permits himself copious purgatives. The conscience of the character will largely define the prevailing qualities of the experience. Bill is not a man who suffers from a self-castigating conscience. Part of my work was to share his conviction, and conviction is a lot easier to live with than doubt. He's a man of unassailable conviction. A very dangerous state of mind, highly enjoyable and strangely relaxing. He does, however, live with a punishing sense of honor, particularly in relation to Priest Vallon, a kind of idealized self who in life and in death confronts Bill with a profound question about his own worth. That question is a weighty one to live with. To my mind, considering the times and the streets that gave birth to him he is— however misguided—an honorable man. And thanks be to Christ he has a sense of humor.

(63)

CAMERON DIAZ:

JENNY EVERDEANE

QUESTIONER: What was your reaction to the sets when you first arrived in Rome?

CAMERON DIAZ: When I first saw the sets I was completely blown away. The harbor and the detail in every building was unbelievable. The texture was so rich. It was incredible to see three or four hundred extras dressed in period costume running around, re-creating day-to-day actions, and the hustle and bustle of the harbor. The scale of it is amazing, it's life-size.

Q: How did you get yourself accustomed to the sets?

CD: I walked around and looked into all the storefronts, at the ground and the stones, and felt the brick. But the Five Points comes to life when the harbor, the Pagoda, and the Brewery are full of people and action.

Q: Tell me a little bit about Jenny, the character you play.

CD: Jenny is a survivor. She's lucky to still be alive, and she's especially lucky to be in her position. She comes from the Five Points, which is the worst slum in New York. She's at the top of the food chain there, which is a really comfortable place to be. She has worked really hard all of her life to get there. She was orphaned at eleven, having come over with her mother from Ireland, and takes up with Bill the Butcher, who has a soft spot for her. She's learned all the tricks of the trade, how to pick pockets, how to be a prostitute, and to do whatever it takes to stay alive. She has learned how to take advantage of the situation rather than allowing it to take advantage of her. But she knows she doesn't want to stay in the Five Points, surrounded by death, murder, and constant terror. It's a tough life, and she wants something more.

Q: What does Amsterdam mean to Jenny?

CD: She's been through everybody in the Five Points. She knows what the men have to offer, and she's never accepted any of them. Her relations with Bill are an exception. He's helped her since she was small, and there's a kindness between them. But in their world there is nothing you can count on. Amsterdam has come to avenge his father's death, and at the same time is climbing the ladder and making his life a little bit more substantial. When Jenny and Amsterdam meet they know they've met each other's match, and they fall in love.

Q: It must be difficult for them to carry on a romance in such a tough neighborhood.

CD: New York was still wild then. There were animals roaming around unpaved roads. As Jenny ventures out of her area, and goes uptown, she becomes more sophisticated in her thievery. She dreams of going to California and making a fresh start.

Q: What was it like, working with Martin Scorsese and this cast?

CD: For me to be working with the actors I've worked with on this movie, and with Marty Scorsese—it is an actor's dream come true. He often uses very technical shots.

One that struck me was a scene in the Pagoda. The camera comes up behind Daniel Day-Lewis, and then goes down below him while there are some men rolling up the carpet, and you see the entire room lit up with four

(65)

OPPOSITE: *Cameron Diaz (Jenny)*

hundred extras, cheering. An unbelievable amount of work goes into a shot like that, but because you're working with Scorsese, and with a crew that's so capable, it happens relatively quickly. Marty has incredible knowledge of film, and he takes all of that information and love of film and puts it in his work.

Q: Tell me about Jenny's look, the costumes, and working with Sandy Powell.

CD: Sandy Powell is unbelievable. Her vision of this film is original, because it takes place in the Five Points, which had never been represented in film before. We often think of people in period pieces as wearing starched collars and very big skirts. But these people didn't have any money, they didn't have anything but their own character. Sandy put a lot of color into the clothes, vibrant, vivid color, which plays a huge part in the texture of all the material. We wanted Jenny to have a certain softness. She wasn't hard despite her difficult life. How good she was as a thief was reflected in how she dressed. She would steal quality pieces and would spend the money to have a shirt made for herself, or take a beautiful Victorian skirt and tear it up. The jewelry showed her status—she always wore some, and it was also her insurance if she ever needed cash. She ran with Bill's crowd, and Bill was the top-notch guy, the fanciest of the fancy in the Five Points. So for Jenny to stand by his side, she had to look good.

Q: Your role is very physical. How did you prepare for that?

CD: There's definitely a lot of roughhousing with the boys, and Leo and I have a few con-

frontations. I've done a lot of physical acting. I even did kung-fu in *Charlie's Angels*. But it's completely different doing it in a corset.

Q: How was it, working with Leonardo DiCaprio and Daniel Day-Lewis?

CD: Working with Leo has been a blast. When we were working together it was as Amsterdam and Jenny. I've known Leo since he was a kid. It's fantastic to watch him play this role. He's a boy becoming a man. He enters the Five Points on his own two feet—that's the only thing he has—to reclaim his father's name. Being the main character, everything pivots around him.

I met Daniel Day-Lewis in the very beginning, before we started shooting the movie, and since then I've been hanging out with Bill the Butcher. He goes so deep into character. He speaks only with the accent of Bill whether he's working or not. He's changed physically and become this other person. He's so dedicated to his work in such an intense way. It's quite frightening but completely admirable.

Q: Is this your first time working in Italy?

CD: Yes, and it's been an amazing experience. It's been our home away from home. We spent so much time here. And we worked on Stage Five, which was Fellini's old soundstage, with our dressing rooms inside. Normally actors live out of big trailers, so it's been amazing to come to a studio every day and go to your dressing room that has real plumbing! When we had to shoot off the lot for a couple of days, we felt insecure. We wanted to go back to the comfort and security of Cinecittà.

ABOVE: *Cameron Diaz (Jenny) and Leonardo DiCaprio (Amsterdam) in the dance scene*

QUESTIONER: Can you tell us a little bit about the character you play in the movie?

LIAM NEESON: I play a guy, called Priest Vallon, who's an Irish immigrant in New York. He's the leader of a gang of similar immigrants called the Dead Rabbits. It's a gang that did exist in the nineteenth century in an area called the Five Points. Vallon is helping his people defend themselves and protect the niche of land that they live on. He's a bit of a warrior in the Celtic mythological tradition. He's looked up to as a fearless warrior/leader, but he has a sense of justice.

Q: What was the situation that the immigrants faced when they came to America in the 1840s?

LN: There was great discrimination against the Irish. There were gangs known as the Nativists, who saw themselves as "pure-blood" Americans. They hated the Irish and immigrants from other countries. The Nativists felt they were rabble and didn't deserve to be allowed to land and set up shop in New York. So there were these people, having made a horrendous journey from poverty-stricken Ireland in these coffin ships—that's what they were known as—to be confronted yet again with another set of obstacles in the form of vicious gangs who were out to kill them. But

the Irish were hard, sturdy people who proved ultimately to be the working-class backbone of this country.

Q: In the film you have a standoff against the leader of a Nativist gang, a guy named Bill the Butcher.

LN: We have a standoff, and I think it's kind of akin to prizefighters who are of the same weight, same experience, equally good. When it comes to fisticuffs, it's just innate respect they have for each other. When they do fight—even though they fight savagely and brutally—they do follow a code of ethics.

Q: When you were approached with this kind of character, how did you research him in order to develop his personality?

LN: Martin's office was wonderful at supplying me with background—pictorial research, lots of books and writings and essays about that period and about life in the Five Points area. So we all did quite a bit of reading. You can do an endless amount of research, but in the end, it was working with the cast, with Martin, and walking onto the sets that did it for me. It's not a computer-digitized set, it's real. They built ten or fifteen blocks, and along with stepping into the wonderful costumes that Sandy

(68)

OPPOSITE: *Liam Neeson (Priest Vallon) with Cian McCormack (young Amsterdam)*

Powell designed, we didn't have to make a huge imaginative leap to enter that world. And with the strength of the script it was fairly easy to kick start the process.

Q: Did you work with Sandy Powell? Did you have discussions as to how the character would look?

LN: I had worked with Sandy on a number of occasions before—*Michael Collins, Rob Roy*—so I know the way she works, and I know she's an extraordinary talent. And Martin did have very definite ideas on what these characters looked like. I tried on the costume, and they tailored certain bits of it, and I put my tuppence worth in, and Sandy did and Martin did, and then we got together with the hairdresser and makeup, to make the whole thing one entity. I felt the coat they made for me, a huge, big, long coat, should be on my character at all times. He would have felt naked without it. The coat became almost like armor, and if you saw that coat you'd know who the character was. Actors have different ways of treating costume and wearing costume. I work from the feet up. I had a good pair of shoes and boots.

Q: What did you think of the sets?

LN: When I arrived in Rome at Cinecittà in mid-January, everyone kept asking me, "Have you seen the sets yet?" The shooting had started many weeks before I joined the film. I remember seeing it for the first time and it really was another world. I have a fair amount of experience as an actor in films and seeing many types of sets, and these were very impressive. You got a sense of the scale of New York in those days, and of how precarious life was. The buildings were wooden shacks, and people lived in them and lived underneath in spaces like rabbit warrens. And there were also two ships that were constructed in the

back, one of which was able to move. I don't think we'll ever see sets like this again.

Q: What was it like working with Martin Scorsese?

LN: First off, it was a real honor to be in his company. He loves actors, he loves their "process," whatever that is, so I immediately felt in safe hands. And his energy is phenomenal. If you're putting in 100 percent you can rest assured he's putting in 300 percent. He's very watchful, and he knows actors—we all like to be watched. He was open to suggestions but at the same time he had a definite idea of how a scene should be played, and the pace it should be played at. He just lived, ate, and breathed the whole film, and it was great to be part of that. He's so passionate, and that gives you a great energy yourself.

Q: What was it like working with Daniel Day-Lewis again?

LN: We've known each other for a number of years, and we have different approaches to the work. Daniel's very intense, and gets into character to an extraordinary level, which is very admirable. He works out a lot in the gym, and I did as well. I found out the time he was going to the gym, which was usually five thirty in the morning. So I went to the gym at four thirty, and as he was coming in at five thirty I was going out. He would always address me by my character's name. We had fun, and we had some very intense fighting to do.

Q: How did you prepare for the fight?

LN: We had a wonderful stunt coordinator, Vic Armstrong, whom I've worked with many times before. I think Martin described what he wanted—very brutal and primordial—and that would be seen in the types of weapons that

OPPOSITE: *Liam Neeson (Priest Vallon) fighting the Native Americans*

(71)

were invented for the fight. He wanted a certain style that was almost balletic yet obviously violent and swift and very decisive—and swirling. I remember the camera did a lot of strange movements. It was demanding because the nature of film is such that you have to repeat something many times, and there are little blood explosions, and they always take a long time to set up and get right. But I love doing that sort of stuff. Daniel loves it too, so we were like two kids in a toy shop.

Q: Do you have a favorite Martin Scorsese film?

LN: I think *Raging Bull* was one of the first films that really affected me in lots of ways. First off, I'm a big boxing fan so I knew quite a bit about Jake LaMotta himself, but I'd never seen a film like this before that kind of touched in so many universal levels, on the nature of man on this planet, and our reason for existing. It was as basic as that, and as complex as that. I've seen all his films, but in that one especially, the performance level from everyone in it was extraordinary. I'd never really seen that style of acting before, that kind of unbelievable commitment from everybody—not just Robert De Niro, who was phenomenal, but Joe Pesci and Cathy Moriarty. It's an extraordinary film on many, many levels.

Q: Scorsese has said that he feels one of the themes in *Gangs* is that the Irish immigration is the first test of what America became, a melting pot.

LN: Yes, I think so. In the year 2002, if someone asked me to describe New York, I would describe it as an elastic band. It keeps getting turned, and turned and turned but it never actually snaps. That period in this city's history [1840s] definitely reflects that. You think something's going to erupt in one area in some way, but it never does, it just keeps changing position all the time. These boatloads of people from all nations arrived and found their niche, and built up from that niche. They spread their wings, and gained confidence. And the country was ready for them.

JIM BROADBENT:

WILLIAM "BOSS" TWEED

QUESTIONER: When you first read *Gangs of New York*, what did you think of the script?

JIM BROADBENT: I thought it was wonderful. The scale of it is awesome—the whole vision of it. I couldn't imagine what it was going to be like. There's nothing predictable about it, and added to that was the fact that Martin Scorsese was directing it. It was a completely entrancing project in every way.

Q: Did the sets meet your expectations?

JB: Coming onto the set was just extraordinary. When I came to the studio for a costume fitting and was taken onto the set and saw the dock and the ships, and the Five Points—I'd never seen anything like it. We don't have that scale of production in Britain.

Q: Did you know much about mid-nineteenth-century New York before working on the film?

JB: No. A lot of invaluable research material was sent to me from New York. It was a fascinating time.

I'm from England, playing a third-generation American. New York was principally Irish, Scottish, English, and Dutch at that time. Everyone in America was an

(73)

ABOVE: *Jim Broadbent (Boss Tweed) at an uptown mansion*
OPPOSITE: *Liam Neeson (Priest Vallon) and Daniel Day-Lewis (Bill the Butcher)*

immigrant. What we now think of as an American hadn't developed yet.

Q: Tell me a little bit about your character.

JB: I play William "Boss" Tweed, who was a real person. He became famous, or rather notorious, about ten years after the period we're dealing with in the film. He was just building his political empire in the 1860s. He ran Tammany Hall, and ten years later he was the most corrupt, ruthless politician in America. He ripped off millions of dollars. Other politicians have tried to emulate him and are still trying, I'm sure. It's a fascinating story. After our period in the film he was finally arrested and died in jail. Political cartoonist Thomas Nast did wonderful caricatures of Tweed, to which Tweed took great exception, because his supporters couldn't read, but they could look at pictures. So Tweed tried to buy Nast off with half a million dollars to go and study art in Europe, but Nast wouldn't have it. After Tweed was put in prison he escaped to Europe. But somebody who had seen a Nast cartoon of Tweed reported him and he was arrested. So Nast got his revenge in the end—but that's another film.

Tweed was a great character—charismatic—and in his own way did a lot for New York. He was a good, practical politician. He had to get people on his side, and at this stage in his career, and in the film, he befriends the gangs. They can buy the votes that he needs. He has to collude with these criminals, which I think he finds quite easy. He's really a gang leader himself—just of a more organized sort of gang.

(74)   **Q:** Were you able to find out enough about Tweed in the history books?

JB: Yes, there's a huge amount of material on him, from newspapers, and also a sort of

RIGHT: *Daniel Day-Lewis (Bill) and Jim Broadbent (Tweed) at Tammany Hall*

biography written in the 1920s. He's still talked about today in New York. During the recent U.S. presidential recount in Florida, *The New Yorker* magazine used a quote by him, which we have in the movie, to the effect that it's not the voters who count but the counters.

Q: How has it been, working with Martin Scorsese?

JB: Actors have various jokes, like, "Is that Scorsese on the phone? Tell him I'm busy." But when it really happens it's really exciting. It's fascinating to work with someone who knows his business so well.

Q: Are there any scenes from the film that stand out in your mind?

JB: There is a wonderful scene down at the port, which was shot in the most extraordinary way. We did long takes coming off the bluff, with one ship moving in the foreground, the army in the background, and the registration of the immigrants on the dock. The camera moves around and picks up the army as they're going up the ramps, off to fight in the Civil War. It's a huge, long take, and I'm just part of it at the beginning. It was wonderful.

Q: What was it like working with Daniel Day-Lewis?

JB: I'd worked with Daniel years ago. I knew that he was going to be a wonderful actor. He's one of those actors you really admire. With Daniel there is always mystery. He has an extraordinary quality.

Q: What was it like to work with Leonardo DiCaprio?

JB: I didn't have many scenes with Leo. He's wonderful, really. Brilliant. Very serious about the work. There was one particularly good scene in the church. Tweed has fallen out with Bill the Butcher, and he turns to Amsterdam. Leo was wonderful. He's very powerful, physically very strong, which gives a good weight to the character.

Q: Did you get a chance to meet with Sandy Powell and talk about what your costume would look like?

JB: Yes. We came to Rome two or three weeks before we started shooting and got fitted for our costumes. Tweed became a huge, fat man by the 1870s, but we're ten or so years earlier, so he wasn't that fat. I wore some padding to give a bit of that weight and to get the feel of him. There's a certain showiness about the character. Sandy is a great costume designer.

Q: Scorsese has made movies about different worlds within New York. What is this world?

JB: This was a lawless anarchic corner of Manhattan which was run by many competing gangs. It's the tale of their struggle for supremacy over each other, and of them being drawn into the bigger gangs of the political parties, and how that affects them and how it affects the city. The Civil War has started, people are being drafted. All of this creates pressure and tension in the story. And there's a love story and a story of revenge woven into that whole tapestry.

There's an awful lot to be gained from watching this movie. I think what fascinated Marty on the set is the history. He had been researching and putting it all together for twenty years. It can't help but make New York even richer to the viewers.

OPPOSITE: *Eddie Marsan (Killoran), Stephen Graham (Shang), and Jim Broadbent (Tweed)*

QUESTIONER: Did the production team provide you with historical research or books to read in preparation for the film?

HENRY THOMAS: It's a period that is glossed over in the history books, and there's not a lot of information on it unless you really look for it. So seeing the sets and learning more about the time as the project got close to being reality made me understand what an interesting time it was in the history of New York and of America.

The one book that I read that was really informative was called *The Rogue's Lexicon*, and it is a dictionary of slang used in the underworld at that time, amassed by the head of police of New York in 1859. It includes all the slang and the jargon used by thieves and pickpockets from England and America. That kind of authenticity is really useful.

Q: Is there any slang that you could use today?

HT: Some of the words that we use in the movie have carried over and become modern expressions, such as "sharp," as in "He looks sharp."

Q: Did someone work with you on dialect and accent?

HT: Tim Monich was our dialect coach, and the "tongue police." He would stop us if we made a slip. The accents are interesting as well, because there is no recorded documentation. This gave some freedom for the actors to pick and choose where the characters came from, since New York is a melting pot with an amalgamation of every accent in the world.

Q: What is Johnny's background?

HT: Johnny is an unfortunate character who's born into a world where he doesn't really belong. It's a hard world, and he's not quite tough enough. He befriends Amsterdam and later betrays him without realizing the implications of what he has done. He's also interesting because he's the kind of everyman to whom the audience will be able to relate. By not really fitting in, he becomes the eyes and ears for the audience to follow into this strange, dark underworld.

Q: Were you aware of the gang situation in New York in that time period?

HT: No, I wasn't at all. In fact when I heard of the *Gangs of New York* project, I thought it must be about the prohibition gangs and bootleggers of the 1920s and 1930s. But this

OPPOSITE: *Henry Thomas (Johnny) after selling a corpse*

ABOVE: *Henry Thomas (Johnny)*

film is interesting because it addresses the foundation the whole city was built upon, down to the fire and the police departments. It was basically any man's town at that time, and there were people vying for the American dream, and going about getting it any way they could. And that's what America is, really, when you get down to it.

Q: What did you learn about immigration and assimilation?

HT: The funny thing about the immigrants who came over was that they didn't come over to become Americans, they came to be Irish people in America, so they grouped together and stayed in these tight-knit groups and gangs. Most of them didn't want to stay here, they just wanted to make enough money to go back home. In fact a lot of the soldiers who fought in the Civil War, a lot of the Irish brigades, were training so that they could go back and fight in Ireland after the American war was over and they had made some money.

Q: Your character is the friend of Amsterdam as a young boy, whose father is the leader of the Dead Rabbits, an Irish gang. Later on, does Johnny identify himself as a Native American?

HT: Johnny is an opportunist, because that's what he has to be in this world to survive. He isn't exceedingly tough. He's not the best fighter, he's not great with a knife. He doesn't have anything to rely on other than his wits and the fact that if he puts his money on a winning horse he'll follow it in across the finish line. And that's what he does. He identifies with whatever group can keep him alive and fed. He has his loyalties, but he feels betrayed once Amsterdam and Jenny's romance starts to take off, and he seeks to get even—not a good move for him.

Q: Another thing that's interesting about your character is that the movie shows the racism and religious intolerance of the time, but Johnny seems to hang out with all sorts of people.

HT: What you're looking at is basically the dregs of society, the lowest animals on the food chain. Through Shang's gang, in the beginning, you first meet Johnny, you also meet Jimmy Spoils, who is black—these guys are the foundation of the gang which is later revived as the Dead Rabbits when Amsterdam comes into the gang. These are people who are doing whatever they can to survive. The company they keep never comes into question, because they're already the pariahs of society. They don't worry about what other people think. It's all about who's on the game, what can they get for this, and where they'll be eating and sleeping tonight. Amsterdam pulls us out of the sty and elevates us for a while.

Q: On this film you've worked with a lot of incredible people. What's that been like?

HT: A film like this is amazing, because we have such a varied and international cast—which is rare. We have the best actors in the world working on this show. It's exciting to come in and look at a call sheet and see Daniel Day-Lewis, Jim Broadbent, Leonardo DiCaprio, and Brendan Gleeson on it. Even some of the smaller parts are played by amazing guys, like John Sessions, whom I wouldn't have had the opportunity to work with or alongside if it weren't a project like this. It's a movie about New York, being shot in Rome with English and Scottish actors playing Americans, American actors playing Irishmen, and a cast of Italian extras playing Americans. So it's a bit of a circus.

Q: Did the director allow you to bring a lot to the table insofar as your character and the ideas that you had for your character?

HT: Absolutely. I think the character was written in one of the earlier drafts as an Italian, but when I first read the script I assumed from the language that he was Irish. So I came in with an Irish accent, and it stuck. It was never really questioned. Over time I realized that he's not only concerned with the details, but more with how the pieces fit into the bigger picture. It's been a real challenge as an actor, because you come to the set with certain ideas about the scene, and you not only have to think for your character but you have to think about what the director is going to want and how that's going to sit with the other characters. It's really an ensemble feel.

Q: What did you think of Dante Feretti's sets?

HT: The sets are so vast. This is the only film I've ever been a part of that you can spend more than half an hour walking through the sets, literally traveling from one end to the other. If you stopped to look at the details, it would take you a few days.

Q: What was it like shooting in Italy?

HT: It's been a little bit strange. But studios are universally similar. There are soundstages, certain people who are always there, a commissary and your dressing room. I feel at home on sets and in a studio format.

Q: How would you describe the film?

HT: It's an old theme with a geographical and historical setting that hasn't been touched on very much by history books or by films. It's a classic tale of revenge set in the founding years of what I think is the best city in the world. You always think of New York as being an international business mecca. And here you see it for what it really was, and what it started out as, and the types of people that pushed it onto the next level. It's not what you would expect, and I think that's interesting.

This is a project that Scorsese has wanted to do for twenty years or so. So it's very exciting to me to be a part of that, and it's fitting that he is the person directing it. He really loves New York, and he's really interested in New York. So I think it's a testament to New York that almost every film that he's done in some way goes back there. It's a city with a lot of interesting facets, and this is another one of them.

JOHN C. REILLY:

"HAPPY JACK" MULRANEY

QUESTIONER: What was your reaction to the Five Points? It's not a place or period many people know about. After reading the script, what did you think it would look like?

JOHN C. REILLY: It's funny, because every time I mention to people that I was shooting this Martin Scorsese film called *Gangs of New York* in Italy, they get this startled expression like, why would you shoot *Gangs of New York* in Italy? And as soon as I got to Rome I realized why, because the craftsmanship there is incredible. I've worked on some pretty big movies and this is insane. They built this whole town with two ships in a harbor. This movie seems like the last of a dying breed. The epic scale of it makes my job really easy. I walk around and I don't have to imagine anything, I'm there. Every detail is accounted for.

I did a little bit of research, so I was familiar with the Five Points, where most of the gang activity takes place in the movie. It was Dickensian. I heard about the misery and the suffering and the immigrants and how bad the conditions were, but until you see it re-created like this, you can't imagine what it was really like. It is startling.

Q: Tell me a little bit about Happy Jack Mulraney, your character. He's a Dead Rabbit, an Irish immigrant at the beginning, and then he goes over to the other side and becomes a cop (albeit a corrupt one).

JCR: At the beginning of the movie I'm part of an Irish gang which is defeated. When you're in a gang that's as fierce as these gangs were at this time, you either join another gang, you

(83)

ABOVE: *John C. Reilly (Happy Jack) as a Dead Rabbit*

get killed, or, as my character was clever enough to figure out, you join the biggest gang of all, the police. He's a practical guy. Everyone in the Dead Rabbits was loyal to the gang, but when our leader was killed everyone had to make their own way in the world. Everyone is corrupt in this movie in some way. I'd like to think that I would make more noble choices than Jack makes but at this time, with the stakes the way they were between these gangs, taking the high road would get you killed. I think he decides to survive.

Q: How did you prepare for the role?

JCR: I looked at a lot of photographs. Pictures of the time are so evocative, and there are a couple of books floating around about the history of the area.

Q: You have some really intense scenes with Leonardo DiCaprio and Daniel Day-Lewis.

JCR: Leo and I knew each other from *What's Eating Gilbert Grape*, which we made when he was a spry eighteen-year-old. So we have a little bit of a history. It's always nice in this business when you get to work with the same people again. It's pretty rare. It was nice to have a friend already on the movie.

I've admired Daniel Day-Lewis from the first time I saw him. He's an incredible actor and a real hero. There was one day when we were shooting this intense scene between Daniel Day-Lewis and me, and it was all I could do to keep myself from giggling and laughing out loud at how lucky I was to be in the room and to experience what I was experiencing.

ABOVE: *Daniel Day-Lewis (Bill), John C. Reilly (Happy Jack) with a rabbit pelt on the table*

Q: What is it like, working with Martin Scorsese?

JCR: One of the biggest surprises for me was how enthusiastic he is about filmmaking itself. Most of the time, when you're working on movies, the director, for good reason, is usually put upon, stressed out, and worried. There's a lot of worry that comes with the job. But one of the wonderful things about Mr. Scorsese is that he feels he's got the best job in the world. His enthusiasm is really infectious. This is not to say that he doesn't have to deal with all the usual struggles of making a film, but he loves it so much. It made me realize that's what it's all about.

Q: Did you talk to him much about your character? Did he offer suggestions?

JCR: By the time I joined the cast of the movie, things were well under way, and by the time I got to Rome, Mr. Scorsese's time was accounted for. It's amazing how much information I got from the short conversations I had with him. I would have an idea about something, and he'd never correct me. He would say what he thought about it. He can communicate a lot to you in a short time without making you feel like he's telling you what to do. He solicits your ideas and then he gives you his, and by the time he walks away you get what he wants.

Q: Did you work with Sandy Powell on the costumes, and did you have some input into what your character would look like?

JCR: As I mentioned earlier, my character starts out at a much more feisty time in his life. In the beginning he's in a gang, so I'm almost like a barbarian. Then the story jumps and I become this corrupt policeman, so I wanted to accentuate a kind of beer belly. The Irish policeman is an American archetype, so I wanted to give a nod to that while at the same time bring some new ideas to it. I did consult with Sandy Powell, who was amazing. With someone as talented as Sandy Powell or Martin Scorsese, you just surrender yourself to them. My character is called Happy Jack because of a scar on his face and a facial paralysis. It looks like he's smiling all the time.

Q: Do you know how that happened?

JCR: If you look at the film you'll see everyone has got some markings from the brutal lifestyle they have led. If you consider the medical attention that was available to them, it's amazing that anyone survived.

Q: How would you describe *Gangs of New York*?

JCR: I can't be so presumptuous to think I know what Mr. Scorsese is thinking about in his films, but he's made some other films about New York—*The Age of Innocence*, *GoodFellas*—and in a way this is a prequel to some of those stories. In *The Age of Innocence*, there are all these hoity-toity rich people. Where did their money come from? Where did that power base come from? It came from these really bloody battles on the street, where everyone is fighting for their piece of the American pie.

In America we're used to our culture moving so quickly that we accept contemporary culture as the way it has always been—because we don't have the sense of history that places like Italy have. But this movie shows our history. I'm sure people will look at Broadway differently after they see this film. They'll look at certain places on the Lower East Side with fresh eyes when they realize what really went on there.

QUESTIONER: Were you familiar with this period of New York history?

BRENDAN GLEESON: I had a layman's knowledge of New York. I had no idea about this period, and I don't think an awful lot of New Yorkers do either. So it was incredible to find this Pandora's Box of humanity, particularly given that the ships were coming over from Ireland. I knew an awful lot about what had driven them onto the ships, and how they fell off halfway over. But I really had no idea what happened when they got here. So it's a great privilege to be here, looking at it.

Q: What was driving all the people from Ireland to New York?

BG: The potato famine decimated the country. There had been warnings about the fact that there was too much reliance on the potato. But the population had exploded—ironically, the famine happened as a result of prosperity. The population had almost doubled from the previous century. The Irish came to America in droves, and their crossing was hideous.

Moreover, some of them were turned back at Ellis Island. It was a nightmare, but they thought there was a pot of gold at the end of the rainbow.

There were a million people who died as a result of the famine and I think a million people left the country. A large portion of the million that were left were dumped off of ships in New York. They went from one hell to another. It's particularly interesting for me as an Irish person to examine this period in history.

Q: Tell us about your character, Monk McGinn.

BG: He's a little bit of a mystery, so to analyze him, in one sense, is to betray him. He's a lone wolf. He's seen a certain amount of struggle back home and he holds himself somewhat aloof from the Irish communities and the Irish gangs. Nevertheless, he operates very well in mayhem, and he has to chase his own demons. He's a consummate killer, if somewhat reluctant in his soul to be what he is. So he pursues a lone furrow throughout the movie, and he carries a torch that maybe he doesn't even know he carries.

OPPOSITE: *Brendan Gleeson (Monk McGinn) looking over the Five Points*

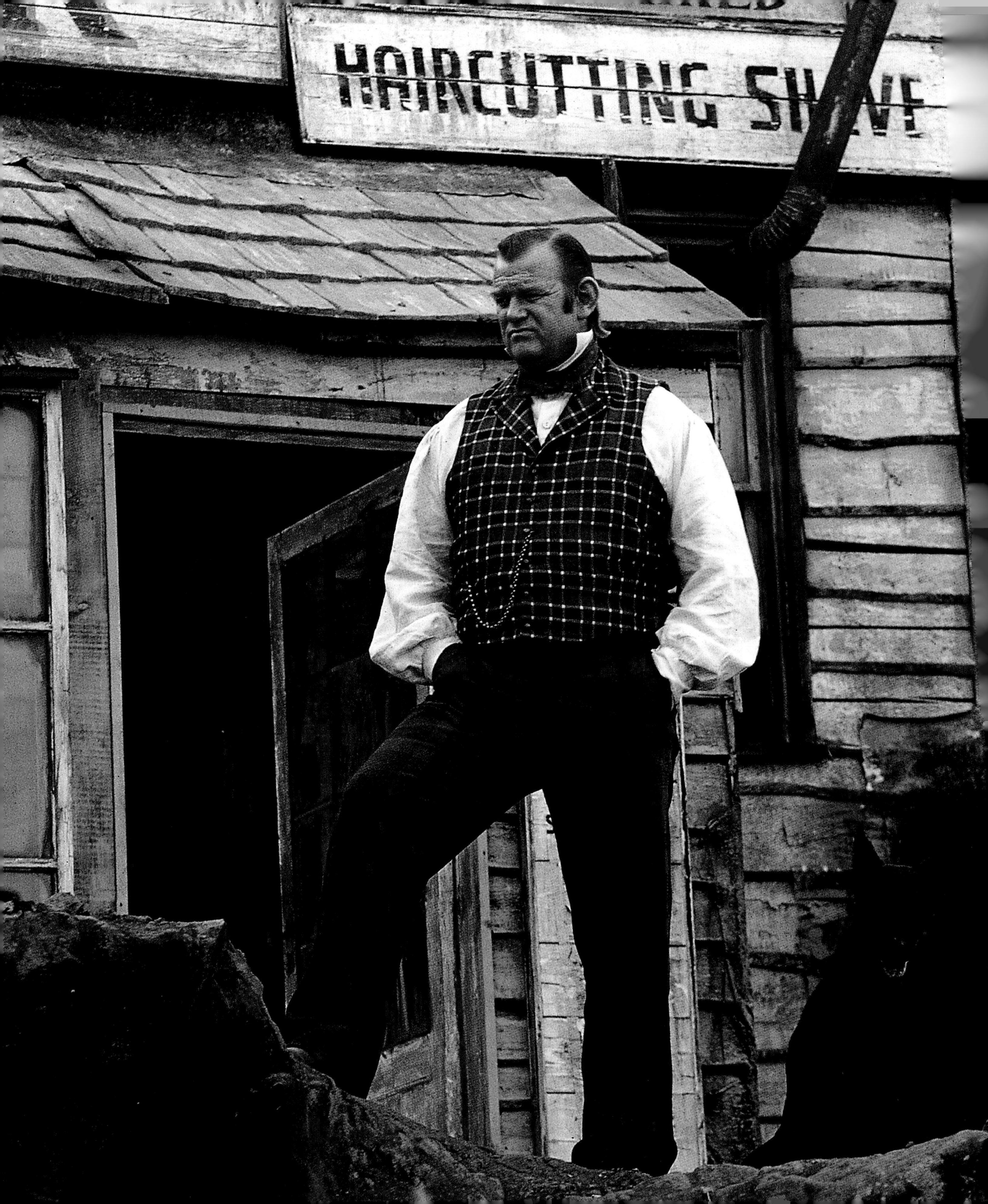
HAIRCUTTING

Q: What is his relationship with Amsterdam?

BG: It would be disingenuous to say he was a father figure because he's not, really, but in another way that's the role he fulfills. On the one hand he keeps an eye on what's going on with Amsterdam, and on the other he insists to himself that this is not his business. His relationship with Amsterdam is conflicted. I don't think Amsterdam knows quite who or what Monk is, or whether he is or is not to be trusted. And Monk would be reluctant to tell him.

Q: Amsterdam convinces him to run for an office that would help the Irish people in the community.

BG: When it comes down to it, Monk does carry the torch, and in a way he examines the whole notion of tribalism, and why people form gangs—if it's just inevitable that people must, of their nature, fight for territorial supremacy or survival. I think he's reluctant because he knows there's something more, there's a different way to do things. He's capable of terrible deeds, and I think he tries to move away from that. In a sense I think Monk is symbolic of the moving on from the situation of battle into the political arena, into a different way of resolving disputes. It's a dangerous role to take, because there's always the kick of a dying horse. Monk in some way personifies the struggle to move Irishmen away from the notion of the gang and the tribe into something a little bit more civilized.

Q: What was it like to work with Liam Neeson?

BG: I worked very briefly with him before, and he's a fantastic presence—a very generous, open individual. From the time that I met him on *Michael Collins* he's always impressed me as somebody to aspire to both as a person and as an actor.

Q: What was it like working with Martin Scorsese?

BG: He's terribly painstaking, but incredibly unpretentious. And it's such an unusual combination to have, somebody who's so meticulous and clear about what we're all trying to achieve, and yet you feel that whatever you can bring to it is more than welcome. It's the way work should be. You learn so much from working with him, and you're surprised constantly by what's going to happen. There's always the search for that spark that'll turn it into something amazing. It's addictive. You just want to do it again and again.

Q: Had you worked in Italy before?

BG: No, I hadn't. I keep remembering John Lennon's line when he was asked why he lived in New York, and he said, if he'd been born in Roman times he would have lived in Rome. And there we were in New York in Rome. It was wonderful to have that sense of history around us in Rome. It doesn't get a whole lot better.

ABOVE: *Gary Lewis (McGloin) with Leonardo DiCaprio (Amsterdam)*

GARY LEWIS:

McGLOIN

QUESTIONER: I was going to ask you about New York City, but you've never been there.

GARY LEWIS: I've wondered about New York for the past so many months, and I've never been to the real place.

Q: Does the back lot at Cinecittà look like what you'd imagined New York to be?

GL: I was bowled over by the sets. I loved wandering about and looking at that place. It's astonishing. My mother told me a story. Her father, my grandfather, went to New York at the start of the Depression in 1929. He had to go and rescue his sister, who had been deserted by her husband. I kind of used that story, even though it was set much later, to get some idea of what it was like for the immigrants coming off the ships in New York Harbor. But then when you come to these sets, you don't have to use your imagination other than to locate yourself in 1845 New York City. The set and the costumes were so supportive.

Q: Did you read about New York at that time?

GL: The production team gave me a wonderful book about the Irish in New York. It's engrossing. I had studied aspects of American history but a little later than the movie's period. So I didn't really know much about the patterns of immigration to the States. So to get that sort of material was wonderful—I lapped it up.

There are definite viewpoints. It's not as if everybody is in agreement, especially about how different people related to others, how the Irish Catholics related to the freed slaves. Some historians highlighted the fact that they were competing on the lowest rung of the economic ladder. They were at the bottom struggling for survival. Others pointed out the fact that out of necessity some intermarried. So all of this background really interested me.

(91)

Q: What was it like for a Scotsman to play an Irishman?

GL: Well, Scotland and Ireland are quite closely linked. A lot of what happens in this movie stems from colonialism and imperialism. Playing an Irishman and coming from Scotland you are very aware of how a lot of the problems in Ireland stemmed from people being forced off the land. And so my character, McGloin, whom Marty wanted to come from the North, had to be a Catholic from, say, Belfast. So he came from a situation where he was in a minority, and life was tough in America, where there was a similar pattern. Like so many who came to the States, he congregated with his ethnic group. The Catholic Church became an immigration institution. So those sorts of things repeated, and you see patterns. A lot of Irish came to Scotland, and in Glasgow, where I come from, a huge section of the population came from Ireland originally—Irish Catholics.

Q: Your character starts out as a Dead Rabbit but then leaves the gang.

GL: Yes. He changes when the leader of the Dead Rabbits dies. The Dead Rabbits comprised Irish Catholics. It makes no sense to talk about the New York Irish as a homogenous unit, because they are descended from Scots, Irish, Anglicans, Presbyterians. The Irish Catholics were on the lowest rank.

Marty had some ideas about why McGloin would change from being a Dead Rabbit to join the absolute enemy camp, the Native Americans. I had different ideas. On one level it's about survival. One of the traditions for a lot of Irish was "The king is dead. Long live the king." My character still practiced his Catholicism in secret. It wasn't a strict Catholicism, it was tribal. It's a product of the fact that life is really brittle, intense, and very unforgiving.

Q: One of the interesting things you encounter at the church is when a black man enters. This scene definitely shows the divide between the races.

GL: There was that tension between the Irish Catholics and the blacks, and I suppose it was born out of economics. It was also political. It's a paradox in that those who saw themselves as Native Americans were so anti-Irish Catholic, the Irish Catholics became anti–anything that was associated with the Natives. The politics were ethnic. And subsequently in American history, Irish workers raided places where black workers were staying because the blacks were lowering the price of labor. When McGloin attacks Jimmy Spoils in the church, he actually appeals to the priest to get rid of the black man.

Q: And earlier on you get attacked by Leonardo DiCaprio's character.

GL: I tried to sell Marty the idea that I win the fight, but he didn't buy it. So Amsterdam kicks my butt in the fight scene. And he kicks my butt again in the church after I insult Jimmy Spoils. He "digs me up"—that's a Glasgow expression. He challenges me because I've changed. When I say, "What's a nigger doing in the church?" he says, "What's a Dead Rabbit doing among the Native Americans?" So the priest whacks me, and Jimmy whacks me, and Amsterdam whacks me again...

OPPOSITE: *Gary Lewis (McGloin)*

ABOVE: *Gary Lewis (McGloin) playing the harmonica with the Native Americans*

Q: Did you get to do all your own fighting, or did they have stunt men?

GL: No, I did most of the stuff, except for a couple of falls. I did most of the fighting.

Q: What was it like, working with Leonardo DiCaprio?

GL: It was great. The fight was the first scene we did together, so there wasn't a lot of hello-

how's-it-going stuff. So it was quite a violent introduction, and then things eased off and became more relaxed.

Q: What was it like, working with Daniel Day-Lewis?

GL: He was Bill the Butcher. I can't remember who Daniel is or even how he really looks. I can't even remember what Daniel sounds like in his ordinary accent, his real voice. But it's wonderful working with Dan. After changing sides I got to be with him a lot.

Q: In the beginning of the film you are with Liam Neeson.

GL: Yes. We all wind up in Paradise Square for the battle. We looked at the fake snow and everybody started to get cold. It was great. I'd never met Liam before. He was such a wonderful figure to see. The two of them, Liam and Daniel, facing each other, was incredible. They traded insults prior to the battle, and they're fearsome guys with fearsome weapons. It was brilliant.

Q: What was it like, working with Martin Scorsese?

GL: The first thing that struck me was how incredibly enthusiastic Marty was all the time. The first time I spoke to him was about guns. When do we have guns? And Marty told a story that happened in New York, when guys started carrying guns, what the implications of that were, how the ante was upped if anybody had a gun. That was the first indication I had of how massive and detailed his picture of all this was.

Q: Does he allow you to bring a lot to the table as an actor?

GL: Yes. The first week I was here I was listening to cassettes with a lot of different accents. Marty didn't want everybody to come from the South of Ireland. So he asked me to be from the North. And I was thinking about music, and I was reading some of the research

stuff, and there was an old song which we still sing in Glasgow, and it was sung in the Five Points, slightly differently. So I thought McGloin must have left the Short Strand, which was a Catholic enclave in Belfast, prior to the 1840s, and he'd have been victimized there, but living near the docks would have given him easy access to a ship. He easily could have encountered at some later time a German harmonica manufacturer who brought harmonicas to the States. So I said to Marty what if McGloin picked up a harmonica from a German sailor and played this song which to this day kids in Glasgow know? So he said okay and sat me on a bale of hay in the port and I played this tune as the Irish immigrants were coming off the boat. So that was a revelation to me as to how a guy who's has such an enormous world and story in his head was still open to you.

Q: What do you tell friends when they ask what the movie is about?

GL: New York is very special as a gateway to America, and this was the first wave of immigration. I was talking to Marty once about history, and the flow, and the patterns. Someone once said that war is an extension of politics by other means. But actually politics is an extension of war by other means. Looking at the period in which the film takes place, the tension between those two outlooks seems to be present, because there's a brutal, intense warfare happening between the gangs. But this tribalism is ultimately superseded when the big guns come. Who's got the big guns? The state. And the way the film covers that enormous scope is wonderful.

IT'S ALWAYS A CHALLENGE, on a period film, to balance the necessity to do something that sounds familiar enough so that it rings true to an audience's idea of class, geography, social condition and at the same time has something that convinces you that you're in another period. Anything happening in 1900 and after is easy to re-create, because we have recordings. And it's also easier because there have been more sophisticated studies done. The study of phonetics didn't really start until the late nineteenth century. Before that, even linguistics scholars were not interested in the sounds of languages and accents.

In the research for *Gangs of New York* I went back to period sources: comic writings, poems, ballads—to get an idea of what New York may have sounded like in 1850. I'm convinced that there was a New York accent back then. I put together what I'd found with the earliest recordings that I have, recordings of people born in the nineteenth century. I have a recording of Walt Whitman, for instance. And you can tell from it that New Yorkers did not pronounce the "r"s yet—New Yorkers even back then were saying "nevuh," and "woild." It's a confluence of English and Dutch.

The big challenge for the actors in this movie is how to sound working-class New York but not have any of the typical ethnic associations of modern-day New York City; how to sound like tough, streetwise New Yorkers, but Anglo-Saxon. When you think of a New York accent today, you think of Italian,

Puerto Rican, Dominican, Irish, and Jewish accents and of boroughs. The boroughs weren't even part of New York yet. So we have to find something that is Manhattan and WASP. From certain spellings—for instance in funny ballads—they were writing words like "off" and "all" as "o-r-f" and "o-r-l."

On the artistic side, Marty was interested in having something eerie and exotic. So putting all that together, I came up with a sound for Daniel, who plays a native-born New Yorker. His is really the prototype speech. He wanted to do something slow, and Marty found that interesting. He wanted to do something very deliberate, thought out, rather than something with that quick New York pace that Marty himself has.

The upper-class New York characters' speech is a little easier to find because I do have recordings of New Yorkers such as Teddy Roosevelt and his daughter.

Then we come to the Irish dilemma. There are only a few characters in the script who are native-born Irish: Priest Vallon, Monk McGinn, and a couple of the other characters. But for instance Leo and Cameron's characters came over to America when they were five and six. They arrived at an area of New York that was largely Irish in population. Leo's character was sent upstate to reform school, filled with a diverse population. Leo needed an American pronunciation that had an Irish feel and rhythm to it. Cameron's character has less of an Irish accent, as she is mobile: she's heard

OPPOSITE: *Leonardo DiCaprio (Amsterdam) with Cameron Diaz (Jenny)*

ABOVE: *Daniel Day-Lewis (Bill)*

well-bred speech and can fit in with more genteel workers uptown. So she sounds a little bit less Irish.

I worked with the cast during pre-production for hours doing lines and reading other materials. We read Walt Whitman with Daniel and we read a lot from the Bible. Daniel incorporated some biblical quotations into the script.

We have almost no actors in the movie speaking with their own accents. We do have a lot of Irish characters, but they're mostly played by non-Irish actors (except for Brendan Gleeson and Liam Neeson). Scottish actors play Irishmen, Irishmen play Americans. John C. Reilly, an American, plays an Irishman. Jim Broadbent, who is English, plays Boss Tweed, an American. We even had Italians playing Irish and a Russian playing a German. It was a big challenge and it was

hard because the cast was large and the actors came and went. Some would arrive in the evening and be in front of the camera the next morning, so we had to work quickly.

Marty really wanted the film to look right, in a way that can only be informed by research plus imagination, and he wanted the same thing with sound. It has to be as true as possible to the appropriate geography, class, social circumstances—all at once. There's improvisation, of course, on any movie. So I became the period policeman. For instance, in an early scene, Leo said, "Okay." They cut, then he ran out of the room and said to me, "Oh, I know, I know, I can't say that." I asked, "What are you talking about?" And he said, "Well on *Titanic* they told me I couldn't say 'okay.'" I said, "'Okay' is a very old American expression. It was used before the Civil War."

FIVE POINTS VOCABULARY

—from *The Rogue's Lexicon* by George Matsell, 1859

AMUSERS: fellows who carry snuff or pepper in their pockets, which they throw into a person's eyes and then run away.

ANGLERS: small thieves who place a hook on the end of a stick, with which they steal from store windows, doors, etc.

AUTUM-DIVERS: pickpockets who practice in churches.

BALLUM-RANCUM: a ball where all the dancers are thieves and prostitutes.

BENE: good, first-rate.

BLUDGET: a female thief who decoys her victims into dark alleys to rob them.

BOARDING-SCHOOL: a penitentiary.

COVE: a man.

CRUSHER: a policeman.

CUTTER: a peculiar instrument that first-class burglars use for cutting through iron chests, doors, etc.

DANCING: sneaking upstairs to commit a larceny.

FIDLAM BENS: thieves who have no particular lay; fellows that will steal anything they can remove.

GANDER: a married man not living at home with his wife.

GROANERS: thieves who attend at charity sermons and rob the congregation, steal the prayer books, etc.

HANDLE: a nose.

HIGH TIDE: plenty of money.

JACK SPRAT: a small fellow.

JIGGER: a door.

LACED MUTTON: a common woman.

LURCH: abandon.

MONEKER: a name.

MORT: a woman.

NIMENOG: a very silly fellow.

PARTIAL: putting one's hand into another man's pocket, stealing.

POLISHER: one who is in prison.

PRIM: a handsome woman.

QUARTER: to give part of the profits.

QUEEN DICK: never; it never happened.

RABBIT: a rowdy (dead rabbit: a very athletic rowdy fellow).

ROUGHS: men who are ready to fight in any way or shape.

SAND: nerve, guts.

SHE-HE: a transvestite.

SNEAK-THIEF: a fellow who sneaks into doors or windows with latchkeys and steals anything he can carry.

STAG: To see, as in "Stag the crusher" ("See the policeman").

STAR-GAZER: a prostitute or streetwalker.

STEPPING-KEN: a dance house.

SWAG: plunder.

TUMBLED: suspected, found it out.

WOODEN COAT: a coffin.

The True Blues

SANDY POWELL:

COSTUMES

MY PREPARATION for *Gangs of New York*, as for any period film, is to look at real things from the time. In this case, it was 1840 to 1860. You look at paintings from the period, and luckily for us the daguerreotype had been invented, so we had photos to look at—lots and lots of them. And Marty's production company had already done years of research. I had a lot of reading material. I read Luc Sante's book *Low Life*, from which I learned a lot about the place.

We went through various stages, and the look ends up fairly stylized although based on historical accuracy. It's a world that we didn't really know about, as there wasn't actually any photographic evidence of the Five Points area of New York. I take the reality a few steps further. In the end, it's kind of a made-up world.

We had to think of different looks for the gangs. But after all, men's clothing is standard—they wore a pair of trousers, a shirt, a waistcoat or a vest, and a jacket and hat. At the beginning, I only dealt with the two main gangs of the movie, the Dead Rabbits and the Native Americans. Further into production,

I felt more part of the world, and things just developed on their own. We could make one group wear the same kind of hat, and another wear the same color vest, or have a stripe. The Dead Rabbits were a real gang, and the one thing we did know was that when they went into battle they had a red stripe along their trousers. We added undershirts that had red stripes, or were plain red.

The women were the most difficult to design for at first, because you look at pictures of Victorian women and everyone knows what they look like. We had to think how we could make the women of this made-up world go with the men, because Martin Scorsese wanted girls in the gangs as well. I wanted to make them look a little tougher, and started again looking through reference material. I found some images of women who actually wore trousers underneath their skirts. There was a group of women in the 1850s who were called "dress reformers." They were like early-day feminists. They tried to change things. The fashion didn't actually catch on, but they were a small group of women cutting up their long dresses, making the bottom bits into trousers and wearing them underneath their skirts. I used that as inspiration. So a lot of the girls have shorter-length skirts with trousers underneath and vests and jackets like the men.

Gang girls

The wardrobe supervisor is in charge of getting all the extras dressed. There were hundreds and hundreds of people who came in early in the morning and got everyone dressed. Some hung up the clothes, others came in the evening to get the extras undressed. The difficult thing was producing the numbers of costumes we needed. The effort was phenomenally huge. We began work in April. I settled in Rome in June, and we started out making prototype shapes. "A" to put on the actors, and "B" to try on extras. We had the small group of people—a workroom with a cutter and some seamstresses. Then by July we started going into factories and having jackets and pants mass produced. Ten months later we were still making things. Everything was made in Italy, and we rented some costumes from England, Italy, and America. The fabrics came mostly from Italy. But I also looked outside of traditional wools, silks, and cottons, and used some African-print fabrics, which I bought in England.

To create the different looks for the main actors, I first spoke with the director. He had quite strong ideas on how he saw Bill the Butcher. He saw him as sort of showing off sartorially, showing off his wealth in his clothing. So I started coming up with a few ideas, and met with Daniel. We tried on some shapes that we had, and it worked. I designed a range of clothes that he then would mix and match.

ABOVE: *Daniel Day-Lewis (Bill) wearing a "vest of certain distinction"*

When we first see Amsterdam, he's arrived in the Five Points after fifteen years in a house of reform. So his beginning look consists of clothes he's been given or found or collected. They don't go together, but they're functional. As he gets more successful, he has more money to spend on his clothing, so he does smarten up, but not to the extent of Bill the Butcher.

Bill

The first time we see Bill the Butcher, he's dressed for battle, which is a bit of a strange look. There is a full-length coat, which has always been in the script. During fitting, we developed a look which accentuated the actor's height and leanness. We made everything fairly tight fitting, and gave him very long, narrow trousers. Later on in the film, he is dressed in the fashion of the period. But again we're using that same exaggeration with narrow legs and sleeves. With more color. He wears frock coats, checked pants, and vests. And hats are very important.

Amsterdam

(107)

With Cameron Diaz, I started as with the other two actors, trying on various shapes that I had experimented with, to see what suited her. Surprisingly, she looked better in simpler things, simple shapes and simple colors. She ended up wearing a lot less than I would have originally hoped. She's the only girl in the film, so I had made hundreds of things for her, but we narrowed her wardrobe down to just a few key items.

Tweed, played by Jim Broadbent, is much more traditional. He's fairly accurate to the period, much more conservative in monochromatic colors—blacks, grays, and browns.

Monk McGinn is a successful gangster/fighter. He has made his money from winning battles for people, and he's one of those guys who shows off his wealth in his clothes, and he's proud of his look. He probably is the most up-to-date dresser, certainly the flashiest.

Boss Tweed

Jenny

(108)

One of the great things about working with Marty Scorsese is that he understands clothes and costumes, and he's got the most fantastic memory. I was really impressed when I showed him reference pictures and he could actually tell the difference between one year and the next.

First we compiled huge books full of reference pictures, photographs from the period, fashion photographs, obscure images from other films—all kinds of things. Then I went through it with the hair and makeup artists and we discussed the look together.

I actually don't start work by designing, I start with the fabrics. The most important thing to me is to be surrounded by fabrics that I like and inspire me. The shape then comes from the fabric. And the drawings are something I do quite a long way down the line. I do little scribble drawings for the people making the costumes, which are more diagramed. I don't actually do the full costume drawings until the end, when I've got the time to do them. There's not enough time to do a beautiful drawing and get the thing made and fitted and on set on time. The drawing's just a record.

We had a wide range of costumes. Apart from the gangs like the Dead Rabbits and the Native Americans—we've got people who live in the Brewery who are slum dwellers, really raggy-looking people. Then we've got politicians and smart people who live in grand houses. We also have things like the Chinese Pagoda scene with Chinese opera performers and jugglers in Chinese costumes. We did costumes for the ballet theater and the play of *Uncle Tom's Cabin*. It's a massive world.

ABOVE: *Extras at New York Harbor*

PAOLO SCALABRINO:

WARDROBE SUPERVISOR

QUESTIONER: What was your job?

PAOLO SCALABRINO: I would fit everybody and get them dressed—thousands of people that we saw daily, all over the studio.

Q: How many extras and people did you have to take care of at a time?

PS: We had an average of four fifty to five hundred a day, which is quite extraordinary. We went through approximately twelve thousand fittings since the beginning of the film. It was a continuous turnover of bodies.

Q: If there were twelve thousand fittings, how many costumes do you think you have?

PS: I think we made three thousand different costumes in our workshop, because we started from scratch. When working with Sandy Powell, who interprets the era and adds her own ideas, it was extremely important, mixing and assembling all the details. We had nearly seven thousand costumes that could be created by assembling the bits and pieces.

Q: How big is your staff?

PS: We had a permanent staff of twelve people. Then we had between eighteen to thirty-two people a day coming in to help dress.

Q: Not many people would have thought that this period was so colorful.

PS: I've admired Sandy Powell for a long time. She manages to be faithful to the historical side and at the same time give it flair. She has also managed to use stuff that's fashionable by today's standards.

Q: Is it the fabric, the texture and feel that then breeds a different look?

PS: We've bought fabrics and stamped fabrics. As the work progressed we invented things, and from there the actual look emerged. You can start with only a color, for example, and add a shape, and everything else happens afterward. The ideas build up as you're going along.

Q: Was there any advantage to being in Italy, where so many fabrics are made?

PS: I would say it was a great advantage, not only for the fabrics. There is a long tradition of incredible craftsmanship here, from the shoemakers to the jewelry makers to the dressmakers. This was a huge-scale production, involving thousands and thousands of people. Normally a production of this size is made in less-expensive countries. But you would never have gotten the style, the detail, and artistry that we achieved.

Q: When you first read the script were you excited, or did it frighten you with the enormous number of costume changes and the numbers of people that would be involved?

PS: I tend to work on big films, so it wasn't that frightening. I'd say I was pleased to be able to accept the challenge.

Q: What did you think of Dante Ferretti's interpretation of the Five Points, when you came on the sets for the first time?

OPPOSITE: *Leonardo DiCaprio being covered in dust*

PS: I remember spending a Saturday morning on the New York Harbor set by myself. I really felt I was in the Harbor. Everything was built when I got here. Dante is a master in every form and every sense.

Q: How did Sandy's vision of the costumes, and Dante's vision of the sets come together?

PS: They complemented each other. I think it's very evident, and whoever sees this film will realize that it's, in fact, a painting.

Q: You were very involved with dressing the different gangs.

PS: It was amusing because there wasn't very much written about them, and no detailed photographic documentation. Of the two main gangs, the Native Americans were more dandified than the Dead Rabbits.

It was amazing that we managed to find the number of appropriate faces we needed in Italy. The research that went into Anglo-Saxon faces was extremely difficult, and it was one of the reasons why we had so many fittings. It was a continual search to get the right looks.

Q: I understand that the director always wanted the costumes to be dirty. How did you meet that requirement?

PS: Well, our problem was solved by the master painters, who painted costumes from morning until they were right. Then over to Makeup to get dirty faces. They're meant to look soiled and have a hobo aspect to them. There were people in the Five Points who didn't wash.

LEFT: *Paradise Square inhabitants*

(113)

ALDO SIGNORETTI:

HAIR

QUESTIONER: There are so many people in this movie. How did you differentiate the looks of all the extras?

ALDO SIGNORETTI: As there are different gangs in the movie, we tried to give a different look for each gang so they could be recognized by their appearance. I especially like the Dead Rabbits, Leonardo DiCaprio's gang.

When the extras are on the set, they create the atmosphere. So how everyone looks is important. We added some of our own ideas to what we found in our research.

Q: Did you collaborate also with Manlio Rocchetti about how the hair fits in with his makeup?

AS: Yes, that's important. Hair, makeup, and costumes together create the look.

Q: How did you determine the looks of Daniel Day-Lewis and Leonardo DiCaprio?

AS: We discussed it and did quite a few tests. When we see Daniel at the beginning of the movie, he's wearing a tight leather cap. For the second part we tried several styles until we found the one that suited his character.

Q: Can you describe Leonardo DiCaprio's look?

AS: He's actually got several looks. The first time we see him he has a little braid on the side. And then he becomes more sharp, so he cuts his hair just a little shorter. Finally, his hair is a little darker, and he looks strong and masculine.

(117)

ABOVE: *Leonardo DiCaprio (Amsterdam) with sharp look*
OPPOSITE: *Hairstyle with braid*

MANLIO ROCCHETTI:

MAKEUP

QUESTIONER: Have you worked with Martin Scorsese before?

MANLIO ROCCHETTI: This is the fourth movie I've done with him, I worked on *The Last Temptation of Christ*, *The Age of Innocence*, and *Bringing Out the Dead*.

Q: What is he like to work with? How does he differ from other directors you've worked with?

MR: On Scorsese's movies, there is the opportunity to do more than makeup to help create the look and the character. In this movie, there are a lot of special effects: scars, wounds, dead people.

Q: How many people did you do makeup for?

MB: Every day there were in the range of one hundred and fifty to two hundred people who needed makeup. It takes about half an hour to make up each person. Some may require two hours. It depends on what role they are playing.

Q: How many people did you have to help you with the extras?

MR: We had an average of fifteen or sixteen extra makeup artists. This is the biggest movie I've ever worked on.

Q: If you have a scene with extras, what time would you get started in the morning?

MR: We would start at six in the morning.

When I was younger we started to do makeup at four in the morning on some movies. But the unions won't allow this anymore.

Q: How did you determine the looks of the principal characters?

MR: You have to think about a character's role and then do some tests. Daniel knew exactly what he wanted, he always had good ideas. He had studied his part for a long time, which helped us find the right look for him. The movie was also a challenge in terms of aging the characters. There is a ten- to fifteen-year difference between the opening scene and the rest of the film.

Q: What types of special effects did you use for the battle scenes?

MR: For the battles we painted some bruises and cuts on legs and arms, but the fish hook trick was the most difficult. This is where a fighter puts two fingers in both sides of the mouth of his opponent and tears his jaw. I had to do a video test first, reenacting the fingers in the mouth, then I made a mechanical head to put over the actor in order to create the special effect of tearing. It worked very well.

Q: Was it difficult to differentiate the various looks of the gangs with makeup?

MR: The difficulty with their makeup was that they had to be so dirty. Even so, Marty was always complaining that they were not dirty enough.

OPPOSITE: *Daniel Day-Lewis (Bill) in the final battle*

SIAN GRIGG:

MAKEUP FOR LEONARDO DiCAPRIO

I DID LEONARDO DiCAPRIO'S makeup on this film. He had asked me to do it months before, and it was one of those projects that we thought might never come to fruition, but it did. The script had evolved since I first read it, and it got a lot more complicated in terms of makeup. There's a scene where Leo's character, Amsterdam, gets beaten up, and Marty wanted five stages of recovery for him. That was a great challenge. The first time you see Amsterdam after he's been beaten and branded, his eyes are swollen shut, which involved the use of prosthetics and a lot of dirt and blood, because he's taken to an underground cave to recover. Gradually you see his recovery, so there needed to be stages to show

the progression of time. One eye starts to open, and then both eyes are open, and then at the end you see him coming out from underground with slight bruising, and the brand mark on his cheek is almost healed.

Every prosthetic is different, and you have to do it on the actor. Leo had never had prosthetics on him before, so that was a new experience for him. It wasn't easy for him to sit still for the three to four hours it took.

When we arrived in Rome, I met with Manlio Rocchetti and we had camera tests so we could gauge what sort of look we were all going for. I looked at how Daniel Day-Lewis was made up and sort of followed his lead to make sure Leo didn't stand out from everybody

(121)

OPPOSITE: *Leonardo DiCaprio (Amsterdam) after beating*
ABOVE: *Recovering from the beating*

else. We were on the same train of thought, so it worked out well. We had done quite a bit of research, as did Sandy Powell, the costume designer. I had a long meeting with her and we talked about the facial hair and whether Leo should have a beard or not. At the beginning of the film he's just come out of a house of reform, so he's meant to look quite broken down and haggard. And then he gets healthier and more fit.

Leo had very good ideas, and between us we worked out what we were going to do. It was a team effort. It's been wonderful to work with such a fantastic team, and watching Martin Scorsese work has been educational. He collaborates with everyone. For instance, he's the one who suggested the five stages of recovery. It was his visual idea.

Leo looks so different in this film. He looks more grown up and rugged than I've ever made him look before. The first time I worked with him he was twenty-one, and now he's twenty-six. This is a different role for him—he plays quite a rough character. It's a fascinating story, and a part of American history that most of us never knew about.

(122)

RIGHT: *Leonardo DiCaprio (Amsterdam)*
recovered with scars from beating

MICHAEL BALLHAUS:

QUESTIONER: You've made several movies with Martin Scorsese.

MICHAEL BALLHAUS: I've done five. This is number six. We missed each other for a couple of years, but now we're back together.

Q: Does it get more complex with each movie?

(126)

MB: This movie is different, it's probably the most exciting project that we've done because of the scale, script, and actors. Martin Scorsese is the most visual director I've ever worked with. It makes my job fascinating to work with

someone who thinks in terms of images and how to tell a story with them.

Q: What was your initial reaction to the script?

MB: I was very excited because of the images, sets, scenes—there are not many movies where you can do this much with imagery.

Q: When you prepared, did you start to research the time period? How did you decide what lighting schemes to use?

ABOVE: *Michael Ballhaus on the set*

MB: First of all, the period dictates what you do with the lights. For this movie specifically, we prepared by looking at a couple of movies set in that period. We found out what the light sources could be, that people smoked a lot, that there is a lot of atmosphere in the air. I used very few filters because it's all smoky. There's fog and smoke everywhere. Because this movie takes place in a part of a town that is very poor and dark, there's very little color.

Q: When did you start working with the production designer?

MB: Dante Ferretti had been working on this movie for almost a year. I saw a lot of his drawings, and we came to Italy in the spring of 2000 with Marty to look at the half-built sets. Dante is such an incredible artist that he doesn't need much guidance. We treated his sets like locations.

Q: Is there any particular setup or set that you enjoyed shooting on more than others?

MB: My favorite was the Chinese Pagoda scene, because it's so rich. We did some shots there that are spectacular.

Q: Are there any shots that you particularly liked?

MB: We did a lot of spectacular wide shots because of Dante's sets. We could photograph almost everything in every direction. We did

some shots at the harbor at night where we started on a close-up of a couple mourning. Then you see coffins, and as the camera is craning up, you see rows of coffins. The camera goes up over a ship and then pans over so you can see the harbor. All shot on the set.

In the Pagoda there was one shot that was very complicated to do, and it's one of my favorite shots. Bill the Butcher is on the stage, and the camera is behind him looking at the audience. He's giving a speech about America. The camera pivots around him and sees him in front and then moves back and sees the stage really wide. It's like seeing the whole Pagoda in one shot from the stage looking at the audience, and then going all the way back and seeing the stage.

There are two other shots that I particularly like. One is a very specific scene which starts on immigrants coming off a ship, being recruited for the military. Then the camera moves alongside, and you see them getting their uniforms, and walking onto the next ship dressed as soldiers, and while they're walking up the steps to the ship you see coffins of dead soldiers being lowered from the ship. It's almost one shot, just intercut with two shots. It's a scene that tells the whole story with images in one shot.

Q: When people ask you what this movie's about, what do you say?

MB: It's about love, about hate, and many of the essential conflicts in life. It's drama, the drama of life.

OVERLEAF: *The Chinese Pagoda scene*

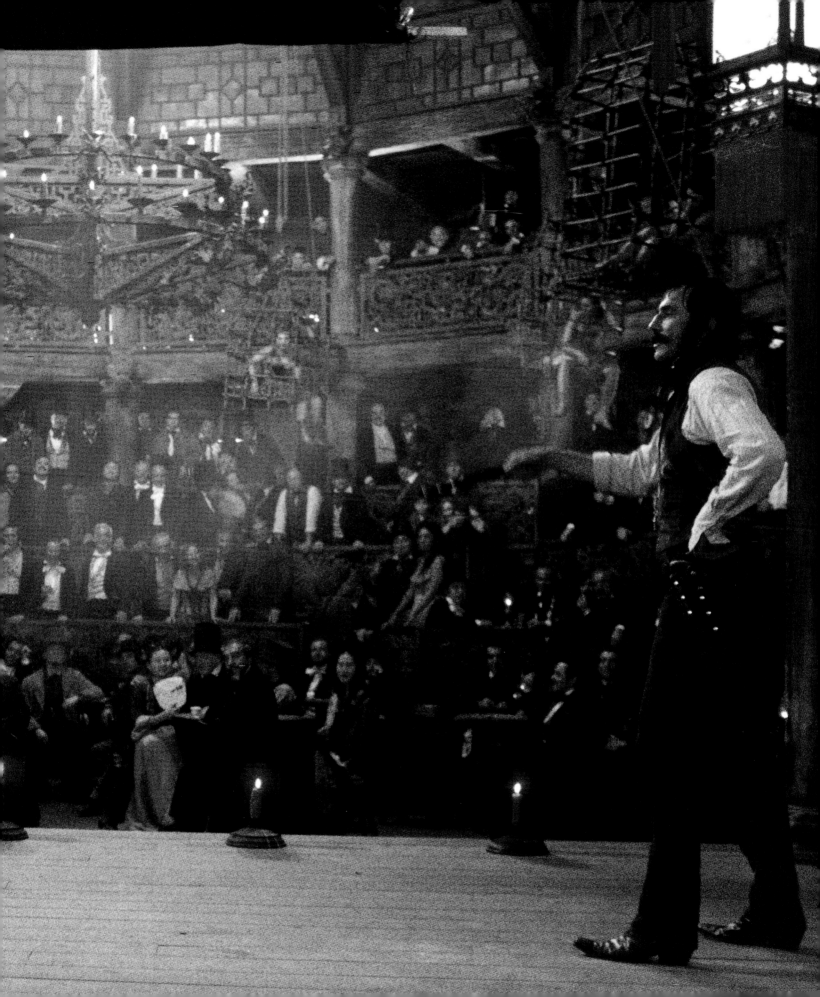

WHEN I FIRST CAME ON THE MOVIE I had no idea why we were making the movie in Rome. So in March of 2000, after I joined Miramax and Marty, I thought I'd better go take a look and see why they chose Italy. Obviously he couldn't make the picture, which was set in 1840 to 1863, in New York, but why Italy? I often pick the movies I do in cities with good restaurants, so I assumed that was part of the reason. When I arrived at Cinecittà (where we shot probably over 95 percent of the movie) the first person I met walking on one of the thoroughfares at the studio was Dante Ferretti, whom I had worked with over twenty years ago on a Marco Ferreri movie with Gerard Depardieu and Marcello Mastroianni. I immediately knew why we were in Italy. The craftsmanship goes back to Michelangelo. There's something in the water, or I suspect it's something in the Chianti. But whatever it is, because of the production design and the craftsmen and the workers, and the dollar-lira exchange, it became quite obvious to me that Rome, Cinecittà, Italy was the right place to make this movie.

I was the first American production person on the ground for a long period of time. I was in Rome six months prior to the arrival of most of the others. I had made movies of considerable size in the past, but had no idea how big and complicated this movie would be when I signed on. On the first day of shooting, the right reason to be in Italy became the wrong reason to be in Italy, because the sets were so large that we had to fill them with approximately 750 extras. The story is about Irish Americans and Anglo Americans, and we were surrounded by Italians, who have a much different look.

To find the extras we went to American army bases and to the embassy. We tried to get blond-haired, blue-eyed people who were living in Italy. They were placed in the foreground, with the dark-haired, dark-skinned people in the background. Instructions were often difficult to convey because of the language barrier. We had enormous scenes of people coming off boats, and Union Army troops.

We had an American stunt coordinator for the run of the movie, George Aguilar. And then Vic Armstrong ran the second and third action units. There was no way that one unit could have finished this movie in a reasonable period of time. Marty would go back and forth on his golf cart and supervise the other units that were shooting. That's the only way we could accomplish all the scenes.

We had costumes from every place that had them—America, France—Italy, obviously—England, Austria. We rented every costume that was available that Sandy Powell thought was right for our period and up to our standards. And then we manufactured a tremendous amount. The wardrobe facility was bigger than an armory. We built dyeing facilities and hair and makeup facilities to cope with the tremendous amount of people.

The beauty of making a movie at a studio is that all of the sets are there. I'm the kind of executive producer who likes to be there

(132)

OPPOSITE: *A caged prostitute at the Chinese Pagoda*

ABOVE: *Rival fire gangs battle it out*

before the crew arrives, to make sure everything's moving well. There are lots of activities to prepare for: sets coming up, dailies, and sets that are finished and can be wrapped. You really want to be the advance guard for Marty. You are the eyes and ears of the director when he can't be there. If there's a problem you call his attention to it, so it can be fixed. Because we had the stars on the lot and the interest of the paparazzi, we had to have a closed set, which was easy to do at the studio. Leo could play basketball, Daniel could

practice his knife throwing, and Cameron could walk around and not be bothered or photographed. It was a great advantage.

In a movie like this there are no easy days. I was in Italy for fourteen months. There are scenes that were more fun to shoot than others. Any scene that had Union soldiers in it I liked. I would take them out and drill them. My fondest story about Marty, who is asthmatic, is that he gave me dispensation to smoke my cigar at night on the set. That was a true indication of how well we get along.

JOE REIDY:

FIRST ASSISTANT DIRECTOR

QUESTIONER: You have done nine films as assistant director with Martin Scorsese. How did this one differ from the others?

JOE REIDY: Although Marty has often worked in the Italian-American world that he was most familiar with, he has explored other worlds in his films. Each time, he immerses himself in the subject; it becomes a part of him, as real to him as something he grew up with. On *Gangs of New York* he was working in a foreign country making a film about New York. I think it put him in this very special place that had nothing to do with Italy. He became totally involved in the film. It was in a totally created world. And although he was working with many familiar collaborators—Dante Ferretti, Michael Ballhaus, Daniel Day-Lewis, and myself—the cast was primarily English, Scottish, and Irish, with Italian extras.

Q: How did you prepare for this film? Were you involved in the historical research?

JR: Marty's research had gone on for twenty years. I wasn't part of that. When I came on, he had already assembled a rather large research library, and had read and absorbed this material. We all had to read the material in order to re-create the world. And it was more than reading. There were visits to the

New York City Fire Museum, for instance. There were a lot of resources. People like technical advisor Luc Sante were helpful. It was more important to study the lifestyle than facts and figures.

Q: I remember Luc Sante saying that he was around to tell you what people in those days did when they had a cold.

JR: Those are the kinds of details we needed to know. He is someone who understood the richness of life, the details, and also the spirit of things. We don't necessarily say we're making a historically accurate film. We've tried to be as accurate as possible of course, but it was more important to have the impression of the life. Luc is someone who has the writer's eye, the poet's eye.

(135)

ABOVE: *Joe Reidy with Martin Scorsese*

Q: Is this the biggest movie that Martin Scorsese has made?

JR: Of the films that I've done with him, yes, absolutely. We had around twenty-five thousand extra man-days, and that's very, very large. Then the size of the sets, and the complexity of the set pieces, and there are many of them. In a smaller story these would have been the climactic event of the film. The prizefight, the fire, the riots, the battles, the Chinese Pagoda sequence. Everything had to be planned and prepared and detailed.

Q: What were the set pieces like?

JR: There was a steady-cam shot inside Satan's Circus. It introduced a number of the characters, including Bill the Butcher and Hell-Cat Maggie. It showed a lot of the life of the time, what a dive like that would be—all in one shot. That was pretty complicated. There were a number of very special or spectacular shots that told the story that were also bravura camera movements, or that had remarkable elements in them. They don't dominate the film or overwhelm the story or the detail that went into the story, or the background or the sets. They're in keeping with the storytelling. But you're also looking at all of the details in the frame and what's actually going on. The camera move or the camerawork itself isn't the most unique element; it's how everything works together.

(136)

Q: How did you get all that detail and life ready for the camera?

RIGHT: *The theater assassination scene*

JR: It started early on in the research phase, because in a specific set piece, we had to know who's there, who's in it, and—beyond the principals—what the extras are like. For a contemporary film you might need twenty-five businessmen or a few tourists, because the world is familiar to the audience. But here, every person has a little story, and it was our opportunity to re-create the detail of the life of that time in the Five Points, a unique place that no one has seen before in a film. Everyone had to be dressed in a special way. Everyone had a little bit of action. So apart from saying how many people were in a place, we spent some time talking about their behavior in advance. We tried to make it as detailed and as specific as possible in every scene. When we shot the Chinese Pagoda scene we had to think about social classes. We would do some research, consult with our technical advisors, and then go to Marty. We wanted to be as historically accurate as possible, and yet not lose the artistry or the story.

Q: Was costume designer Sandy Powell involved in this process?

JR: She had specific looks for specific kinds of people, and sometimes she would say that we needed to see more of a certain type of person. That kind of collaboration was very helpful to Marty.

Q: What kinds of businesses were in the Five Points?

JR: In preproduction, Chris Surgent, the second assistant director, and I came up with lists of scenarios of what types of work people would be doing in Paradise Square and what average people would be doing if they were not just walking around. That formed a sort of a framework. The wrong behavior draws attention to itself and detracts from the principal action, so sometimes we had to be much simpler. We had to remember that this was New York—it wasn't the New York of today, but it has more in common with it than we had expected. We had to use our New York sensibilities, because it was a crazy and chaotic place then, as it is now.

Q: What was it like, staging the battle scenes and working with an action unit director?

JR: Battle scenes are like any stunt work in that you have to do them very carefully. Safety is important, and difficult here because we were working in several different languages at the same time—English, Italian, and Croatian. We had a lot of stunt people and stunt people in training. We had to go very slowly. The costumes and the weaponry were so unusual and had their own characteristics, making everything a little tricky. Vic Armstrong, our action-unit director, had done medieval and other period scenes before. His experience with hand-to-hand combat using swords, knives, and clubs was very helpful. And we had outstanding stunt coordinators in George Aguilar and Claudio Pacifico. There were rehearsals and a lot of warmups to learn the hand-to-hand combat moves safely.

Vic Armstrong was someone Marty had wanted to work with for quite a while, but he had not done a film that required Vic's expertise. Vic would carry out Marty's ideas from the shot list and help us stage the overall look of the master scenes. Marty was inspired by other films that he knows well. The assistant directors and Vic also had seen a lot of films that we used as reference, such as

(138)

ABOVE: *Daniel Day-Lewis (Bill) makes his entrance at the fire*

Chimes at Midnight. We also watched many of the Russian masters who specialized in montage, like Eisenstein in *October*, *Strike*, and *Potemkin*, and some American films, such as *Big Country*, for part of a fight scene and for a very specific special effect with the sword. The movie *San Francisco* had a totally different kind of sequence, with an earthquake, but its shooting style was helpful.

Marty does not just shoot anything. He's always very clear. And every shot has to mean something, has to convey a feeling or information, or be part of an editing scheme. So when Vic was shooting the second unit, Marty was able to see video playback, or to join him and watch him work because we were at the same

studio. This saved us a lot of time. They worked very well together.

Q: How did Marty work with the actors?

JR: The most important thing for Marty is creating an atmosphere in which the actors can work. So my first responsibility was to help him create this atmosphere. Marty helped prepare the actors by making all the research available to them. They worked on their accents with Tim Monich, or they had fight instruction with George Aguilar and Dominick Vandenburg, a former member of the French Foreign Legion. As we approached the beginning of photography he began to rehearse the scenes that we'd be doing, in shooting order.

There was always smoke in the room and some gas lamps of the period. All of those elements helped the actors get into their roles. Marty wanted to keep the atmosphere going for the actors. He loved it when the actors in Daniel's gang were sitting around playing cards and horsing around between takes (like their movie characters). He liked the crew to be quiet if the gang men needed to make noise.

Q: What was the importance of the sets?

JR: Dante and Francesca did a lot of research, but Marty also wanted Dante to have some artistic freedom. Marty would often ask, "Dante, can you do something special for me here?" Dante would have a certain devilish look and say, "I'll try." For example, we didn't have accurate pictures of the Old Brewery and what went on inside. We only had some descriptions from newspaper articles, so Dante had some freedom in re-creating it. His pièce de resistance is the Pagoda.

Marty had held this project in his heart for twenty-five years, and he had a burning passion to tell this story. That permeated every decision he made and every action we took. He always feels that way about his films. I think what made this one different is that it's a story that he had longed to tell for so long that when he was finally on the set and his dream was about to become a reality, he had to stop and think. Even in the excitement of the moment, he always stopped to think about what was right for the scene, what was right in this moment, and how to make whatever he was doing at that moment unique, special, and better.

Another important feature of the film is the source music. He wanted music that would have been appropriate for the Irish, the African Americans, and for the time. We found good music advisors in Rome who love Irish music and know it well. We had African music and songs. Certain lines of songs had to appear on camera—the song in Satan's Circus for example, *New York Gals* sung by Finbar Furey, was of the period and sung in the Five Points.

One of the most special shots in the movie was what we called the Anthill shot. It was a cutaway of the inside of the brewery. It showed the principal actors coming out of the underground tunnels as well as the life of all of the people inside the brewery. This was an instance where Marty went over the specific behaviors of the people in each of the rooms in that cutaway. We had a list of potential actions and cast them specifically. He had envisioned this shot for twenty years. In Luc Sante's book *Low Life* there's a diagram of a New York tenement—I believe from a nineteenth-century newspaper—that showed what went on inside. We used that as an inspiration for the shot. When we see the end frame of this shot we see a whole impression of the place. Each element was detailed and gone over—it wasn't just generic background action. I had to have a separate story in each frame to make it work. It took many meetings over a course of months to arrive at what the shot ended up looking like.

ABOVE: *Interior of the Old Brewery with its honeycomb structure*

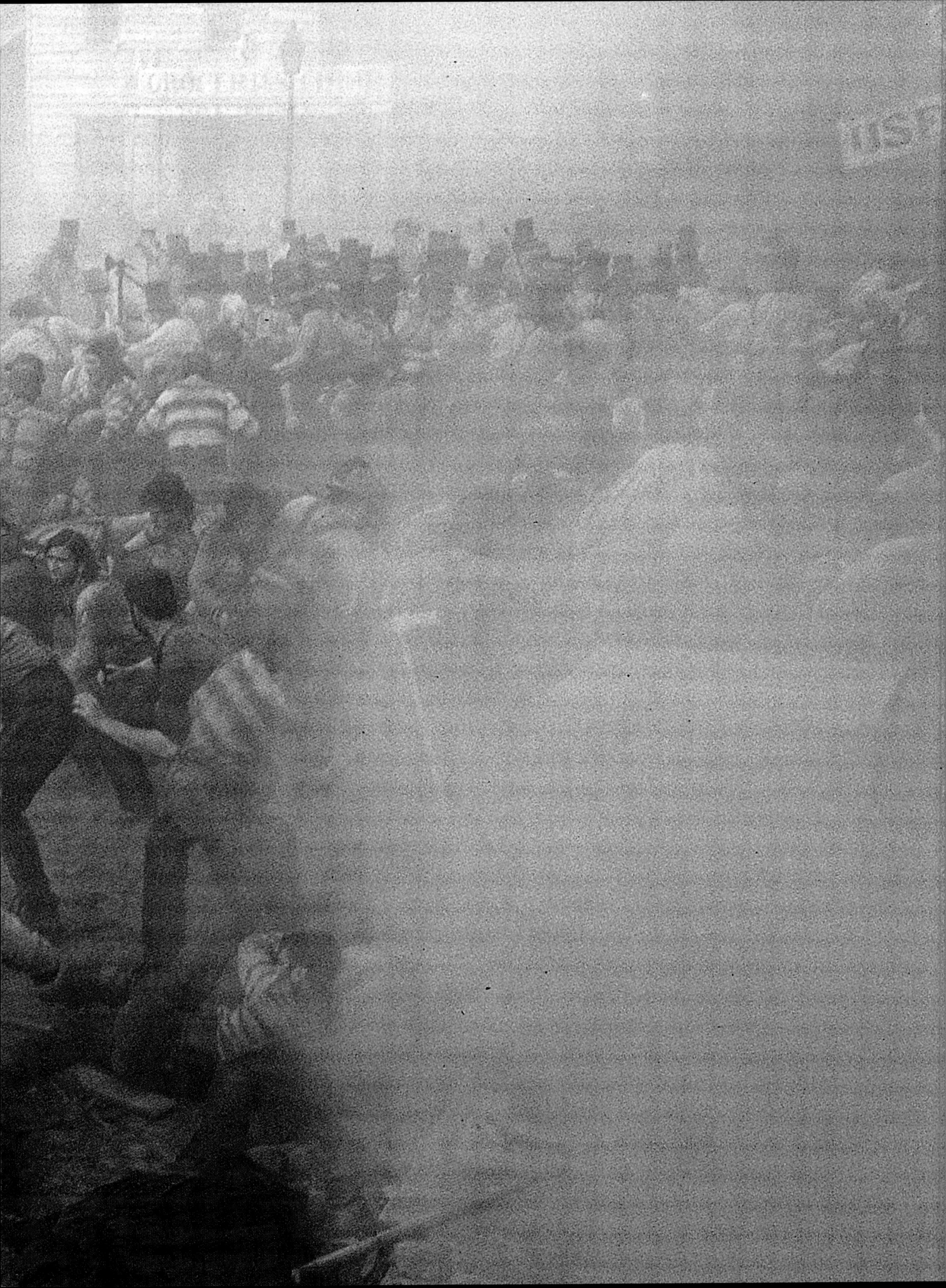

ACTION UNIT

VIC ARMSTRONG:

ACTION UNIT DIRECTOR

Hong Kong and couldn't do it. He's an absolute joy to work with and he's a movie encyclopedia. When we were walking around the sets one day and getting ready for the first fight, he was actually quoting me shots I'd done on *Henry V* that I couldn't even remember.

Q: How exactly did your collaboration work?

VA: Collaboration is the secret of the business of working with a first unit director and action unit director, and Marty is wonderful. No matter when you call him, no matter how stressful the situation is, he'll always think about the question, come up with an answer, take your advice, assimilate that advice, and then come up with a solution that is great for the show. I really enjoyed it when he came onto my set, and I think he enjoyed it as well. He has a great sense of humor.

Q: You worked with Florian, the son of Michael Ballhaus, Scorsese's director of photography.

QUESTIONER: What was your job on the set?

VIC ARMSTRONG: Action unit director. I took care of all the action and the fighting. Marty had a great deal of work with the actors and storytelling, and we have two major fights in the movie: the 1840s gang battle between the Dead Rabbits and the Native Americans and the Draft Riots in the 1860s. There's a cross-section of people in the riots: soldiers and protesters on Broadway, and gangs in the Five Points.

(144)

Q: Had you worked with Martin Scorsese before?

VA: I hadn't worked with Marty before. I was offered *Cape Fear*, but unfortunately I was in

ABOVE: *Leonardo DiCaprio with Vic Armstrong and Martin Scorsese on the set*

ABOVE: *Daniel Day-Lewis (Bill) and Leonardo DiCaprio (Amsterdam) in their final confrontation*

VA: Working with Michael Ballhaus was wonderful. He's such an experienced gentleman, and I was lucky to have Florian, who has the same sense of humor as me, and the same work ethic. We had a really great relationship. My daughter is one of the stuntwomen on the film, so it is sort of a family affair.

Q: Which of the action scenes stands out in your mind?

VA: I think the most interesting battle scene is the first one, because there are no guns, only medieval-type weapons set in a Dickensian time. It was quite difficult to come up with different ways of killing people, maiming people—all the usual fun stuff—and just coming up with visual ideas to keep the audience interested—not just bludgeoning people.

Q: Are there any particularly exciting stunts in this movie?

VA: There are a lot of unique stunts and some great fighting in this movie. George Aguilar is a wonderful stunt coordinator. He set the style and tone, and trained the actors. The actors are

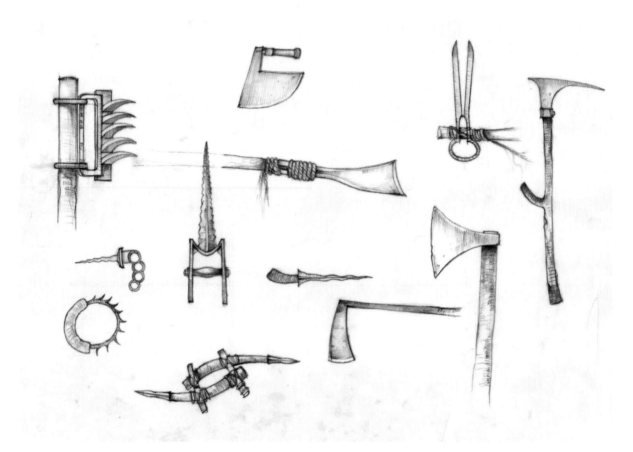

ABOVE: *Weapons designed for the movie*

ABOVE: *Liam Neeson (Priest Vallon) in the opening battle scene*

incredibly devoted, and they gave it absolutely 100 percent. So I think it's going to be realistic in the respect that the guys were really into it. We tried to stay away from "film-y" things but at the same time make the action extravagant enough to be entertaining. The sets are fantastic. Dante Ferretti has great flair, and the whole movie has an extravagant look to it.

Q: If someone asked you what this movie's about, how would you describe *Gangs of New York*?

VA: I'd say it's Charles Dickens in New York with a *Mad Max* type of action and slant on life.

(147)

ABOVE: *Leonardo DiCaprio (Amsterdam) and Gary Lewis (McGloin) in their boxing scene*

GEORGE AGUILAR:

STUNT COORDINATOR

MY JOB AS STUNT COORDINATOR means choreographing fight scenes. *Gangs of New York* is different from Scorsese's other movies because it's a period and action film. I had worked with Marty on *Bringing Out the Dead*, which was his previous picture and totally different from this one. He's very inclusive, and listens to ideas from everybody while trying to keep things historically accurate. He doesn't go for just what looks best—he sticks to making things real.

Gangs of New York was a huge job mostly because of the number of people involved. The battles had, instead of fifty against fifty, three hundred against three hundred. At rehearsal we divided our three hundred into little platoons like an army, and put somebody in charge of each group. It made it a lot easier than trying to talk to three hundred people at once.

We had done research on the fighting styles, techniques, and weapons they used at the time, because fighting then was so different from modern-day fighting. The stances are different. They used different parts of the body, and fighting was a lot less structured. For instance, a fistfight wasn't just a fistfight—there was eye gouging and ear biting.

We rehearsed early on with Leo and Daniel and got a look that we all were comfortable with. They did all of their fighting themselves, it was mostly hand-to-hand fighting.

The weapons of each gang had their own look. The Rabbits were more primitive, so their weapons were garden-variety weapons: shovels, picks, and axes. The Natives were a little more stylized: they had scythes and strange-looking weapons that you rarely see in movies. The opening scene looks at once medieval and futuristic—you don't know what time frame you're in.

The stuntmen were predominantly Italian. But when we had huge calls, there were Americans, Czechs, Slovaks, Croatians, and British. The toughest part of having an international crew is communication. You have to take your time and make sure everyone understands.

My favorite scenes are probably the first battle between Vallon and Bill the Butcher, for the sheer scope of it—and the boxing scene between McGloin and Amsterdam. It's the first time you see the old boxing technique.

Leo also enjoyed fighting, and he's very good at it. Cameron had a lot of stunt stuff during the Draft Riots. I'd worked with her once before and she's incredible. Physically she's as talented as anyone I've ever seen.

It's tough to define *Gangs of New York*. It's an epic in that it's a big-scale movie. It's not really a love story, but there's a love story in it. It's not an action movie, but there's action in it. It's not really a drama, but there's drama in it . . . so I think it encompasses everything.

(149)

QUESTIONER: You've worked with Marty for a long time on many kinds of films. How is this film different from the other films you've worked with him on?

THELMA SCHOONMAKER: It was a great pleasure to be working on such a big canvas: battle scenes, riots, but also a very intense personal story. Of course the big challenge has been to balance the historical story against the personal story.

It's been fascinating to discover so much about the period and to find out what a horrible state certain parts of New York City were in around the time of the Civil War, and how that impacted the city so terribly, with this enormous Draft Riot exploding, which most people aren't even aware happened. It's been a very different film for us in many ways. We've done historical films before, but nothing on this scale, with major battles, riots scenes, and all. It's been a tremendous amount of fun to be exposed to all of those new challenges.

Q: Marianne Bower was talking about these folders that Marty created for the actors and the cast. Was this part of your preparation?

TS: Actually not in this case. On other films we've worked on—for example *Kundun*, I did learn a great deal about the Tibetans and Tibetan history. But for this film it was really better for me not to know too much, so that when Marty and I were looking at dailies [the scenes shot the day before] or working on a scene, I was seeing it almost as the audience would see it. And then together we would discover if there was any more information he needed. It's always better for me not to participate during the shooting or the preparation of the films, in order to have a colder, more objective eye. In fact I love to go on the set to watch Marty and the actors work, but it's better for me not to go, because if I'm there, and the crew is saying, "Oh, wait 'til you see this beautiful tracking shot, we've just laid track for two miles and It's gonna be great"—it's much better for me not to have my mind pre-influenced by that, but just to see it up on the screen.

Marty talks constantly to me during dailies of his feelings about what he's shot, about the performances of the actors, and how he wants to shape the scene. I take extensive notes and then begin carving the scene out with that in mind, and my own feelings of course.

(154)

ABOVE: *Thelma Schoonmaker editing the film*

Q: Do you always go on location when he's shooting?

TS: Actually no, I've missed both times, in Morocco—on *Last Temptation* and on *Kundun*. Because we were developing the film in the lab in New York, it was better for me to be here and see the dailies immediately in case there was a camera problem or something, so I could tell the crew. But fortunately with *Gangs*, because we were shooting at the great Cinecittà Studios, I was able to go and have a wonderful location experience in Rome, which I think my crew, and all the production crew, enjoyed thoroughly.

Q: Did you find it different working in Italy?

TS: It's a different work ethic. Fortunately, I had two of my best assistants with me, so we could structure the editing room the way we wanted to. Italians think we're nuts for working such long hours. They like to go home to their meals and are shocked by Americans eating in the editing room. Of course, having just worked on the documentary about the Italian cinema, to be on the lot where so many of those great movies were made was a wonderful experience.

Q: What about when you shift from production into post-production?

TS: During production our days are driven by the pressure of the dailies pouring out of the lab, getting them synced up and screening them for Marty. Once we got back to the States it became strictly about the editing, and it was a very much quieter, more concentrated experi-ence, with Marty able to sit in the editing room and evaluate what he'd shot, and how it was working and the first cuts that I'd done.

Q: Did you work together with him, or did you assemble something, and then show it to him?

TS: It varied, of course, from scene to scene, but generally he has a very strong hand in the editing. He's a great editor, Marty. He cut *Mean Streets* by himself. He could cut all his films by himself, frankly, and he taught me everything I know about editing.

He tells me how he thinks the editing should go, and then I put together a first cut. He comes in and works with me from that point on. He's very much engaged in the edit-ing. I think all great directors have to know a lot about editing. Marty also knows an immense amount about camerawork, and designs the camerawork on his films.

Q: What were some of the biggest challenges of this particular movie?

TS: Well, we had a lot of fun with the open-ing battle sequence and the Draft Riots scene. Marty had experimented with different camera speeds, and so putting together the montage in the battle scene was challenging. But there are other things in the film that presented different challenges. For example, the climactic scene in the middle of the film at the Chinese Pagoda. Just because there was so much footage, you had to get on top of it all. It was extremely rich. And once we got it in shape, we've hardly ever gone back to touch it.

BRUTAL MURDER OF A NEGRO MAN IN CLARKSON STREET BY THE RIOTERS, WHO STRIPPED OFF HIS CLOTHES AND HUNG HIM TO A TREE, AFTERWARDS BURNING THE BODY, ON MONDAY, JULY 13.

ABOVE: *Goya-esque engraving of the Draft Riots from the* New York Illustrated News, *July 25, 1863*

Q: This film has certain graphic imagery, like the newspaper headlines and engravings. Is that different for you?

TS: I think Marty felt strongly about including the engravings of the actual Draft Riots, terrible images like the lynching of blacks, to make the audience understand that this really happened. The images are stunning. Michael Powell once said Marty's use of violence is akin to Goya's *Disasters of War*, a famous series of etchings in which Goya graphically portrayed war atrocities. Goya felt compelled as an artist to document them, but also to let the world know what was happening. So it was interesting for me when Marty showed me one particular engraving which struck me as looking like a Goya.

Q: Could you talk just a little bit about ADR [Additional Dialogue Recording], and how the mix works?

TS: We've done a lot more Additional Dialogue in this film than we normally do, partially because there are so many accents in this movie we have to re-record just to make things a little clearer. When we finish editing the film, the dialogue and ADR editors, the effects and foley editors take our cut and start building many tracks of dialogue, ambience, sound effects, explosions, gunfire, people screaming, all kinds of things. The music editor builds the composer's music to fit the film. Then we go to a mixing studio and start combining all these many tracks—there can be as many as 200 tracks on a complex scene—into "stems" or 8-track elements for each area (dialogue, sound effects, music, etc.) Tom Fleischman then weaves all these 8-track elements together to create drama, emotion and excitement in the action scenes.

It's a very important part of filmmaking, because you can create a different feeling about a scene by how you mix the music, or certain sound effects. Frank Warner, our sound editor for *Raging Bull*, taught us that sometimes the most powerful thing you can do is to take the sound out at a dramatic moment, and then bring it back in for effect. Marty is exacting in what he wants in a mix. I remember once Tom had done a very beautiful fade-out and Marty said: "Yes, but I heard you fading." He wanted the fade to be almost invisible.

Q: What are Foleys?

TS: In the early days films were silent, but they were always accompanied by music—a piano, or a string quartet. Sometimes they even had quartets on the set to put actors in the right mood. And in big cities there were often people behind the screen doing sound effects—cracking a whip, or firing a gun at the appropriate moment.

After sound came in, a man named Jack Foley originated the idea of amplifying the sounds human beings or objects made by recording the sounds of a person opening a door, or footsteps on a gravel path separately and adding them into the soundtrack to enhance it. These sounds are now called "foleys".

Q: How do you work out the rhythm and pacing? When you finally have the movie together and you may want to make something a little quicker, or slow it down?

TS: Rhythm and pacing is everything. For building character, for example, how often you use a close-up or a medium shot—which actor you are on at a certain time can completely change an actor's performance. Rhythm is one of the most important things in editing, we're always striving to achieve the right dramatic impact.

Q: And what would you say was your biggest challenge on this movie?

TS: I think to get the historical story and the personal story in balance. To make the historical background hook up with our characters properly and in the most dramatic way. Marty's been thinking about this material for so long. It's a fascinating chunk of New York history, neglected by most historians. And it all happened in the area where he grew up.

INT. UNDERGROUND CHAMBER

VALLON a man in black, is shaving while his son, AMSTERDAM, watches in the shadows. He finishes shaving and hands the razor to Amsterdam, who begins to wipe the blade on the bottom of his jacket.

VALLON (*Sharply*)
No, son. Never. (*More gently*) The blood stays on the blade.

He helps Amsterdam slide the blade back into the pouch.

VALLON (*CONT'D*)
Someday you'll understand.

AMSTERDAM (*V.O.*)
Some of it I half remember. And the rest... the rest I took from dreams.

He fastens a white priest's collar around his throat.

VALLON
Michael, the Archangel, defend us in battle, be our protector against the snares and the wickedness of the Devil.

He hangs a St. Michael medal around Amsterdam's neck.

VALLON (*CONT'D*)
Now, son. Who's that?

(160) AMSTERDAM
Saint Michael.

VALLON
Who is it?

AMSTERDAM
Saint Michael.

VALLON
And what did he do?

AMSTERDAM
He cast Satan out of Heaven.

VALLON
Good boy!

Vallon nods slightly, and Amsterdam blows out the candle.

INT. UNDERGROUND TUNNEL AND ROOMS

Amsterdam clutches his father's hand as they emerge from the chamber and move in and out of candlelight along a tunnel cut into the earth. Vallon holds in his other hand a distinctive iron Celtic cross. The haunting music rises over—

Human and animal sounds. A Madonna and Child crudely painted on a wall in a chamber where McGLOIN hones blades sewn into his boots while HAPPY JACK studs a belt with broken glass. As Amsterdam passes, McGloin unexpectedly gives him a friendly wink.

Happy Jack and McGloin fall in behind Vallon and Amsterdam. The battle hymn continues as they walk on.

Happy Jack reaches down and gives the boy's hair a friendly tousle. Amsterdam yanks his head away. The three grown-ups laugh briefly. They proceed into—

Another chamber where a man stuffs a hat with scraps of leather to make a helmet. Another paints ritual markings on his face. A girl dusts a man's long beard with gunpowder. A woman attaches a set of iron claws to her fingers. As Vallon passes this room, these warriors fall in behind them. The rhythmic music and chanting is joined by—

INT. OLD BREWERY—DAY

Blacksmiths hammer at crude weapons. Amsterdam glimpses faces in the shadows, peering out from behind ancient brewery machines. He finds himself standing next to **JOHNNY**, a boy around his own age.

JOHNNY
Amsterdam!

AMSTERDAM
Hello, Johnny.

JOHNNY
What's the battle?

AMSTERDAM
Natives against the Dead Rabbits.

JOHNNY
Which are you?

A warrior passes by carrying an enormous pike decorated nearly from blade to butt with dead rabbit pelts.

AMSTERDAM
What do you think? Dead Rabbits.

He hurries to catch up with the gang. Johnny follows. As the gang marches on, we drop back to see how cavernous this place is in a cross-section of the building—hundreds of people and animals living together in squalor. Ahead, the black-

smiths are handing out weapons to the line of gang members as they pass. Amsterdam gets closer. People make way for them. Ahead, an imposing figure stands in the dark by the door.

VALLON
Well, Monk? For the last time, are you with us or not?

MONK
For the last time, Vallon: I'm with you if the money is right, and if it's not...

VALLON
I'll give you ten per notch.

MONK
Ten?

VALLON
You have my word.

MONK
Ten per notch?

VALLON
Per new notch.

MONK
Then I'm your man.

Monk grasps a notched war club, kicks at the door, and light crashes in like a wave. Vallon heads into it. Amsterdam, unsure, follows after him, swept along, and Monk follows him, towering over him like the Holy Ghost.

(161)

EXT. PARADISE SQUARE— CONTINUOUS—DAY

Patches of snow on the ground of a place as strange and bleak as an alien planet. Vallon steps out of the Old Brewery, followed by Amsterdam, Monk, and the others. He sends Amsterdam to watch from one of the sidewalks.

Silence as they assemble outside the dilapidated building. On either side of it wind alleys and streets lined with dirty shacks. Perhaps this is England in the Middle Ages, or some post-apocalyptic town not worth fighting for. Pigs rut in the snow.

Another gang appears, almost twice the size of Vallon's—armed like Visigoths with hand-forged clubs and pitchforks. A man in a long coat, lean and fierce, steps forward. He has mismatching eyes—one of them glass, engraved with an American eagle. The other surveys Vallon's gang.

BILL THE BUTCHER
Is this it, Priest? The Pope's new army? A few crusty bitches and a handful of rag-tags?

VALLON
You swore this was a battle between warriors, not mobs. So warriors was all I brought.

Fifty more Celts from other sects, distinguished by their colors, emerge from hovels and streets and fall in behind Vallon, the gangs now equal in number.

IRISH GANG LEADERS
The O'Connell Guards—the Plug Uglies—the Shirt Tails—the Chichesters—the Forty Thieves—

When they're done, everyone waits for Bill to speak.

BILL THE BUTCHER
Bene.

Bill opens his long coat. Inside, from a leather belt, hang a cleaver, knives, and other butcher's instruments. Bill selects his weapons, a cleaver and a big knife.

BILL THE BUTCHER (CONT'D)
By the ancient laws of combat, we are met on my challenge to reclaim the Five Points for them born rightwise to this land, from the foreign invader who's encroached upon our streets. The last time we met I was shamed! But in shame or glory, we won't never rest until last of him's been drove into the sea!

The Natives shake their weapons and roar.

VALLON
By the ancient laws of combat, I accept the challenge of the so-called Natives, who plague our people at every turn. We seek no quarrels, but will run from none neither, and the hand that tries to lay us low will be swift cut off!

The roar is deafening. Every weapon is hoisted and bristling. Smoke rises from the beard of the man who dusted it with gunpowder.

BILL THE BUTCHER
May the Christian Lord guide my hand against the gangrenous creep of your roman popery.

VALLON
Prepare to receive the True Lord.

The air is suddenly full of battle cries as the two gangs hurl across Paradise Square. Through fleet images and sensory impressions we see a flurry of knives and sharpened buckles, glass-studded leather and fists.

Amsterdam glimpses his father in the middle of the fray. Monk dispatches Natives with his war club. Hell-Cat Maggie flies into a Native and pins him to the ground.

HELL-CAT MAGGIE
Whadya got two of, that you only need one?

As her iron talons dive at the man's face, Amsterdam looks away—and sees Bill, wading through the combat, wielding his cleaver, cutting down one Dead Rabbit after another. On the rooftops, kids watch, including Johnny.

The sounds of the battle fade except for the relentless slashing as the camera rises above the square and the heaving shadows of bodies falling and rising.

Suddenly we're descending again to the ground, moving through the fighting men to Amsterdam's eyes.

He glimpses his father battling Natives. In intermittent flashes he sees: Bill coming at him, the glint off his knife, his father turning too late, the hand plunging down, once, twice, three times. Vallon falls, the knife sticking out of his chest.

Bill drops to his knees and gathers Vallon in his arms.

BILL THE BUTCHER
Here! Look to me! Who is this? Who is this under my knife?

The Natives and Rabbits turn and look at the tableau of Bill holding the bloody priest. They still their weapons. Johnny watches from a rooftop. Bill lays Vallon out on the ground and strokes his face.

BILL THE BUTCHER (*CONT'D*)
Easy now. It won't be long.

Amsterdam runs hard across the square, almost magically parting the crowd as he goes. He reaches the dying man and buries his face in his chest.

AMSTERDAM
Father...!

VALLON
Oh, son...I can't cross the river with steel through my heart.

Amsterdam doesn't understand, but Bill does.

BILL THE BUTCHER
Stand back.

Bill pulls the knife out and there is a spurt of blood. He lays the blade on Vallon's chest.

AMSTERDAM
Father, father...! Please! Get up, get up. Kill them!

VALLON
Oh, my son, don't never look away.

BILL THE BUTCHER
Soon be over, Priest.

VALLON
Finish it.

He dies. Amsterdam bursts into tears and buries his face in his father's chest.

BILL THE BUTCHER
You may need this across the river.

Bill steps away from the body.

BILL THE BUTCHER (*CONT'D*)
Ears and noses are the trophies of the day. But no hand shall touch him. No hand shall touch him. He'll cross over whole. In honor. **(163)**

Monk steps through the trophy-hunters, kneels by Vallon as if paying his respects, then reaches inside his coat.

MONK
Not before I take what's owed.

AMSTERDAM
No—!

Bill pulls Amsterdam aside.

BILL THE BUTCHER
It's fair. Indelicate, but fair.

From where the boy is, it's hard to tell exactly what Monk's taking, He gets up holding the razor pouch.

MONK
My sympathies.

He leaves. A nearby Native nods at Amsterdam.

NATIVE AMERICAN
What'll we do with this one?

Bill looks down at Amsterdam.

BILL THE BUTCHER
Give him to the Law. See that he gets a good education.

NATIVE AMERICAN
Okay, boy. Say goodbye to your father.

Two Natives come toward Amsterdam. Amsterdam grabs the knife off Vallon's chest and jumps over the body. He brandishes the knife at the Natives and runs.

The two Natives take off after Amsterdam.

NATIVE
Hey!

ANOTHER NATIVE
Hey!

NATIVE
Come back here!

ANOTHER NATIVE
Get him!

NATIVE
Get after him!

ANOTHER NATIVE
Come here, boy!

NATIVE
Don't let him get away!

Amsterdam is very fast and nimble as he runs across the square toward the Old Brewery. He skips, ducks, and twists through the battleground, but the men are gaining on him.

Suddenly Johnny runs out into the square and throws himself in front of one of the Natives. The Native goes sprawling, knocking Johnny over too. But Johnny is tough and spry; he rolls with it and is back on his feet running after Amsterdam.

As he runs, Amsterdam turns to see what's happened. Johnny is close behind him and the Natives are closing in on them both.

JOHNNY
Hurry! Over here!

The boys run into the Old Brewery.

INT. OLD BREWERY— MOMENTS LATER

The boys run through followed by the Natives, then split to find their own hiding places. Amsterdam leaps down into the warren of tunnels and the camera plunges in after him.

He pulls ahead of us, then disappears into the darkness. In a moment, the Natives overtake us, then they, too, disappear into the darkness ahead.

NATIVE AMERICAN #1
Come here, boy! You're going to Hellgate, son.

NATIVE AMERICAN #2
There he is! Let's get him!

BILL THE BUTCHER (O.C.)
Priest Vallon died a noble death—

AMSTERDAM
Let go of me!

There are sounds of a struggle and the boy's voice crying out.

EXT. PARADISE SQUARE—NIGHT

Bill addresses the Natives and Dead Rabbits. They are putting Vallon's body on a wagon.

BILL THE BUTCHER
Priest Vallon was of impure blood, but it ran redly and spread bravely. He will be buried in honor. But his Dead Rabbits is done and outlawed. Let no one even speak their name from this time forth, or suffer my displeasure.

The camera rises over the narrow winding streets and ramshackle wooden buildings of the Five Points like crumbling ruins of a lost civilization. Rising higher reveals taller stone buildings to the north, and beyond that, wilderness.

A title appears: **NEW YORK CITY, 1844**

CALVINIST
In this place, you have grown from a boy into a man...

INT. ROOM HELLGATE BRIDGE PRISON—DAY

Tight on the face of a young man. Behind him, on an otherwise bare wall, hangs an unadorned cross.

CALVINIST (V.O.)
Put to death then what is earthly in you. Immorality, impurity, passion, and vengeance. In these you once walked. Now you renounce them. The Lord has forgiven you. So you must also forgive.

The young man nods, renouncing and forgiving. As the Calvinist hands him a Bible—

Another title appears: **15 YEARS LATER**

EXT. HELLGATE BRIDGE PRISON—DAY

A guard unlocks a gate, above which ironwork informs all who pass, THE WAY OF THE TRANSGRESSOR IS HARD.

CALVINIST (V.O.)
You go forth to a country torn apart by civil strife...

Amsterdam and the Calvinist embrace at the door. Amsterdam walks away.

CALVINIST (V.O.) (CONT'D)
Lend your hand to the work that yet remains, that this war may end, and the plague of slavery that brought this conflagration down upon us, vanish forever from the earth.

He passes two Chinese convicts burning rubbish outside the prison gates. He exchanges a look with one of them. Behind him the gate closes. Amsterdam immediately tosses the Bible off the bridge. The Bible sinks into the swirling water of the river.

EXT. NEW YORK HARBOR—DAY

A wave of sick and disoriented Irish immigrants disembarks a sailing ship.

NEWSBOY
New York Tribune!

RECRUITER
Join the Army, lads! Three square meals a day and good pay in your pocket.

AMSTERDAM (*V.O.*)
When the Irish came, the city was in a fever. Since the time of the Great Famine, they'd come streamin' off the boats. They got a right warm welcome.

Coffins, too, are off-loaded: relatives who died on the journey. As the lucky ones take their first step on American soil, they're met by a trio of men offering them handshakes, warm soup, and cards that read, "Vote Tammany."

A much smaller boat docks. Amsterdam climbs from it and is caught up in the arriving masses trundling their belongings. Suddenly, out of nowhere, a paving stone hits a woman, knocking her to the dock in front of her children. A small group of Native Americans, some recognizable from the battle with the Dead Rabbits, jeer.

NATIVE AMERICAN
There's more of that awaiting you in the Points, you Irish bastards.

NATIVE AMERICAN (*CONT'D*)
Go back to Ireland, you dumb micks!

NATIVE AMERICAN (*CONT'D*)
You'll remember that, you bog-Irish gyps.

NATIVE AMERICAN #2
Get back on the boat, Paddy!

NATIVE AMERICAN #3
Go back to where you came from!

Amsterdam comes past the fallen woman as others tend to her. He looks at the Natives as he is swept along by the crowd.

AMSTERDAM (*V.O.*)
I only came two hours down river from Hellgate, New York, but they all took me for an immigrant. Why not? There was Irish in all our throats to varying degrees. And to the Natives, we was all the same.

The biggest of the Tammany men, mistaking him for an immigrant, offers a handshake and a bowl of soup.

TWEED
Tammany's here to take the chill off your soul and the weight off your heart.

(*To Amsterdam*) Welcome to America, son. Your long, arduous journey is over.

(*To the crowd*) Vote Tammany!

NATIVE AMERICAN
America for Americans!

EXT. OLD BREWERY—DAY

A clergyman stands next to a beggar girl, one hand atop her head, the other clutching a Bible.

Her hand is upturned waiting for a gratuity as he addresses a crowd that's only mildly interested in what he has to say.

AMSTERDAM (V.O.)
The Five Points hadn't changed much since I was eight years old. Murderers' Alley, Brickbat Mansion, the Gates of Hell. Every year the reformers came. And every year the Points got worse, as if it liked being dirty.

REV. RALEIGH
...this poor child. She lives in squalor in this God-forsaken den of vice and misery behind me.

AMSTERDAM (V.O.)
...They said it was the worst slum in the world. To us it was home.

REV. RALEIGH (O.C.)
...foul haunt of degraded men and women.

Amsterdam comes through the crowd, notes the banner draped above the Old Brewery door—"Future Home of the Five Points Mission, Rev. Raleigh, Pastor, Praise God"— passes some Ladies of the Mission, and disappears inside.

INT. OLD BREWERY AND TUNNELS—DAY

As Amsterdam comes through, cops with torches hunt the Old Brewery's darker recesses for squatters.

SQUATTER
Where am I gonna go?

POLICEMAN
Move! The Reverend wants you out of here!

REV. RALEIGH (O.S.)
...We will nourish their souls with God's abiding compassion, a glorious resurrection will spring from the filthy depths to which these miserable creatures have fallen. In God, they will find their true home...

Amsterdam descends and moves through the tunnels. Reaches a crossroads, leans against the earthen wall, then takes ten short "eight-year-old-length" paces back, and sets his candle on the ground. He scrapes at the dirt. Feels for planks.

Pries them loose and climbs down into another, lower tunnel. This one leads to an underground chamber.

Amsterdam kneels with a candle in a corner and digs at the earth. His hands find a small medal on a chain. He rubs at it and an image appears in the flickering light: Saint Michael dispatching Lucifer to Hell.

Then he brings out the knife that killed his father.

AMSTERDAM
Michael, the Archangel, defend us in battle, be our Protector against the snares and the wickedness of the Devil. Father...Father...Give me the strength for what I have to do.

JOHNNY (O.S.)
Who are you?

Amsterdam spins around, slipping the knife into his jacket.

Johnny, grown up, and a very tough looking black kid, **JIMMY SPOILS**, are standing at the entrance of the chamber. They both have knives out.

(167)

JOHNNY
I said, who are you? What are you doing here?

Amsterdam looks at the boys, sizing them up.

AMSTERDAM
I just like it down here.

JOHNNY
See what's in his pockets.

Johnny and Jimmy Spoils approach Amsterdam, knives out.

AMSTERDAM
Now look, boys, I don't want a fight.

JIMMY SPOILS
Don't worry, son, you couldn't give us one.

Jimmy Spoils lunges at Amsterdam. Amsterdam catches his knife arm and head-butts him in the face. Jimmy Spoils goes down and out, blood streaming out of both nostrils.

Amsterdam snatches the knife out of his hand before he hits the ground, turns Johnny's thrust, and grabs him by the throat, pushing him back against the wall, his knife an inch from Johnny's eye. Johnny drops his own knife.

JOHNNY
Don't kill me.

AMSTERDAM
(Lightly) All right.

(168) Cautiously he steps back. Johnny spots the Saint Michael's medal lying in the dirt. He looks at Amsterdam with a flash of recognition.

JOHNNY
Where'd you get that?

Amsterdam doesn't reply. He picks up his medal, folds it in a scrap of blue cloth, and puts it in his pocket. Jimmy Spoils groans and rolls over.

JOHNNY (CONT'D)
Jesus, I think you killed him.

Jimmy Spoils lurches to his feet, feeling at his face.

JIMMY SPOILS
I ain't killed. I feel good.

AMSTERDAM
I said I didn't want a fight.

JOHNNY
(Genuinely puzzled) Why not? Look how good you done.

EXT. PARADISE SQUARE—DAY

Amsterdam walks away from the Old Brewery. Johnny is hurrying to keep in step with him. (Perhaps we see Jimmy Spoils in the B.G. behind them, going his own way)

JOHNNY
You're the Priest's son, aren't you?

AMSTERDAM
You! Get away from me, understand?

JOHNNY
You don't remember me, do you? I'm the one that tried to help you—When the Natives took you.

Amsterdam looks at him.

AMSTERDAM
That was you?

JOHNNY
I thought you was killed.

AMSTERDAM
No. Just locked up.

JOHNNY
This long?

AMSTERDAM
I kept trying to escape. They add on time for that.

JOHNNY
What're you doing back here?

AMSTERDAM (Dry)
Guess I just missed the place.

JOHNNY
You got a place to stay?

AMSTERDAM
No.

JOHNNY
I got a place.

AMSTERDAM
What about somethin' to eat?

JOHNNY
Oh, that you got to work for.

EXT. BROADWAY—NIGHT

Fireworks explode in the sky and rain down behind the silhouette of Bill the Butcher, flanked by a small army of Natives, coming through a crowd of ragged-looking troops, fitted out in tatty Union uniforms, standing under a banner proclaiming the Irish 69th.

A great banner is strung across the street, one rope coming out of a window in the Tribune Building, the other tied to a tree across the street. It reads "**The President's Proclamation. Slavery Abolished. States In Rebellion**"

AMSTERDAM (V.O.)
In the second year of the great Civil War, when the Irish Brigade marched through the streets, New York was a city full of tribes…war chiefs— rich and poor.

MAN IN CROWD
Lincoln will make all white men slaves!

AMSTERDAM (V.O.)
…It wasn't a city really. It was more a furnace where a city someday might be forged.

BILL THE BUTCHER
That's the spirit, boys. Go off and die for your blackie friends.

MAN IN CROWD
Down with the abolitionists!

Bill and McGloin look at the banner.

BILL THE BUTCHER
We should have run a better man against Lincoln when we had a chance.

McGLOIN (Reading the banner)
He's trying to say we're no different than the niggers now?

BILL THE BUTCHER
You ain't.

WOMAN IN CROWD
God bless the Union Army!

MAN IN CROWD
Three cheers for Lincoln!

(169)

McGloin grabs a black man and violently shoves him to the ground.

MCGLOIN
Go back to Africa, nigger!

MAN IN THE CROWD
Leave him alone!

AMSTERDAM (V.O.)
The angriest of the talk was of the new Conscription Act, the first draft in Union history.

MCGLOIN
No nig noggery! No nig noggery here! None!

Bill takes out one of his knives. He throws the knife through the air. The perfectly-aimed knife clips the rope tying the banner to the tree and the whole thing flops down against the side of the building. The Natives cheer.

INT. TAMMANY HALL—DAY

The camera races along an ornate corridor past portraits of important-looking gentlemen and into—

AMSTERDAM (V.O.)
New York loved William Tweed. And hated him. And those of us trying to be thieves...well, we couldn't help but admire him.

INT. TWEED'S OFFICE—DAY

(170) A flurry of feathers as canaries, frightened by the noisy entrance of the Natives, bat against their cages.

Tweed and his aide are startled too, and turn to face the gang.

TWEED
Mr. Cutting. Gentlemen. I'm...honored.

He offers Bill his hand, but Bill lets it hang there. McGloin taps at the bars of a cage, panicking the birds even further.

TWEED (CONT'D)
Sir? Excuse me. I think you're frightening them.

BILL THE BUTCHER
Don't mind him, he used to be an Irishman.

McGloin glances across to Bill, who says without saying, Leave the birds alone.

TWEED
Thank you. Now, perhaps Mr. Killoran can show the boys around while we talk in private.

Killoran looks less than thrilled with the assignment.

INT. TWEED'S OFFICE— LATER—DAY

The canaries have calmed, and remain so, until, every so often, another burst of fireworks flares the window.

TWEED
You may or may not know, Bill, that every day I go down to the waterfront with hot soup for the Irish as they come ashore.

Tweed holds out an open box of cigars. When Bill doesn't accept, Tweed sets one down next to him.

TWEED (CONT'D)
Part of building a political base.

BILL THE BUTCHER
I've noticed you there. You may have noticed me.

TWEED
Indeed I have. Hard not to.

BILL THE BUTCHER
I don't get down there as much as I'd like. Too much humanitarian work of my own these days.

TWEED
Throwing torrents of pavers and withering abuse at every single person who steps off those boats—

BILL THE BUTCHER
(On "person") If only I had the guns, Mr. Tweed, I'd shoot each and every one of them before they set foot on American soil.

INT. TWEED'S OFFICE—LATER

The tenor in here has changed, darkened. As Bill speaks, there's a flashcut to each street he mentions—

BILL THE BUTCHER
Mulberry Street and Worth. Cross and Orange and Little Water. Each of the Five Points is a finger, and when I close my hand the whole territory is a fist. I can turn it against you.

TWEED
But we're talking about different things, Bill. I'm talking about civic duty. Responsibilities we owe to the people. Schools and hospitals, sewers and utilities; street construction, repairs and sweeping. Business licenses, saloon licenses, carting licenses...streetcars, ferries, rubbish disposal. There's a power of money to be made in this city, Bill. With your help, the people can be made to understand that all these things are best kept within what I like to call the Tammany family. Which is why I'm talking about an alliance between our two great organizations.

BILL THE BUTCHER
You're talking about muscle work.

TWEED
That, too. Muscle to match our spirit.

BILL THE BUTCHER
You own the crushers. Get them to do it.

TWEED
The police? Oh, Jesus, no. Jesus, no. The appearance of the law must be upheld...Especially while it's being broken.

A burst of fireworks lights up the night sky, and—

EXT. STREET—NIGHT (2ND UNIT)

The sparks cascade down onto the roof of a building—

AMSTERDAM (V.O.)
We always liked a good fire in the Points. You could generally pick up a little swag and if the cops came along you really got a show...

MAN IN THE CROWD
Fire! Fire!

TWEED
Vote Tammany!

AMSTERDAM (V.O.)
...The municipal police fought the metropolitan police. The metropolitan police fought the street gangs...

TWEED
Hurry up, men, before the Black Joke get there!

AMSTERDAM (*V.O.*)
...There were thirty-seven amateur fire brigades, and they all fought each other.

EXT. SIDE STREET—NIGHT

Tweed runs down the street at the head of his fire brigade, wearing his fireman's coat and Tiger-insignia helmet.

WOMAN IN CROWD
The Black Joke are on their way, Tweed, and they'll beat the shite outta ya!

EXT. BUILDING—NIGHT

MAN IN THE CROWD
Anyone know if the Flanagans are still inside?

Flames devour the building. We pan right to find the Americus Fire Brigade coming around the corner, headed for the front of the building.

We pan left to find the Black Joke Fire Brigade barreling toward the front of the building with Black Joke Chief McAuley at the head.

TWEED
It's the Black Joke! Go get 'em, boys!

The two brigades come crashing together in front of the building and start brawling, completely ignoring the fire.

(172) **MAN IN THE CROWD**
Give those Bowery Boys hell!

Stepping clear of the melee, Tweed and Killoran carry a barrel toward the fire plug, where an anguished **RESIDENT** is wringing her hands.

TWEED
Any habitants inside?

RESIDENT
No, praise God, but all we own is.

TWEED
Then we had better wait for reinforcements.

He and Killoran put the barrel on top of the fire plug.

TWEED (*CONT'D*)
In your next time of trouble, ma'am, call on Tammany first.

He gives the woman one of his "Vote Tammany" cards and sits on top of the barrel.

Young thieves are looting the building, throwing furniture out side windows to others down below who run off with it.

We find Johnny leading Amsterdam into the crowd.

JOHNNY
Quick, before there's nothing left!

ANOTHER MAN IN THE CROWD
Go back to the Bowery, you bums!

ANGUISHED MAN
Stop them, for God's sake. They're taking everything.

Amsterdam hesitates. He glances at the families huddled across the street watching their building being burned and looted.

JOHNNY
I thought you said you was hungry!

Johnny runs across the street and into the burning building. Amsterdam runs in after him.

As the fighting rages and the building burns, the Black Joke chief emerges from the imbroglio and approaches Tweed.

TWEED
Evening, McAuley.

BLACK JOKE
William Tweed, we are here to quench this blaze.

TWEED
Well, sir, the human soul is bung-full of laudable ambition.

BLACK JOKE
May I point out this building is burning to ashes?

TWEED
May I point out this area is the province of my own Americus Fire Brigade, and that you lot belong on the Bowery?

BLACK JOKE
May I point out you're outmanned, outmaneuvered and, in a moment, outfought.

TWEED
Am I? Let's ask my new friend.

A face suddenly swirls through a curtain of flames: Bill the Butcher hanging off the side of another arriving Americus Fire Co. wagon, like a demon.

BILL THE BUTCHER
There's the Black Joke. Let's take them on the cobbles. Go spill some claret, boys! Go on, Shorty, have a nice muss! Go!

MAN IN THE CROWD
Clear the way for Bill the Butcher!

INT. BURNING BUILDING

The vision of the Devil is Amsterdam's, his first look at Bill the Butcher in fifteen years. As young thieves ransack the building around him, he watches Bill and his Natives and the Americus firemen climbing down off their wagon below.

AMSTERDAM
Grab what you can, Johnny!

EXT. BURNING BUILDING

As Bill's men disembark, the Black Joke firemen stop fighting and back away, intimidated. Tweed gets up off the barrel.

TWEED
Right, boys! To work!

The bruised and bloodied men of the Americus Company hobble off the battlefield, hitch a hose to the plug. A primitive pump sputters water.

BILL THE BUTCHER
What's the use? Fire's near burned anything of value inside.

It's true; the place is almost completely engulfed in flames. As the Americus firemen rush toward it, Tweed calls out:

TWEED
Boys! Forget that one! Next building over! Mustn't let it spread!

The building he's pointing to isn't even connected; it's across the alley and in no danger at all. The firemen charge it, ax through its doors, climb through its windows.

TWEED (*CONT'D*)
Take what you want from that one.

(173)

Bill signals his men to follow the firemen. A stunned resident appeals to the gang coming past him.

RESIDENT
What are you doing? There's nothing wrong with that one. That's my build—

Someone slugs him and he goes down.

BILL THE BUTCHER
(*Calling out*) For Christ's wounds, McGloin, fight the fire from the front and take the loot in the back! These men need room to work!

McGLOIN
Right you are, Bill!

TWEED
Punctuality, Bill. You'll need to work on that. First rule of firefighting.

INT. BURNING BUILDING

Johnny rummages through drawers, unconcerned the room is burning down around him. He finds a small music box and puts it to his ear as timbers crash down, cutting off his only way out. Suddenly there is a groaning crash and he is nearly crushed by flaming timbers. Surrounded by fire, he panics and yells.

In the next room, Amsterdam is opening and closing drawers. He finds a jewel box tucked away in the back of a drawer full of clothes. He smashes it open against the corner of the bureau. A fistful of old heirloom jewels scatters all over the floor. He grabs a couple of brooches but before he can do more he hears Johnny yelling and looks around.

Johnny on the other side of the flames, trapped.

Amsterdam hesitates between going after the jewelry and helping Johnny, then growls and crams the brooches in his pocket and responds by... leaving. Johnny wails and coughs.

Amsterdam reappears moments later covered in a blanket and braves the wall of flames.

Inside the burning room now with the terrified Johnny, he wraps them both in the blanket and crosses back through the flames to the corridor.

The flames lick around the uncollected jewelry on the burning floor.

EXT. BURNING BUILDING

As Bill watches his Natives, running in and out of the building, carrying their swag, something unexpected catches his eye. He sees a figure shrouded in flames, helping the young thief out of the burning building, laying him down on the street. It's Bill's first view of Amsterdam, even though he doesn't know it yet.

EXT. ALLEY—LATER

Johnny huddles under the blanket, sipping water from Amsterdam's cupped hands. It almost resembles a holy rite.

AMSTERDAM
You want more water?

JOHNNY
(*Shakes his head*) You get any swag?

AMSTERDAM
No. But the way I figure it you owe me half of what you got.

JOHNNY
It ain't so much.

AMSTERDAM
I ain't proud. Give it to me.

Johnny gives Amsterdam half his swag. He keeps the music box. Amsterdam lets him.

JOHNNY
Let's find supper, then I'll take you around to meet the boys.

AMSTERDAM
All right.

They get up.

JOHNNY
They won't be half-jiggered when I walk through the door with the living son of Priest Vallon—

Amsterdam catches Johnny's arm.

AMSTERDAM
I'm nobody's son. I come back 'cause I got no place else to go. But I'm not looking for no trouble and I don't mean to find none on account of you. If that's not so clear I can drag you right back in that fire and watch you burn.

JOHNNY
It's clear... Only what do I call you?

INT. SHANG'S HIDEOUT— LATER—NIGHT

Swag from the burning building on a plank table in an almost-bare room. A pair of hands sorting through it all, arranging it in piles. Other members of the young, ersatz gang look on. It's all pretty much junk.

JOHNNY
His name is Amsterdam.

Shang, the sorter, as he looks across at Amsterdam—

SHANG
What do you know of him, bringing him in here?

JOHNNY
He's a right gent. Educated. Been to boarding school. Ten years and up at boarding school. Hellgate.

The others, hearing this, regard Amsterdam, sitting quietly in a corner, with a measure of respect. He's a real gangster who's done time.

AMSTERDAM (*To Jimmy Spoils*)
How's the beak?

JIMMY SPOILS
Ain't so bad.

There is an element of mutual respect in this exchange, interrupted by—

SHANG
You. You get anything? Give it up or get out.

Amsterdam comes over and puts down the two brooches he salvaged and the stuff he got from Johnny.

SHANG (*CONT'D*)
Right. Here's the rake. Everything comes here. We fence it, Johnny takes our tribute to the Natives—we chop up the winnings, each to his equal portion, amongst the gang. Does that meet your approval, Hellgate?

AMSTERDAM
My approval...? What's the matter, Jack Sprat? Can't you think for yourself?

Sudden quiet.

SHANG
You're out of place talking like that.

AMSTERDAM
Set me straight.

Shang pushes noisily away from the table. Johnny steps in the way. Amsterdam backs down, letting Shang save face.

AMSTERDAM (*CONT'D*)
You're right. I didn't mean to give no offense. You're the chief here. Your rules suit me just fine.

HAPPY JACK (*O.S.*)
You boys settle with me before settling with each other.

Amsterdam turns to the voice and immediately recognizes the half-paralyzed face of the ex-Dead Rabbit coming into the room, now wearing the uniform of a cop.

HAPPY JACK
I come for my due and proper.

He approaches the table and notes the jewelry amidst the rest of the swag.

HAPPY JACK (*CONT'D*)
Now, this ain't a bad haul.

He pockets Amsterdam's brooches, assorted rings, the best of what's there.

(176) **HAPPY JACK** (*CONT'D*)
…You know, when folks start in to sayin' where the country's goin' to Hell, I always tell 'em, "Look at all the hard work these fine young lads of ours is doin' down in the Five Points."

He holds up a glittering pendant.

HAPPY JACK (*CONT'D*)
Ah, now this is just the thing for Mrs. Mulraney.

SHANG
All right, Jack, all right, just leave us somethin' to quarter to the Butcher—

Jack cracks him across the knees with his nightstick. Shang goes down. Silence as he looks around to see if anyone else wants some of that. He sees Johnny's music box. Johnny reaches for it. The nightstick cracks across his hand. As the box falls to the floor, its lullaby begins to play. He picks it up and examines it carefully.

HAPPY JACK
Not my favorite tune…

He tosses it back to the floor and the music stops.

HAPPY JACK (*CONT'D*)
Thank you, boys. Keep out of trouble, now.

Amsterdam watches Jack's every step as he walks out. As Jimmy helps Shang up, Amsterdam is still looking over where Jack left, listening to the cop's footsteps echoing on the cobblestones outside.

AN IDEALIZED IMAGE OF A YOUNG WOMAN
crossing Paradise Square like some kind of angel in Hell.

INT. STOREFRONT—DAY

The vision is Amsterdam's perspective through a window, clouded around the edges like a old picture frame. As the woman disappears, he turns away and watches Johnny fencing the gang's swag. The music box melody is cut short as—

EXT. PARADISE SQUARE—DAY

They come out the door into the chaos and cacophony of the Five Points, a strange world overflowing with lowlife: hawkers and whores and beggars and gangs.

JOHNNY

...Streets here always are lively of an evening. The city comes here to sport.

AMSTERDAM

The swells come down here?

JOHNNY

Aye, that they do.

AMSTERDAM

Who are the gangs around now?

As Johnny leads Amsterdam across the square and describes the gangs, we see them in vignettes engaged in the individual scams they favor, each freezing on action into a sepia-toned illustration—

JOHNNY

The Daybreak Boys and Swamp Angels work the river, looting ships. The Frog Hollows shanghai sailors down around the Bloody Angle. The Shirt Tails was rough for a while but they've become a bunch of jack-rolling dandies, lolling around Murderers' Alley looking like Chinamen. Hell-Cat Maggie tried to open her own grog shop, but she drank up all her own liquor and got throwed out on the street. Now she's on the lay for anything from poultry rigging to the ken's crack. The Plug Uglies got their own language no one can understand and love fighting the cops. The Night Walkers of Ragpickers Row work on their backs and kill with their hands. The Little Forty Thieves used to be something until they got took over by One-Lung Curran and his Gophers. They're so scurvy only the Plug Uglies will talk to them, but who knows what they're saying? The Slaughter housers and the Broadway Twisters. They're a fine bunch of bingleboys. And the Little Forty Thieves—I used to run with them for a while, till they got took over by Bendrick the Cockroach and his red-eyed buggers. Bendrick carries a germ. If you try to leave the gang, they say he hacks up blood on you...

TRUE BLUE AMERICAN

The limejuicers are nothin' but a bunch of rapacious grab-ups, and it's time they were sent back to where they came from...

JOHNNY

The True Blues say they're a gang, but all they really do is stand around on corners damning England.

TRUE BLUE AMERICAN

Oh, open your eyes and see them for what they truly are...

AMSTERDAM

Any of them got the sand of the Dead Rabbits?

A vignette of the great battle between the Native Americans and the Dead Rabbits freezes into a sepia illustration, the knives and clubs and fists caught in mid-action. Johnny's face comes through it, superimposing, staring at Amsterdam.

JOHNNY

You don't say that name. The Dead Rabbits died with...(*Catching himself*) They been outlawed.

AMSTERDAM

When I was in the blockhouse the Chinks told me that the Natives celebrate their victory over my father every year. Is that true?

(177)

JOHNNY

Aye, that they do. And it's quite the affair. The Butcher himself's got to invite you or you don't go.

EXT. DON WHISKERANDO'S BARBERSHOP—SAME TIME

Above, on a hillock, stands Monk, surveying all he sees below, like Zeus. He can see both young men moving through the crowds, but isolates the one, the stranger.

JOHNNY (*V.O.*)

The Natives run the territory, all right—overground and underground. They're tolerant to a degree, and you don't have to run with 'em to show your face in broad daylight—

EXT. PARADISE SQUARE— CONTINUED

Johnny and Amsterdam walk along...

JOHNNY

...but in all the Five Points there's nothin' that runs, walks, or cocks his toes up don't belong to Bill the Butcher.

...Johnny bumps right into the young woman we glimpsed before.

JENNY

Look where you're going, Johnny!

Johnny smiles, abashed by her beauty and her proximity. He hunts in vain for something to say. She smiles and moves by—and the action suddenly slows—as Amsterdam watches the movement of her long fingers. She looks over at Amsterdam. He is impressed, tacitly sizing her up.

JENNY (*CONT'D*)

You look stunned and poorly, sir. But count yourself lucky that's all you are if you stand fast beside this one.

Neither of them replies. They are both staring at her.

JENNY (*CONT'D*)

Quite a pair of conversationalists, aren't you?

AMSTERDAM

Maybe not, but we're deep thinkers.

JENNY

(*Laughs*) Gentlemen, I leave you in the grace and favor of the Lord.

With that she walks off lightly. Johnny stares after her. So does Amsterdam.

AMSTERDAM

Is that the one you were telling me ab—

JOHNNY

That's her. Jenny. The finest bludget in the Points.

AMSTERDAM

She is a prim-looking star-gazer. Only I'd check my pockets if I was you. I do believe she lifted your timepiece.

Johnny checks and realizes his watch is gone.

JOHNNY

Oh, I let her take it. I let her do it all the time. (*Feeling in his pockets*) Sometimes she leaves me notes.

He feels in his pockets and comes out with a slip of paper. He reads it.

AMSTERDAM

What's it say then?

Johnny shows Amsterdam the note.

JOHNNY
"Beware of Strangers"

Amsterdam smiles. Johnny balls up the note and throws it away. Amsterdam slings an arm around his neck.

AMSTERDAM
Come on, let's go steal something.

INT./EXT. SATAN'S CIRCUS— LATER—DAY

Kids with a gunnysack come past a window. A moment later, Amsterdam and Johnny appear and stop in front of it.

JOHNNY
(*A little awkwardly*) I got to go inside.

AMSTERDAM
What for?

JOHNNY
I got some business to attend to. I'll see you later.

AMSTERDAM
(*As Johnny walks away*) Where we going to meet?

But Johnny's already inside, leaving Amsterdam alone on the street. He stares curiously, surprised by the brush-off. Then his eyes move to the door of the place. There's a Devil puppet from a Punch and Judy, nailed to it.

Inside, we see the kids from before handing over their sack to the barkeep. It seems to be alive. The man weighs it using his arm for a scale and pays the boys with pennies. As he turns away,

the camera follows another barkeep down a long bar, emptying the residue of glasses into a bucket, then dumping it into the all-sorts barrel where several men—and one woman—push and shove and suck it up through hoses. Putting an ear down as payment next to a jar of ears.

BARKEEP
Hey, Maggie. Right ear or left ear?

HELL-CAT MAGGIE
Aw, give us a drink, ya idjut. (*Drinking*) Ah, you're a great bunch of boys...!

Johnny comes past. Following him, the camera suddenly dives to glimpse a terrier in a pit, over to glimpse the gunnysack being emptied of rats, and back up as Johnny passes a large and loud group of men placing bets.

GAME MASTER
Towser against the Vermin! The count to beat is twenty-five rodents in three minutes! Gentlemen, betting is closed!

Are the enumerators satisfied? Fifty!

ENUMERATOR
Yes!

GAME MASTER
Let 'em go!

This is the base of operations for the Native Americans. Part saloon, dance hall, gambling den, whorehouse, slaughterhouse. Johnny comes past sides of beef on hooks, then past a small stage and singer few pay attention to, before his path is blocked by McGloin.

McGLOIN
Where you going, boyo?

JOHNNY
Here to pay tribute to Bill.

McGLOIN
Are you now?

The Irish ex-Dead Rabbit, now a Native, holds out a hand.

McGLOIN (CONT'D)
Give it to me, I'll give it to him.

JOHNNY
No thanks. I'll pay him myself.

McGLOIN
Will you now? What do you want to keep...the money or your teeth, boyo?

McGloin puts his hands up and slaps/pushes at Johnny. Johnny's hands go up as well, but before they can get into it, Bill, in a far corner of the room playing cards with three of his Natives, glances to the noise.

BILL THE BUTCHER
John! Welcome, welcome.

McGloin steps aside. Johnny approaches Bill. A collection of American flags hangs on the wall behind him.

JOHNNY
From me and my lads, sir.

Johnny sets down the contents of his pockets to show they're equal. Bill rakes one pile closer with a knife, leaving the other for Johnny, then leans slightly to see around him.

BILL THE BUTCHER
Mate of yours? Where's he from?

Johnny sees that Amsterdam has come in and is standing now across the room.

JOHNNY
Oh...He's not from around here.

Bill considers both boys a moment, then gestures to the figure in the shadows to come forward.

BILL THE BUTCHER
(To Amsterdam) You! Yes...! You!

As Amsterdam takes a few slow steps into the light toward Bill, he takes in the scene—Bill in all his power and glory, flanked on all sides by looming, enormous, deadly looking thugs.

BILL THE BUTCHER (CONT'D)
That's close enough.

Bill looks him over carefully. Amsterdam's eyes shift slightly to a framed portrait and candle set up like a shrine next to the Butcher. The portrait is of Priest Vallon. Amsterdam is surprised and disturbed to find his father's picture hanging in a place of honor on Bill's wall.

BILL THE BUTCHER (CONT'D)
Your friend can't look me in the eye. That's not an admirable characteristic.

JOHNNY
Nobody can look you in the eye, Bill. Not when you're playing cards.

Bill follows Amsterdam's sightline to the portrait. Then glances to one of the card players—

BILL THE BUTCHER
This is whist. This is a gentleman's game. Make a gentleman's bet.

(180)

CARD PLAYER
I'm betting large, Bill.

BILL THE BUTCHER
That ain't large.

The player pales. Then pushes everything he has into the pot. As his hand slides back, there's a sudden thwack and a yelp of pain.

Johnny flinches. So does Amsterdam—but less noticeably. Bill has driven his dagger (O.S.) through the player's hand, leaving on the table the coin he was trying to palm back. He looks impassively at the player, who is in agony.

BILL THE BUTCHER (CONT'D)
Please—don't make that sound again, Harvey.

The player shakes his head, nearly fainting. Bill's eyes move back to Amsterdam even though he's addressing Johnny. Bill takes half the money Johnny's given him and gives him back the rest.

BILL THE BUTCHER (CONT'D)
I like a man who's willin' to burn for his swag. How do you fare on water?

Johnny frowns, doesn't get it.

BILL THE BUTCHER (CONT'D)
Come closer, John. Closer. I ain't gonna bite. Close.

Bill's eyes stay on Amsterdam as he speaks softly into Johnny's ear.

BILL THE BUTCHER (CONT'D)
There's a PortaGeezy ship lyin' low in the harbor, quarantined three weeks and choked with swag. They lift quarantine tomorrow. Get there before the Daybreak Boys strip her, and maybe you and we'll talk some more.

JOHNNY
(With only the slightest hesitation) Consider it done, sir.

Amsterdam is watching all this carefully. Bill pats Johnny on the shoulder and sends him on his way. As Amsterdam starts to follow, he calls out...

BILL THE BUTCHER
And you. Whatever your name is. What is your name?

AMSTERDAM
Amsterdam, sir.

BILL THE BUTCHER
Amsterdam? I'm New York. Don't never come in here empty-handed again. You got to pay for the pleasure of my company.

AMSTERDAM
(Nods, low) Bene.

As Johnny and Amsterdam start to leave.

BILL THE BUTCHER
(Calling out) Take him for a boat-ride, John. Who knows but he might save your life again.

Amsterdam looks back at Bill, as if he is grateful for the opportunity, knowing inside he's being "watched"...

INT. SPARROW'S CHINESE PAGODA—DAY

Hands unfold a page torn from a Bible, a note in Chinese symbols scrawled over a faded illustration of the Apocalypse.

AMSTERDAM (V.O.)
Every year the Natives celebrated the killing of

my father all over again, at Sparrow's Chinese Pagoda. The drum rolls and the Butcher drinks a glass of fire...

As Amsterdam waits for the Chinese proprietor to read it, mahjong players regard him suspiciously. This room interests Amsterdam. He carefully studies it like a thief cases a bank, taking in the locations of its stairs and doors. The Chinese hoodlum shows him a secret panel.

INT. SPARROW'S CHINESE PAGODA—LATER

Money changes hands at a fan-tan table. Beyond the Chinese gamblers, Amsterdam can be seen engaged in quiet conversation with a Chinese hoodlum in the large, almost deserted room.

INT. SPARROW'S CHINESE PAGODA—LATER

AMSTERDAM (V.O.)
When you kill a king, you don't stab him in the dark. You kill him where the whole court can watch him die.

Amsterdam walks away from the bar in slow measured steps, counting to himself like a duelist. Fifteen paces, he turns. A shot glass is set down in foreground. Liquor's poured into it. A match is lit, brought close, and the liquor ignites.

INT./EXT. RECRUITING OFFICE.—DAY

(182)

Pictures of fingers pointing at food promise illiterate, destitute immigrants a better life in the Army. The long lines of men stretch out into the street where a drum and fife lead newly recruited Union soldiers off to war.

RECRUITER #1 (O.C.)
Enlist! Join up! Serve your country!

RECRUITER #2 (O.C.)
Come on in, out of the draft, boys.

RECRUITER #1 (O.C.)
Join up now and get the bonus.

RECRUITER #2
Volunteer and get your fifty dollar bonus.

OFFICER
We need 30,000 volunteers and we're prepared to pay six hundred and seventy-seven dollars per volunteer. Please read this. Thank you. Would you like to take one of these please to fill out? Three square meals a day. Three square meals a day—

RECRUITER
—Young man. Enlist and serve your country. Three square meals a day, gentlemen. If you're interested, I suggest you read this and consider joining up.

AMSTERDAM (V.O.)
Everywhere you went people talked about the draft. You could buy your way out for 300 dollars, but who had 300 dollars? We didn't know anything about the South. We only knew the Bowery, Mott Street, and Murderers' Alley. And we never dreamt the war could touch New York.

As Amsterdam walks by he glimpses Jenny, dressed completely differently, her head hidden by a bonnet, strolling toward him past a soldier.

JENNY
Good afternoon, sir.

As she approaches him he realizes who she is and steps back, hands raised, giving her a wide berth.

AMSTERDAM
You...! Don't run into me.

JENNY
(*Laughs*) Fair enough.

Jenny immediately trips over a paving stone and goes sprawling into his arms. Suddenly they are face to face.

AMSTERDAM
(*Unamused*) I said, don't run into me.

JENNY
I'm sorry...!

They straighten up. They both search through their pockets and belongings, keeping an eye on each other.

JENNY (*CONT'D*)
Everything in place?

AMSTERDAM
It seems so.

JENNY
Then I leave you in the—

AMSTERDAM & JENNY
—grace and favor of the Lord—

AMSTERDAM
—yes, thank you.

Amsterdam nods. Jenny moves on. As Amsterdam watches her go the sternness in his face relaxes a bit and he smiles.

He takes out the folded blue cloth where he put his father's medal. Unfolds it.

It's empty.

AMSTERDAM (*CONT'D*)
Oh, the dirty Mab!

He sees Jenny just boarding a street coach. He darts after her and hops aboard just as the coach starts driving away.

INT. STAGE—MOVING

Amsterdam stays at the back of the crowded coach so the girl won't see him. A passenger offers her his seat. She smiles demurely as she sits and arranges her hands genteelly on her lap. The passenger is beguiled.

PASSENGER
I hope you won't think me rude if I speak. I wouldn't want you to think me forward.

JENNY
Well, sir, that depends on what you say.

As they converse in low tones, Amsterdam watches from the back of the coach: Her hands, which appear to be folded on her lap; a "third" hand moving slowly out from her wrap toward the passenger; brushing past his jacket—past his thigh—up toward his fine gold pocket watch—hesitating there—then continuing up toward his trouser pocket—

PASSENGER
Would you call me reckless if I said you were the prettiest girl in New York?

JENNY
Only New York?

(183)

The passenger is in Jenny's thrall. He has no idea what's going on. But Amsterdam knows. He watches every silken, surreptitious move of Jenny's hand with professional interest.

PASSENGER
May I know your name?

Her hand hovers above his pocket, waiting for the sway of the coach to mask her movement—

JENNY
(*Sweetly*) Not if I don't tell it to you.

She stands up as the coach jostles to a halt, her hand sliding the man's wallet from his trousers as he recovers his balance. She slips it under her wrap and steps down to the street. He steps down after her.

PASSENGER
May I walk with you a little then?

JENNY
(*Very sweetly*) No.

She walks away. He watches after her. As the coachman reins at the horses and the coach moves on, Amsterdam jumps down.

EXT. BROADWAY ALLEY—DAY

First making sure no one's looking, Jenny moves her body a little and the porcelain hands come off under her long coat. She stashes them and continues on her way. But somebody is looking. Amsterdam follows her.

EXT. UPTOWN STREET—DAY

As he keeps her in view up ahead he also looks around at his surroundings. He's never seen this part of New York; never knew it existed. The houses are grand and the people on the street well-dressed—unlike him. Some even walk dogs—on leashes. It's another world.

EXT./INT. UPTOWN MANSION—DAY

Jenny sheds her coat, revealing the maid's uniform she's wearing underneath, strides up to a back door of a mansion, and opens the unlocked door.

Amsterdam appears a moment later and peers through a window as she climbs a staircase inside.

AMSTERDAM (*V.O.*)
For every lay, we had a different name. An Angler put a hook on the end of a stick to drop behind store windows and doors. An Autum Diver picked your pocket in church. A Badger gets a fellow into bed with a girl then robs his pockets while they're on the go. Jenny was a Bludget—a girl pickpocket—and a Turtle Dove. A Turtle Dove goes uptown dressed like a house-maid, picks out a fine house, and goes right through the back door. Robs you blind. It takes a lot of sand to be a Turtle Dove.

As her legs disappear from his view, he moves to another window and watches, fascinated, fragments of everyday rituals of a world he's never seen:

In a series of dissolves: Servants come into a high-ceilinged dining room with silver platters; a family unfolds linen napkins under a crystal chandelier; etched goblets are filled; silverware, clutched in thin, white, bejeweled hands; the low murmur of conversation in a cultivated accent he's never heard before.

Jenny slips out of the servants entrance of the mansion. She gets two steps before Amsterdam appears out of nowhere, grabs her, and spins her around.

AMSTERDAM (*CONT'D*)
I'll have my medal back.

Jenny's face contorts with frightening animal fury and she immediately knees him in the balls with all her strength.

He groans and lets out a gasp of intense pain, and almost lets go of her, but incredibly he manages to hold on, too tough to release his grasp. He pushes her back against the wall, pressing his whole body against her to keep her knees and legs in place.

AMSTERDAM (*CONT'D*)
(*Still in considerable distress*) Don't do that again.

She immediately tries to do it again but she can't get any leverage. She struggles literally like a wild animal, but he's way too strong for her.

JENNY
Take your hands off me...! They'll bag the both of us!

AMSTERDAM
Just give me the medal!

There is a sudden sound at the servants' entrance and they both instinctively flatten against the wall, instantly silent. **A SERVANT** pokes his head out of the door to see what all the noise is about. They are just out of his eyeline. He goes back inside.

Amsterdam turns once more to Jenny.

AMSTERDAM (*CONT'D*)
Now then—

He finds she has a knife at his throat.

JENNY
Go back to the Points and leave me to my business or I'll open your throat, so help me God.

AMSTERDAM
All right.

He catches hold of her hand and tries to press the knife into his own throat.

AMSTERDAM (*CONT'D*)
Go on then.

Jenny resists—thrown off guard. She doesn't actually want to kill him.

JENNY
(*Shaky*) I would...!

AMSTERDAM
Go on then!

They are very close. It's very intense, almost sexual. He pushes harder. The skin is pierced and a drop of blood runs down the blade. Jenny is alarmed, scared—Amsterdam keeps pushing until suddenly she relents and he yanks the knife away.

They look at each other. Something in her has surrendered to him, and it's left her breathless.

AMSTERDAM (*CONT'D*)
Now, give me that medal.

Jenny's hand goes to the collar of her uniform. She pulls the fabric down, exposing her throat.

Around her neck are twenty stolen chains and necklaces from the mansion inside.

JENNY
Take it. I can't remember which is yours.

AMSTERDAM
Suppose I help myself to everything.

JENNY
Suppose you do.

Very carefully Amsterdam reaches out to her exposed throat and deftly selects his father's St Michael medal. With one hand he undoes the clasp and slips it from around her neck. She is looking him in the eye the whole time.

He slips the medal in his pocket and reaches toward her throat again. She flinches just a hair. He takes the rest of the necklaces and tucks them back down inside her blouse. Then he neatly rearranges her collar.

Her eyes haven't left his face. She's impressed.

AMSTERDAM
Can I walk with you a little, then?

Jenny nods.

EXT. UPTOWN STREET—DAY

As Amsterdam and Jenny walk along a tree-lined street, other people—rich people—stroll past with gold-tipped walking sticks and silk parasols.

JENNY
They leave their doors unlocked and walk around unarmed. They live like they're not in New York.

There's no comparison between the people here and those in the Points. They almost seem like a different species.

AMSTERDAM
I never been north of Saint Patrick's before.

JENNY
I wouldn't do it too often. You'll be collared for sure in that get-up.

She touches the shoulder of his frayed jacket. A cop, in fact, is eying Amsterdam right now, making sure he and the girl keep moving.

AMSTERDAM
What could a fellow earn up here in a day? Maybe you and me could pal in together.

JENNY
Oh, I think you're a bit rough for this sort of game. Besides, I work alone.

AMSTERDAM
Alone? How much do you quarter to Butcher?

JENNY
Me? Nothing.

AMSTERDAM
Nothing?

JENNY
The Butcher and me have a special arrangement.

Amsterdam stops walking. Looks at her.

JENNY (*CONT'D*)
You're looking at me like a gypsy. You want something more than a look it'll cost more than the price of that medal.

AMSTERDAM
I'm not interested in that kind of romance.

Jenny laughs outright.

JENNY
Oh, I see. A man of God.

AMSTERDAM
Do you know your Bible?

JENNY
By rumor and reputation only.

AMSTERDAM
I must be about my father's business.

JENNY
A priest, I'm sure.

AMSTERDAM
Yes.

She looks at him, puzzled. She frowns. She's very stirred up by him and she doesn't like it.

JENNY
I don't want to see you again.

AMSTERDAM
I don't blame you.

EXT. NEW YORK HARBOR— NIGHT

Close on the undertaker from the prologue, fifteen years older now, doing business, trying to get distraught relatives to sign up for better coffins to replace the plain pine boxes their soldier sons and husbands are arriving in. An undertaker walks with a woman in mourning.

AMSTERDAM (V/O)
I never liked the harbor after dark. And now each night they brung ashore the bodies of the soldiers. It was a mournful sight. But we had business of our own.

UNDERTAKER
...It's the least we can do for these poor brave lads...Now, if you'll just give your son's name and regiment to the chief mate, I'll try to make all the necessary arrangements. It is scant comfort, I know, but so many mothers have not even the solace of knowing where their sons have fallen. I lost my own eldest at Antietam. But his mother and I were unable to recover his remains. God is good, madam. It's only a matter of time...the war can't last forever.

Shrouded in fog, Army personnel supervise the off-loading of more soldiers killed in action. The civilians surround those with the lists, and every so often another new, mournful wail cuts through the night. The camera rises above the fog and dark water toward spots of moving light far offshore—

JOHNNY (V.O.)
And God moved upon the waters—

AMSTERDAM (V.O.)
Sit down, Johnny, before you fall overboard.

JOHNNY (V.O.)
The Daybreak Boys catch us on the river they'll cut our throats...

AMSTERDAM (V.O.)
I'll do it myself in a minute if you can't keep quiet.

EXT. HUDSON RIVER— CONTINUOUS—NIGHT

(187)

Two rowboats gliding across black water, almost entirely veiled by thick fog.

The hull of a large ship suddenly looms up.

JOHNNY (*V.O.*)
Hard starboard, Jim—

JIMMY SPOILS (*V.O.*)
What? Which way's starboard?

JOHNNY (*V.O.*)
Left! Left!

JIMMY SPOILS (*V.O.*)
Which way's left?

Too late. The lead rowboat bangs against the ship hull like a loud knock on a door.

EXT. SHIP—NIGHT

A rope ladder clinches against the ship's rail. The gang climbs up onto the deck, Johnny behind Amsterdam. Shang indicates silently where they should go. All around them lie smashed-open crates.

SHANG
The Daybreak Boys already been here. There's nothing left. Let's go back—

JOHNNY
Shhh—

As he moves around the deck then, looking for something worth taking, Amsterdam looks at his hand. Blood drips from it. He touches the railing with his clean hand, and it comes away with blood, too. He looks up to the sound of a door creak and sees a huge shadow looming up behind Jimmy.

AMSTERDAM
Jimmy!

Jimmy turns. The ship's captain stands behind him. Jimmy hits the deck. The musket barks. The shot flies wide. A lantern shatters. The captain collapses dead, a knife sticking out of his back.

SHANG
That'll bring the harbor cops for sure.

Jimmy yanks the knife from the captain's back, wipes it on the captain's pants and sticks it in his own belt. He and Amsterdam exchange a look, then he follows as the gang hurries back down the ladder into the rowboats—except for Amsterdam, who looks around, frustrated.

AMSTERDAM
Jesus! They killed everybody. There's nothin' here but a bunch of dead sea-crabs.

He grabs hold of the body and drags it toward the railing.

JOHNNY
Shove off.

JIMMY SPOILS
Stop—Where's Amsterdam?

The captain's body suddenly slams against the side of the rowboat. Shang, panicked, pushes it into the water. As Amsterdam is climbing down the rope ladder—

AMSTERDAM
No, you damn fools, take him!

SHANG
What in hell for?

AMSTERDAM
Never mind what for, you bastard, just don't let him sink.

(188)

Amsterdam jumps down into the boat, reaches into the water, and hoists the dead man aboard.

EXT. MURDERERS' ALLEY—NIGHT

At the end of a dark, cobblestoned alley, Amsterdam negotiates a sale of the corpse to some medical students.

AMSTERDAM
I said no less than fifteen.

SHANG
Right.

MEDICAL STUDENT
Is this fresh?

AMSTERDAM
Four hours most. Much obliged, gents.

A LURID SEPIA ILLUSTRATION

of a gang selling a corpse to vampirish-looking medical students replaces the real scene. The caption reads: Ghoul Gang Slaughters, Then Sells to Medical Science—A Fresh Outrage of the Five Points.

INT. SATAN'S CIRCUS—DAY

Bill studies the published illustration in his hands. Waiting for his reaction, Johnny and Amsterdam exchange an anxious glance. Bill points to the words—

BILL THE BUTCHER
What's it say there?

AMSTERDAM
It means—

BILL THE BUTCHER
I didn't ask the meaning, I asked the word.

AMSTERDAM
Ghoul.

Bill's never said, or even heard the word before.

BILL THE BUTCHER
Ghoul. That's a good word.

He smiles. Looks at Amsterdam and Johnny.

BILL THE BUTCHER (*CONT'D*)
(*Reading with some difficulty*) "Ghoul Gang Slaughters, Then Sells to Medical Science—A Fresh Outrage of the Five Points." That's a notice you could be proud of. You two ain't done so bad.

AMSTERDAM
Thank you, sir.

JOHNNY
Thank you.

Johnny smiles, enormously relieved, and looks at Amsterdam. Amsterdam's face is nearly unreadable.

McGLOIN
(*Almost to himself*) Low thing, to do that to a body. Low.

BILL THE BUTCHER
(*Points to Amsterdam*) Why? This bene young cove shows enterprise, McGloin. Unlike you. He could have left that ship with nothing. Instead he makes *The Police Gazette*. A periodical of note.

(189)

Bill slaps the newspaper enthusiastically.

McGLOIN
(*With real feeling*) Body's meant to stay beneath the earth, wearin' a wooden coat until the Resurrection.

Everyone looks at McGloin curiously, including Bill.

JOHNNY
(*Uneasily*) Well, here's the ned for it.

Johnny empties his pockets of money and puts it down next to some bloody slabs of meat.

BILL THE BUTCHER
(*Sharply*) Don't put that money in the meat. I don't know where it's been.

Bill starts counting it. He glances from McGloin to the boys.

BILL THE BUTCHER (*CONT'D*)
(*Mildly*) Don't fret that body, McGloin, for Christ's sake. These two are just a pair of bog-eaten Irish sons of bitches same as you and it don't seem to bother them none. But maybe they don't share your religious scruples.

McGLOIN
Maybe they're just a couple of Fidlam Bens.

There is some scattered laughter from a few of the Natives. Johnny tenses. Amsterdam meets McGloin's gaze steadily. Bill just watches and waits, immediately interested.

(190) **AMSTERDAM**
(*Laughs*) I been called a lot of things mister, but I ain't never been called... (*fumbles for the wording*)

McGLOIN
Fidlam Bens.

AMSTERDAM
Fidlam Bens, right... Well, if I knew what in the Hell that meant, I might be inclined to take offense.

The air grows thicker. McGloin takes a step toward Amsterdam.

McGLOIN
A Fidlam Bens is a fellow steals anythin', dead or alive, 'cause he's too low to work up a decent lay for himself. Count that careful, Bill, just count that careful.

JOHNNY
I'm tellin' you—That's all there is. That's all they give us.

Amsterdam puts a hand on Johnny's arm to stop him. He takes a step toward McGloin.

AMSTERDAM
Now, "chiseler." If you had said "chiseler." There's a word I understand. Now, is that what you're callin' us?

The room is dead still. Bill is watching them with keen interest.

McGLOIN
I can think of a number of things to call you, boyo.

AMSTERDAM
Yeh, but I asked if you was callin' us chiselers.

McGLOIN
Supposin' I am, grave robber?

AMSTERDAM
Well, then we got business.

McGLOIN
That we do.

They turn away and take off their jackets. The Natives start clearing away the tables, some of them laughing. Bill smiles with them, but seems less certain of the outcome. McGloin raises his fists. Amsterdam does the same. The smirking grows as the gang members gather round to watch...

McGloin showboats for them, throwing a few punches. Amsterdam parries with surprising skill, catching him a few times. As McGloin gets frustrated he lashes out with his foot. Amsterdam reacts viciously and the traditional fist fight explodes into a savage street brawl. Amsterdam fights with a repressed fury, like a man possessed. In a flurry of knees, elbows, and fingers he sends McGloin crashing into the card table, knocking everything over. He slithers astride the Irishman, about to fishhook him, when the other Natives stop laughing and pull him off. Bill's the only one still smiling.

BILL THE BUTCHER
All right, that'll do. That'll do.

AMSTERDAM
Have you got anything to say now?!

The men struggle to get Amsterdam off McGloin. He tries to recover his breath. Bill comes forward with a knife, eying the boy.

NATIVE
That's enough, kid.

NATIVE (*CONT'D*)
You're gettin' too old for him, McGloin.

The room is still and tense. Silence. Amsterdam collects himself, not sure of what Bill might do. Bill slaps a slab of meat into Amsterdam's hand, and then raises it to a wound on Amsterdam's cheek. The room sighs. And Amsterdam smiles. Bill nods in approval.

BILL THE BUTCHER
I thought you told me you could fight, McGloin. All these years I took you for a giant...

The others start to laugh now.

BILL THE BUTCHER (*CONT'D*)
McGloin, how would that head look without the ears and the nose on it?

McGLOIN
You better leave that head alone, Bill.

BILL THE BUTCHER
I think I'm gonna trim the ears and the beak off of that head. Make a nice pot of soup of that head.

NATIVE
You can find a tastier head than that, Bill.

ANOTHER NATIVE
I ain't got the stomach for no...no Irish stew.

BILL THE BUTCHER
The mighty McGloin almost fishhooked by a sprat.

Amsterdam looks around like a caged animal, still consumed by the violence. The Natives slap him on the back and hand him a drink. As he slowly calms down, his eyes meet Bill's. Bill smiles and raises his glass in a toast. Taken by surprise by the gesture, Amsterdam responds instinctively, raising his own glass, almost smiling back.

Bill comes slowly forward, rights the card table, picks up the portrait of Vallon with surprising gentleness and returns it carefully to its place of honor. The smile disappears from Amsterdam's face, as the laughter continues all around him.

(191)

INT. SLUM BUILDING (OLD BREWERY)—DAY

Tribune publisher Horace Greeley and some wealthy uptown citizens follow their tour guide, Happy Jack, through a dank and overcrowded building.

HAPPY JACK
Fleeing the Great Irish Famine, they cross the Atlantic with pennies in their pockets and hope in their eyes, searching the horizon for a glimpse of land and salvation. A glimpse of America.

Faces peer out of the darkness at Greeley and the others, like animals in cages, with hatred in their eyes.

HAPPY JACK (*CONT'D*)
Ah, but only shattered dreams await them. Pauperism and dereliction. Drunkenness and depravity. Molestation and murder, kind sirs and ladies.

EXT. PARADISE SQUARE— DAY—SAME TIME

Amsterdam walks alongside Bill as the usual Native bodyguards, Johnny, and a marked McGloin follow. Johnny is watching Bill talk with Amsterdam.

BILL THE BUTCHER
...The Daybreak Boys run the East River; the Swamp Angels handle the West. Irish gyps. Part of the Irish plague. The Lord rested on the seventh day but before He did, He squatted over the side of England and what come out of Him was Ireland. No offense, son.

AMSTERDAM
None taken, sir. I grew up here. All I ever knew of Ireland was in the talk of the others at the orphan asylum.

(192)

BILL THE BUTCHER
And where on that excrementitious isle were your forebears spawned?

AMSTERDAM
I been told Kerry, but I lost the proof of it in my language at the asylum.

BILL THE BUTCHER
I was raised in a very similar establishment. Now everything you see belongs to me, to one degree or another.

As he speaks, we see quick vignettes to small-time crime—

BILL THE BUTCHER (CONT'D)
The beggars and newsboys and quick thieves here in Paradise. The sailor dives and gin mills and blind tigers on the waterfront. The anglers and amusers, the She-Hes and the Chinks. Everybody owes, everybody pays. Because that's how you stand up against the rising of the tide. Isn't that right, boys?

THE NATIVES
Yeh, Bill, that's right...

A quick cut of some kids throwing a brick through a shop window and grabbing stuff—

BILL THE BUTCHER
Oh, I hear the sound of breaking glass and it's like a beautiful young mort's fingers running down my spine.

EXT. SLUM BUILDING / PARADISE SQUARE—DAY

A tour group emerges from the building. A group of sick Irish immigrants shelter in the doorway.

SCHERMERHORN
Conscription may be no bad thing, Mr. Greeley—at least the Army would provide these poor wretches with three square meals a day—

GREELEY
—You must find all this most unsettling, Miss Schermerhorn.

MISS SCHERMERHORN
On the contrary, Mr. Greeley, I find it most illuminating—

HAPPY JACK
Commissioner Brunt said you wished to view the Points in all its splendor and squalor. "Spare nothing concerning the conditions," said he—

SCHERMERHORN
Nothing but our safety, Constable.

MRS. SCHERMERHORN
I am sure we can be in no danger while in the Constable's company, my dear.

HAPPY JACK
Quite so, madam. Witness—

Jack takes out his watch and chain and carefully hangs it on a lamppost.

HAPPY JACK (*CONT'D*)
Shall we continue on?

HORACE GREELEY
You dare leave it there?

HAPPY JACK
Safe as a vault, Mr. Greeley, since all knows it's mine.

Leading them on, he steps over a body in the street, a cholera victim, as if it were a puddle of water. The Schermerhorns stare as they walk around it.

MISS SCHERMERHORN
Is that man drunk, or—

HAPPY JACK
Dead as Good Friday, Ma'am.

Miss Schermerhorn controls her reaction with admirable fortitude. But looking back up from the body she takes a sudden step backward and involuntarily grips her father's arm. Standing before her is a man with a beat-up face—McGloin—flanked by Bill, Amsterdam, Johnny, and the Natives.

BILL THE BUTCHER
Day to you, Mulraney.

HAPPY JACK
Boys.

BILL THE BUTCHER
Slum Sociable?

HAPPY JACK
Fact-finding, Bill. Reforms-studying. May I present—

BILL THE BUTCHER
(*On "may"*) The Schermerhorns of Fifth Avenue scarcely require an introduction from you, Jack.

HAPPY JACK
—Mr. Schermerhorn, indeed, and their daughter...And this gentlemen is Mr. Horace Greeley—

BILL THE BUTCHER
(*On "is"*) Ah, Horace Greeley, the great publisher. Honor and a pleasure, sir.

HAPPY JACK
—of the *Tribune*...

BILL THE BUTCHER
I'm William Cutting.

Bill offers to shake hands. Miss Schermerhorn steps forward and complies with some spirit.

MISS SCHERMERHORN
How do you do, Mr. Cutting?

There are "How do you do's" and handshakes all around.

HAPPY JACK
Mr. Cutting is one of the Five Points local—

MRS. SCHERMERHORN
(*Overlapping*) Pleasure to meet you, sir.

HAPPY JACK
(*Overlapping*)—leaders.

BILL THE BUTCHER
(*Overlapping*) Mr. Greeley.

GREELEY
(*Overlapping*) Pleased to meet you, Mr. Cutting.

BILL THE BUTCHER
...Sirs, ladies, the Five Points welcomes you. You are welcome to these streets, and will pass in safety.

HAPPY JACK
I'll see to their safety, thank you, Bill.

Bill just smiles in his face. The group passes by. Amsterdam watches Happy Jack as he goes by.

(194)   **HAPPY JACK** (*CONT'D*)
(*To the Schermerhorns*)...the criminal's braggadocio, you see...

MR. GREELEY
He knows who I am.

HAPPY JACK
Oh indeed, sir. You're well known in these parts.

MR. GREELEY
I must say, I find that strangely flattering.

Amsterdam spits after Happy Jack. Bill looks at him.

AMSTERDAM
(*Covering*) I don't like crushers.

BILL THE BUTCHER
Well, draw it mild, son. Happy Jack don't fill his lungs with air without I tell him he may do so.

They turn. Monk is coming directly toward them down the street. Bill is suddenly battle-ready; Monk likewise. They eye each other as they pass.

MONK
Do you think my watch would be safe on that lamppost, Bill?

BILL THE BUTCHER
Why don't you hang it up there and see?

MONK
Someday.

BILL THE BUTCHER
Someday.

MONK
(*Nods at Amsterdam*) This a new lad?

BILL THE BUTCHER
Just another bastard son of Erin I've folded in the warmth of my embrace.

They pass by each other like two cobras sizing each other up but deciding not to strike. Bill walks on with his Natives in tow and Amsterdam at his side.

As Amsterdam comes past Monk, the big man's hand cuffs at his cap. Everyone in the street suddenly bristles, ready for a brawl. Amsterdam steps back, grabbing at his hat. Monk remains calm.

MONK

Just wanted to see your face. No harm intended.

Bill and his retinue walk on. Amsterdam falls in step with them, then looks over his shoulder. Monk is standing in the same spot, watching him.

INT. TWEED'S OFFICE—DAY

Tweed sits in a wooden box like a primitive sauna. Around him stand two petitioners and some assistants.

DR. GLEASON

My plague box fends off pestilence. Its elixir combats ill-humors—

KILLORAN

We can't have every citizen of the Five Points boxed up like cargo.

TWEED

Cholera, Mr. Killoran! An epidemic! We must think about our constituents, especially the immigrants. Can't have them all dying off, least not before election time.

Climbing out of the box he's quickly swathed in towels.

TWEED (CONT'D)

Dr. Gleason, this is Mr. Baff. Mr. Baff is a friend of Tammany, a friend of mine. He will provide conveyance of your elixir, Doctor, but without your box. You will each bill the city five thousand dollars a month for supplies and services—

(*Their faces light up.*) Of which you'll receive ten percent. (*Their faces fall.*) Mr. Killoran will work out the details. That's how we do things around Tammany, gentlemen.

Bill! Come in! Thank you, gentlemen.

As Killoran leads the doctor, Baff, and the assistants out, Bill, Johnny, and Amsterdam come in.

TWEED (CONT'D)

Who's this then?

BILL THE BUTCHER

Some bright young lads of mine.

TWEED

Bright enough to see themselves out and shut the door behind them?

INT. TAMMANY HALL—LATER

A bust of Tamanend, the legendary Delaware Indian chief, sits on a pedestal at the end of a long corridor. Amsterdam and Johnny wander through.

He notices Johnny staring at him.

AMSTERDAM

Either you got somethin' on your mind, Johnny, or you're startin' to get feelings for me. Now which is it?

JOHNNY

Bill's taken quite a liking to you...I was a bit... If you're up to something, bene, only I don't want no part of it.

AMSTERDAM

I was in Hellgate for sixteen years. I'm just trying to make my way is all, just like you. Unless, of course, you've got a better notion?

JOHNNY
No.

Amsterdam does not respond. Instead he continues along the corridor, looking at the artifacts devoted to the history of Tammany: All manner of rings and medals with strange secret-society markings in glass cases. An illustration of men dressed like Indians posing outside a craftsman's shop called the Society of St. Tammany's First Wigwam. Portraits of white men with head-dresses, Grand Sachem-this, Grand Sachem-that. A stuffed, snarling Bengal tiger in a prowling pose. He gestures for Johnny to look. Johnny looks.

AMSTERDAM
This is a gang.

INT. TWEED'S OFFICE— SAME TIME

Alone in the room, Tweed and Bill confer.

TWEED
Bill, I can't get a day's work done for all the good citizens coming in here to fret me about crime in the Points. Some, I'm horrified to say, have gone so far as to accuse Tammany of connivance with this so-called rampant criminality. What am I to do? I can't have this. Something has to be done.

BILL THE BUTCHER
What'd you have in mind?

(196) TWEED
I don't know, I think we have to hang somebody.

He says it as if he's talking about what shirt he should wear tomorrow.

TWEED (CONT'D)
No one important necessarily. Average men will do. Back-alley amusers without affiliations.

BILL THE BUTCHER
How many?

TWEED
Three or four.

BILL THE BUTCHER
Which.

TWEED
Four.

BILL THE BUTCHER
(Aghast) Four good earners!

TWEED
No, Bill, no need for that; just as long as they're guilty of something.

BILL THE BUTCHER
I expect to be reimbursed for this.

EXT. FISH MARKET, WHARF—DAY

ASST. HANGMAN
You stand convicted varyingly of—

(reading) Lewdness, jack-rolling, sneak-thievery, chloral-hydrating, sodomy, strangulation, and enthusiastic corruption of the public good.

A round of applause for the accomplishments of the four condemned and manacled wretches. The crowd of a hundred or so gathered in the muddy courtyard are in a carnival spirit. Hot-Corn girls and vendors of all variety hawk their wares.

The condemned men are led to the gallows steps, where they encounter a receiving line of lowlife well-wishers headed by Bill, who shakes each of their manacled hands.

BILL THE BUTCHER
(*Variously to the men*) Good man. Chin up. We'll remember you. You're a fine bunch of gallows fruit. Say hello to Amsterdam—Nearly fishooked McGloin the other day—

McGLOIN
Nearly!

CONDEMNED MEN
(*To Amsterdam*) How'd y'do?

AMSTERDAM
(*Shaking hands*) Pleased to meet you.

BILL THE BUTCHER
See you dressed for the occasion, Arthur.

The last **CONDEMNED MAN** is wearing a fancy silk scarf around the collar of his threadbare jacket

CONDEMNED MAN
Always try to look my best, Bill.

Bill fingers a golden locket hanging around the Condemned Man's neck.

BILL THE BUTCHER
(*To Condemned Man*) Take a dollar for the locket?

CONDEMNED MAN
(*Resentfully*) It's me Mum's.

BILL THE BUTCHER
Dollar and a half?

CONDEMNED MAN
Done.

Bill takes the locket and pays the Condemned Man, who bites into the coins to make sure they're good, then pockets them.

BILL THE BUTCHER
I'll miss you, Arthur.

(*To another condemned man*) See you in the hot country, Seamus.

As the men are led up the steps to the platform. Bill gives a nod to a strangely dressed man, **MONSIEUR NEW YORK**, the hangman. He returns Bill's salute.

AMSTERDAM
Who's that nimenog?

BILL THE BUTCHER
Why, that's Monsieur New York. Finest hangman in the North. If their necks don't break on the first drop he don't eat meat for a week.

The Assistant Hangman cinches the nooses around the condemned men's necks.

ASST. HANGMAN
Got any last reflections?

The condemned hooded men all turn toward each other variously. No one has prepared anything.

CONDEMNED MAN 2
Not with this hood on I don't...!

The crowd chants, "No hoods, no hoods!" The Assistant Hangman removes the hoods. The crowd cheers. Condemned Man 2 steps forward.

CONDEMNED MAN 2 (*CONT'D*)
Is my son present? Where is my little man?

Amsterdam follows the man's look into the crowd, and catches sight of a **SMALL BOY**, around eight, standing in front of his **MOTHER**, looking up at Condemned Man 2. Her hands grip the boy's shoulders tightly.

CONDEMNED MAN 2 (CONT'D)
Farewell, dear boy. I never struck a foul blow or turned a card. May God greet me as a friend.

He steps back. The long trapdoor opens. The four ropes snap taut and the crowd roars its approval.

Amsterdam looks at the boy as he watches his father die; the roar of the crowd in his ears is like the roar of the Natives 15 years ago when Amsterdam knelt beside the dead Vallon.

INT. OLD BREWERY/ MISSION—NIGHT

A choir of twenty kids in rags, guided by some Ladies of the Mission, sings a hymn as Rev. Raleigh looks on proudly. Ship lanterns and candles try to illuminate the cavernous place. The missionaries have taken it over and thrown out most of its transients. Now it's filled primarily with whores and young men from gangs, differentiated by their colors. Rev. Raleigh glances at them uneasily.

EXT. PARADISE SQUARE— NIGHT

Street kids run from the spray from a hose on the back of a horse-drawn cart. On one side is painted "Anti-Pestilence, Cholera-Thwarting Solution." On the other, "A Public Service of Tammany."

AMSTERDAM (*V.O.*)
That night the reformers held a dance. That was the Five Points, all right. Hangings of a morning. Dancin' of an evening.

Johnny and Amsterdam, Shang, Jimmy, and the others dodge the spray as they cross the street. Johnny carries the music box. We catch them mid-conversation.

JOHNNY
I can tell by the way she smiles at me...

AMSTERDAM
She smiles at a lot of people, Johnny.

A soldier leaning on a crutch, missing one leg, tries to block their path.

LEGLESS SOLDIER
Penny of gratitude for a fighting Irishman, young sirs.

Amsterdam stops.

AMSTERDAM
You're from Kerry.

LEGLESS SOLDIER
I am, sir.

Amsterdam. Gets a coin out of his pocket and gives it to the soldier.

AMSTERDAM
It ain't much.

LEGLESS SOLDIER
Thank you, sir.

Amsterdam moves on. Johnny falls in step.

INT. OLD BREWERY/ MISSION—CONTINUED

Off by herself, Jenny watches a distraught woman dragging her child out of the choir line as the rest keep singing.

REV. RALEIGH
Madam, please. We welcome Christians of every stamp, but there's no need to frighten the children with a great big crucifix showing Christ dripping blood from His wounds.

DISTRAUGHT WOMAN
Yes, there is.

As she takes her child out, Amsterdam and the others come in and scan the place. Johnny spots Jenny across the room. She smiles at him, then sees he is with Amsterdam and frowns.

REV. RALEIGH (O.S.)
Ladies and gentlemen, we are delighted to see so many young faces at our first annual Mission dance...

SHANG
Boys, this'll be a real ballum-rancum, eh?

REV. RALEIGH (O.S.)
...and we are particularly happy to greet our Roman Catholic friends who join us here tonight.

INT. OLD BREWERY/ MISSION—LATER

The boys have been guided to one side of the room. Reverend Raleigh moves along the smaller group of girls (and She-Hes) lined up on the other.

WOMAN #1
Good evening, Reverend.

WOMAN #2
Good evening, Reverend.

JENNY
(To one of the She-Hes, jokingly) Looks as though you should have shaved closer.

He stops in front of Jenny.

REV. RALEIGH
Miss—

JENNY
Everdeane.

REV. RALEIGH
Miss Everdeane.

He offers her his arm, leads her to a small wooden chair in the center of the room, and hands her a small pocket mirror.

REV. RALEIGH (CONT'D)
And the evening's regent chooses her evening's partner. Now, the gentlemen. Over here, if you would, please.

The boys are shepherded into a line behind the chair. Amsterdam is swept along with the rest. The rest of the ceremony is played out in **THE MIRROR** in Jenny's hand. As she raises it, the first boy appears alongside her profile in foreground. She shakes her head, no. The next candidate appears and is similarly rejected. And the next.

Johnny steps into the reflection, trying to look confident. Jenny hesitates, then shakes her head, no. Johnny isn't sure he saw right. He waits. She shakes her head again. The Rev. Raleigh gently moves him along. Amsterdam steps into view. She looks at him for a long time. He starts to move away—She turns around sharply.

JENNY
That one.

Amsterdam stops where he is. He's not sure how to take this. Neither is Johnny.

REV. RALEIGH
Our queen has chosen.

He applauds. The Ladies of the Mission—and no one else—join in. He gestures to a small band. A waltz version of "A Mighty Fortress Is Our God" begins to play. He helps Jenny up and leads her to Amsterdam.

REV. RALEIGH (*CONT'D*)
Sir? Your Lady.

(*And, as an aside*) Regular services this and every Sunday, at dawn's light, eight and ten.

AMSTERDAM
Go to hell.

Johnny watches from afar as Jenny places Amsterdam's arm around her waist. He turns and walks out with the music box.

Amsterdam and Jenny start dancing after a fashion. A few other couples pair off.

At first Amsterdam and Jenny don't look at each other, looking only over each other's shoulders. Their tone is quite serious. As before, there is something intense between them right away that is more than either one of them bargained for.

AMSTERDAM (*CONT'D*)
What are you doin'?

JENNY
What?

(200) **AMSTERDAM**
I said, why'd you pick me?

JENNY
That's none of your business.

AMSTERDAM
Well, would you mind tellin' me—

He steps on her toe.

JENNY
Ow!

AMSTERDAM
I'm sorry.

He immediately does it again.

JENNY
Ow!

AMSTERDAM
I'm sorry—! I'm not much of a dancer.

JENNY
Just try to keep calm.

Amsterdam tries unsuccessfully to do better.

AMSTERDAM
I'm sorry. I've never been to a stepping-ken before.

JENNY
(*Surprised*) Never?

Jenny looks at him curiously. He tries to answer, and literally cannot come up with anything to say. Jenny sees he'd rather not discuss himself and doesn't press the point.

JENNY (*CONT'D*)
Well, it's best not to look down. And, you can hold me tighter if you like.

He holds her tighter. They keep dancing. He does slightly better.

AMSTERDAM
Why didn't you dance with Johnny?

She looks at him for the first time. Pause.

JENNY
Because I'm not in love with him.

Pause. They look at each other. She holds him even closer. His arms go around her tighter. Their bad dancing has improved somewhat.

In the candlelight, their movement becomes split, sequential, like an old Gjon Mili photograph, their bodies creating a rush of yellow light across the screen.

EXT. WATERFRONT DOCKS— NIGHT

There are reflections in the water of torches from a Negro burial ritual in the distance. Amsterdam and Jenny are sitting on the pier, kissing. He kisses her mouth, her face, her neck.

AMSTERDAM
(*As he kisses her*) I don't want this. I'm not wanting this. (*Fumbling at her corset*) How does this open?

JENNY
It takes too long to lace it up again; we'll be here all night.

He keeps kissing her. She squirms around, very turned on.

JENNY (*CONT'D*)
(*Breathless*) Sure, all right, I'll take it off.

She hurriedly removes the pins and her long hair cascades down her body. They kiss again. He

begins to unbutton her blouse, from the bottom up, revealing a scar just below her waist.

JENNY (*CONT'D*)
(*Slightly embarrassed*) There was a baby…They cut it out—I'm sorry.

Amsterdam makes a gesture, i.e., "You don't have to apologize."

JENNY (*CONT'D*)
(*A bit shyly, perhaps*) Have you got any scars?

AMSTERDAM
(*Hesitates*) One or two.

She slowly begins unbuttoning his shirt, from the top down. The shirt parts, revealing several long, jagged scars on his chest and stomach. She never expected to see so many of them. It's a map, in bas-relief, of almost-countless knife fights.

She almost gasps, then looks at him as if to say "What happened to you?" He starts to speak, at a loss where to begin, then gives up trying. She shakes her head and smiles; she already knows the whole story.

He watches her face as her fingers gently trace the scars, one to the next, like rungs on a ladder. She looks back up and they kiss more passionately.

His hand undoes the top button on her blouse, and, as it parts, he sees a familiar gold locket against her neck.

AMSTERDAM (*CONT'D*)
What's that?

JENNY
This? It's a gift from Mr. Cutting.

(201)

Amsterdam shifts away from her a fraction of an inch.

AMSTERDAM
A gift?

JENNY
(*Pointedly*) Yes. A gift.

Brief pause.

AMSTERDAM
Is it your birthday?

JENNY
No.

AMSTERDAM
What did you give him, then?

JENNY
The answer to that has nothin' to do with you.

He just looks at her, expressionless.

JENNY (*CONT'D*)
Don't tell me you're angry with me.

AMSTERDAM
No. I'm through with you.

Jenny reacts like he's just slapped her. She tries unsuccessfully to laugh it off.

JENNY
You're quicker than most fellows.

(202) Generally they wait till afterwards.

AMSTERDAM
Well, I ain't interested in the Butcher's leavings.

She starts to speak, then stops herself. She gets up, shaking her head, and starts buttoning her blouse. She is nearly in tears. Her hair is all over the place. She stoops down to find her lost pins.

Amsterdam watches her. She is having so much trouble finding the pins that he finally makes a movement toward her. She twists away violently. Giving up the search for the pins she walks away, managing her hair as best she can. Amsterdam buttons his shirt, watching her go.

INT. SATAN'S CIRCUS—DAY

The place is almost empty: a few Natives playing cards; a destitute family waiting for a gift of meat as Bill expertly dresses the carcass of a pig. Amsterdam stands next to him wearing an apron and holding a knife.

BILL THE BUTCHER
You get to know a lot butchering meat.

We're made up of the same things. Flesh and blood. Tissue. Organs.

I like to work with pigs: The nearest thing in Nature to the flesh of a man is the flesh of a pig.

AMSTERDAM
Pig, eh?

BILL THE BUTCHER
(*Gives some meat to the mother*) There you go, mother.

DESTITUTE MOTHER
God bless you, Mr. Cutting.

BILL THE BUTCHER
(*As she walks away*) She ain't really my mother.

AMSTERDAM

I was goin' to ask...

Bill shows Amsterdam where each organ is located with his knife, on the hog (which we don't see) and on him.

BILL THE BUTCHER

This is the liver. This is a kidney. This is the heart. This is a wound. The stomach will bleed and bleed. This is a kill. This is a kill. This is a kill.

Now he's sticking the knife into the carcass with fluid speed. Amsterdam looks at the knife in his own hand, then at Bill. His eyes fall on the colored handbill on the wall.

15th Commemoration of The Great Battle of 1844
A Celebration of the Stirring Native Victory

INT. SATAN'S CIRCUS—NIGHT

Two boxers hammer at each other in a makeshift ring. A bell rings and a Card Girl steps in carrying a sign marked "Round 44." Amsterdam, Johnny, Shang, Jimmy Spoils, and the others move through the large, boisterous crowd collecting bets.

JIMMY SPOILS

I never seen so much cabbage in my life!

SHANG

He just took another one in the mush!

AMSTERDAM

Bill says keep clear of the pikers. Fifteen to one, Johnny: Bug-Eye Moran. Did you get that? Write it down.

Shang and Jimmy move off. Johnny starts to follow.

JOHNNY

Yes, sir, straight away, sir.

Amsterdam catches his arm. Johnny shakes it off.

AMSTERDAM

Johnny—nothin' happened with her. We only talked awhile—We never even—

JOHNNY

(*On "happened"*) That's all right. I got no claim to her—It's all right, it's got nothin' to do with me.

AMSTERDAM

Look, Johnny, she belongs to the Butcher! We've both of us got to keep clear of her.

JOHNNY

The Butcher's the Devil Incarnate, all right? He's had every girl in the Points. She don't belong to him. We do.

BILL THE BUTCHER

(*From across the room*) Amsterdam! Here to me, son, I want you!

Johnny disappears into the throng as the bell rings for another round. Amsterdam stares after him as the crowd cheers, then turns to go to Bill.

AMSTERDAM (*V.O.*)

Everyone was working for the Butcher. We ran his errands, made his money, took a piece, and said "Thank you, sir..."

The fighters limp back into the ring. Suddenly another brawl breaks out as two groups of police—state and municipal—stream in to break up the match. Bill watches in stunned fury as his evening's entertainment—and business—is disrupted.

Tweed, sitting right next to him, notes Horace Greeley and the journalists present, gets up, steps forward, then turns around so he appears to be leading the cops. He "arrives." Bill stares at him, flanked by all the police. A newspaper artist immediately begins sketching a picture of the man "leading" the cops.

GREELEY
Gentlemen, it's a raid!

AMSTERDAM (V.O.)
...Even Tweed.

TWEED
That's it, gentlemen, the fight's over!

AMSTERDAM (V.O.)
...Even me. My father's son.

TWEED
Sorry, Bill. The city ordinance against boxiana is a blight, I grant you, but some appearance of order is in—order. Even in the Points.

Tweed calls out to the crowd. Bill barks at him:

TWEED (CONT'D)
That's it, gentlemen, fight's over!

BILL THE BUTCHER
I'm losing revenue while you speechify!

(204)   Half the spectators throw chairs at Tweed. It's bedlam. The two factions of police start fighting not only with the crowd but with each other. Tweed sighs. Amsterdam appears at Bill's side. Bill snaps at him:

BILL THE BUTCHER
Get out there and collect those bets!

AMSTERDAM
How do I collect if no one won the fight?

BILL THE BUTCHER
This counts as a "No Decision." You got that covered, right? Didn't anybody pay off the police?

TWEED
We paid the metropolitan police! These are the municipal police!

BILL THE BUTCHER
(To Tweed) You're gonna pay me every cent I would've made in here tonight!

TWEED
I can't pay off a fight that never finished!

BILL THE BUTCHER
Look at this, God damn it, this is chaos!

AMSTERDAM
Mr. Tweed! Suppose we—

TWEED
Who asked you?

BILL THE BUTCHER
Let him talk, he don't answer to you!

AMSTERDAM
The law don't allow no boxing in the city, is that right?

TWEED
In the city, yes.

AMSTERDAM
Well, where does the city end?

Amsterdam makes a gesture, i.e., "problem solved." Bill and Tweed look at him blankly.

EXT. BOXING RING—DAY

The same bare-knuckled fighters battle it out in a proper ring. The same Card Girl DISSOLVES through the boxing action carrying a sign that reads, "Round 72."

REFEREE
The winner in the seventy-second round—one minute, thirteen seconds...

Amsterdam, seated with Bill, notices Jenny working the crowd.

She comes past Johnny and stops to say a friendly word. He's wary at first but finally responds with some warmth, and there is some kind of affectionate exchange between them. They move off together.

As Jenny walks through the crowd, she notices Amsterdam, sitting next to Bill—glancing over. She continues walking away. Amsterdam looks away.

P.T. Barnum rushes into the center of the ring. The crowd roars its indignation.

P.T. BARNUM
The winner—gentlemen!—the winner by a knockout, the incumbent Native American champion—High Water Dobbs—(cheers and boos) Who has beat the Hibernian challenger, Beltless Tom O'Shannon, in one minute and thirteen seconds of the seventy-second round! (cheers and boos) While I have your kind attention, may I remind you of the further wonders that await you at my museum, located on Broadway—(a loud chorus of boos) P.T. Barnum's Gallery of Wonders,

from worlds Natural and Unnatural, from Nature and from Myth.

Everyone jeers, Tweed and Bill included. Amsterdam does not join in.

P.T. BARNUM (CONT'D)
I would also like to acknowledge our great debt to the man whose vision and enterprise made possible the staging of this noble combat in these awe-inspiring—and entirely legal—surroundings—

Bill smiles at Amsterdam and pats him on the shoulder.

P.T. BARNUM (CONT'D)
Mr. William Cutting!

Bill stands and accepts great cheers from the huge crowd.

Suddenly he reaches down and pulls Amsterdam up with him. Amsterdam reluctantly climbs into the ring with him.

The waves of cheers and Bill's arm around his shoulder jolly him out of his distemper, and he finds himself smiling as the crowd roars and hats fly into the air. Shang and the boys cheer loudest of all.

Amsterdam scans the crowd for Jenny or Johnny but can't find them.

We begin to pull wide, showing Bill and Amsterdam, the crowd, the boxing ring, the raft they're all on—half a city block long—the sparkling Hudson River it's floating in the middle of, and the wild northern reaches of Manhattan in the distance.

(205)

AMSTERDAM (V.O.)
It's a funny feeling being took under the wing of a dragon. It's warmer than you think.

EXT. NEW YORK HARBOR—DAY

Another wave of Irish immigrants trundle their belongings across the docks. Waiting for them, of course, is hot soup served up by Tammany representatives. Tweed points to the ragged people coming off the sailing ship.

TWEED

There's the building of our country right there, Bill. Americans aborning.

BILL THE BUTCHER

I don't see no Americans. I see trespassers. Paddies who'll do a job for a nickel what a nigger does for a dime and a white man used to get a quarter for—then moan about it when you treat them like niggers.

AMSTERDAM

Bill's got mixed feelings as regards the Irish.

TWEED

Maybe he should look a little closer.

BILL THE BUTCHER

(Sharply) This ain't no joke. What have they done? What have they contributed?

TWEED

Votes.

Amsterdam looks out at the Irish immigrants thoughtfully.

BILL THE BUTCHER

They vote how the Archbishop tells them. And who tells the Archbishop? Their king in the pointy hat what sits on his throne in Rome.

TWEED

Then we will rival Rome for their loyalty and affection. Soup for the hungry, alms for the poor,

medicine for the sick, muscle for the recalcitrant. Mother and father, crusher and church to them all. Deliver these good and fervent folk to the polls on a regular basis and there'll be a handsome price for each vote goes Tammany's way.

BILL THE BUTCHER

My father gave his life makin' this country what it is. Murdered by the British with all his men, on the twenty-fifth of July, Anno Domini, 1814. Now you want me to help befoul his legacy by givin' this country over to them what's had no hand in the fighting for it? Why? Because they come off a boat, crawling with lice and beggin' you for soup?

TWEED

You're a great one for fighting, Bill, I know. But you can't fight forever.

BILL THE BUTCHER

I can go down doing it.

Amsterdam has been following all of this very closely. Bill turns to leave. Amsterdam falls in behind him.

TWEED

And you will.

BILL THE BUTCHER

(Stops) What did you say?

TWEED

I said you're turning your back on your future.

Bill has an arm on Amsterdam's shoulder.

BILL THE BUTCHER

Not our future.

Amsterdam glances back at Tweed. The Natives stride past several tables where officials naturalize the immigrants, having them raise their right hands and repeat the oath of citizenship. Next to those tables are others where recruiters stamp at forms—

RECRUITER
That document makes you a citizen. This one makes you a private in the Union Army. Now go fight for your country.

ANOTHER RECRUITER
Sign here, son. Or make your mark.

RECRUITER
There's your musket. Make sure you keep it dry on the boat. Same for the cartridge case!

NEW RECRUIT #1
Where we goin'?

NEW RECRUIT #2
I heard Tennessee.

NEW RECRUIT #1
Where's that?

Another line of immigrants who have just arrived and been naturalized, inducted, and put in uniforms, board another ship that will carry them off to war. Off that ship, more coffins are being hoisted onto the docks.

NEW RECRUIT #3
Do they feed us now, you think?

STEWARD
Free up the gangway. Free up the gangway!

INT. BOWERY THEATRE—
NIGHT

Close on the face of President Abraham Lincoln.

LINCOLN
My children! My children! We must heal the division between us!

It takes a moment to realize his beard is stuck on with spirit gum and that he's just an actor— Harry Watkins—arms outstretched as if crucified. The stage is ablaze with candlelight.

LINCOLN/WATKINS
This war must cease! North and South must stand united!

He's answered by catcalls and whistles. All the gangs in the Five Points are in attendance. Amsterdam and Bill are hurling rotten fruits and vegetables. They are shouting at the stage, looking at each other and laughing at each other's remarks. (The dialogue should be somewhat staggered, full of interruptions and hiccups— since they are listening to each other and trying to get their sentences out at the same time.)

AMSTERDAM
More division! More fighting! The more fighting, the better we like it! We like fighting!

BILL THE BUTCHER
Burn the rebels alive and use the niggers for kindling! Free the niggers and enslave the Paddies!

As they hurl the rotten fruit, we see that Watkins is hovering on a rope like an angel, twenty-five feet above the stage, where a tearful tableau of *Uncle Tom's Cabin* is being enacted.

AMSTERDAM
What happens at the finish then?

BILL THE BUTCHER
Then we have ourselves a rowdy-dow.

Ain't you never been to the theater before?

AMSTERDAM
No.

LINCOLN/WATKINS
(*Ignoring the jeers and projectiles*) Mr. Legree, lay down your whip!

Miss Eliza, join hands with Mr. Shelby! And Topsy, dear little Topsy, cradle Uncle Tom's head.

NATIVE AMERICAN
(*As Uncle Tom stirs to life*) Leave the nigger dead!

BILL THE BUTCHER
Down with the Union!

AMSTERDAM
Down with the Union!

As Amsterdam joins in the general laughter, we see a man in a velvet waistcoat make his way along their row to a chorus of boos from those whose view he's blocking. The next actions play out like steps of a ballet:

The man's hand sliding under his jacket; Amsterdam turning; the hand reappearing with a pistol; Bill oblivious; Amsterdam seeing it; the pistol pointing at Bill's head;

ASSASSIN
For the blood of the Irish, Bill!

Amsterdam lunging over the seats, grabbing the man's arm; the gun firing with a puff of smoke; the bullet piercing Bill's shoulder, exiting the other side; striking the Native next to him in the ankle.

As Amsterdam wrestles with the would-be assassin, Bill bellows in pain like a big game animal felled, sinking to his knees, clutching at the messy wound.

The audience is in an uproar. Uncle Tom rises quickly from the dead and hurries offstage with Mr. Shelby and Topsy while poor Harry Watkins twists from his rope harness high above the stage.

Amsterdam grips the wrist of the hand with the pistol, trying to keep it from pointing at him, and twists it toward the assassin. It fires, tearing into the man's waistcoat.

McGLOIN
Stifle that rat bastard down!

The audience falls silent, waiting to see if Bill gets up or not. Fighting the pain and the flowing blood from his wound, he rises from his knees and stands tall and puts his hat back on his head.

Ignoring Amsterdam, he turns to the dying assassin, who is clutching at a string of beads and mumbling a prayer to himself with his last breaths.

BILL THE BUTCHER
(*In great pain*) Whose man are you? Speak smart, and speak up.

He steps on the assassin's wound. The man writhes in agony, but keeps mumbling, still clutching his beads. Bill reaches down and roughly pulls at the man's fingers to reveal his talisman: a rosary. The man keeps mumbling.

BILL THE BUTCHER (*CONT'D*)
(*To Amsterdam*) You! Boy! What's he saying?

Amsterdam is momentarily taken aback. He looks down at the dying man.

AMSTERDAM
(*Troubled*) He's makin' his peace with God.

BILL THE BUTCHER
The hell with that. He makes his peace with me.

Bill takes the gun out of Amsterdam's hand and levels it at the assassin.

BILL THE BUTCHER (*CONT'D*)
I'm hearing confession tonight you mother whoring Irish nigger. Whose man are you? We speak English in this country, whose man are you? You see this knife? I'm going to teach you to speak English with this fucking knife. Whose man are you? Whose man are you?

The assassin shudders and dies.

BILL THE BUTCHER (*CONT'D*)
Well, that don't tell me very much.

He pulls himself together and looks to his audience.

BILL THE BUTCHER (*CONT'D*)
(*Aloud, to the crowd*) Shame about that fine waistcoat…! I don't think it can be mended! Will I keep it as a souvenir?

The crowd roars its approval. Some Natives strip the vest from the dead man. Bill notes poor Edwin Forrest still dangling above the stage.

BILL THE BUTCHER (*CONT'D*)
Where's Legree? Where's Mopsy? (*They're cowering in the wings*) Tragedians! Continue! Intermission is over!

The crowd cheers. Bill stands tall, in great pain. His eyes meet Amsterdam's. Slowly and without irony he takes off his hat and bows low to him. He puts his hat back on just as the Natives swarm him with congratulations and accolades and he is carried away by them. Amsterdam, mortally confused by what he's just done, slowly backs away through the crowd.

At the back of the theater, he finds his way blocked by Monk.

MONK
Now, that was bloody Shakespearean.

AMSTERDAM
What?

MONK
Do you know who Shakespeare was, sonny?

Amsterdam, very disoriented, shakes his head.

MONK (*CONT'D*)
Well, he's the fellow wrote the *King James Bible*.

AMSTERDAM
Mister, I don't know what in the hell you're talkin' about—

He tries to get around Monk, but Monk grabs him and slams him against the wall.

MONK
That's because you're a dumb, ignorant, barbarous Irish whelp. Just like your father.

Amsterdam tries to push Monk away, but Monk is too strong.

MONK (*CONT'D*)
Tear my head off and destruct the world. Just like the rest of the stupid Irish in this country. That's why I never ran with your dad. He always wondered why I wouldn't run with him. I never told him in so many words, but I'll tell you: When the Irish get together, they turn stupid. All they do is fight. I'd rather do that on me own. He never understood that.

AMSTERDAM
I don't know what you're talkin' ab—

Monk says something in Gaelic. Amsterdam stares.

MONK
It means: If you're not strong, you better be smart. Now, I don't know if you're being too clever or too dumb. But whichever it is, just remember that for all his faults, your father was a man who loved his people.

Monk releases him. Amsterdam runs away from him and stops, backed against the wall, alone, breathing heavily, his mind in a whirl at what he's done.

BILL THE BUTCHER (O.S.)
Amsterdam...! Come here to me, my boy! Amsterdam...! I'm New York! New York is calling you...!

The crowd roars.

INT. SATAN'S CIRCUS— LATER—NIGHT

A pair of scuffed shoes hammers out syncopated rhythms on broken glass—an early version of tap dancing.

It seems as if everyone from the theater has repaired here to celebrate Bill's deliverance from the clutches of death. It's a dark, drunken scene.

(210)

BILL THE BUTCHER
Look at that. What is that? Rhythms of the Dark Continent tapped out in a fine American mess... a jig doing a jig.

He tosses Amsterdam the bullet that hit him.

BILL THE BUTCHER (*CONT'D*)
Little keepsake.

Amsterdam is getting drunk, deep in a stew of his own confusion, trying to hide his state of mind from the others. He turns his head as Tweed and Killoran arrive and push their way toward Bill. Three whores gather around Tweed and Killoran as they talk.

TWEED
Bill. Thank God you're all right. I heard the news and came over as quick as I could.

BILL THE BUTCHER
Was it the news you was hopin' for?

You're as timely as the Angel of Death.

TWEED
(*Reproachfully*) You're not suggesting that I would stoop to what you're suggesting...!

BILL THE BUTCHER
Oh, stop your boo-hooin'. Turns out he was just an old Bowery Boy, tryin' to settle ancient scores. Now I've got a hole in my shoulder and it hurts. So have a drink and shut up, or shut up and get out.

TWEED
I believe I'll have a drink.

BILL THE BUTCHER
Careful, Tweedy, the mort's Frenchified.

The crowd laughs.

TWEED'S WHORE
No, no, I'm clean! I'm clean...!

Tweed and Killoran head for the bar, followed by the whores.

POV AMSTERDAM: A woman's hands unbutton Bill's shirt from the bottom up. Jenny tends to Bill's wound

Jenny pries a sufficiently drunk whore off Bill and takes her place next to him with a bowl of clean water. Bill looks up at her.

BILL THE BUTCHER
Jenny...

JENNY
Bill.

Amsterdam is passed out, flanked by a whore on his arm, but upon hearing Jenny's voice he raises his head to look at her. She briefly stares back. Amsterdam comes to and casually brushes the whore off of him. He watches as Jenny tends to Bill's wound, cupping a hand under the bullet hole catching spirits from a pitcher, rinsing the rivulets of blood. She applies a clean white bandage.

JENNY (*CONT'D*)
It's not my best wrap yet...

BILL groans.

JENNY (*CONT'D*)
It's got to be tight.

BILL THE BUTCHER
(*Smiling*) Loves to make me cry.

JENNY
(*Laughing*) You can take it.

Amsterdam hides his disgust, but can't keep from watching Jenny tenderly care for Bill. A whore tokes on an opium pipe and hands it to Amsterdam. Jenny stares at him. He takes a drag, and Bill approves.

BILL THE BUTCHER
There's my boy.

When Amsterdam looks at Bill, Jenny deliberately cradles him in her arms, feigning affection.

BILL THE BUTCHER (*CONT'D*)
(*Patting her*) Mmm, it's all right, it's all right.

Amsterdam lurches from his chair, raising a glass. He stares a moment at the spectacle of Bill and Jenny embracing.

AMSTERDAM
To the Butcher!

Jenny leers at Amsterdam. Touché.

AMSTERDAM (*CONT'D*)
We're all much obliged. Forever.

The tension has risen between Amsterdam and Jenny, and **AMSTERDAM** raises his glass to toast **BILL**.

BAR PATRON (*O.C.*)
Bill the Butcher.

TWEED
To the Butcher.

Amsterdam stumbles to the bar. Jenny's eyes follow him, and she quietly approaches Johnny.

(211)

JENNY
Why don't you get out of here, Johnny. Go on, go.

Taking her balms and bloodied bandages, she moves past Tweed at the bar—

TWEED
Lovely as always, Miss Everdeane.

JENNY
How nice to see you again, Mr. Tweed.

POV AMSTERDAM: Jenny walks up the stairs.

CHINESE WHORE
Come upstairs with me, Bill.

BILL THE BUTCHER
Have I ever had you before?

CHINESE WHORE
No.

BILL THE BUTCHER
So you don't call me by my Christian name.

Amsterdam lurches to his feet, pretty drunk. He walks past all of them, in plain sight, and follows Jenny up the stairs.

INT. UPSTAIRS— SATAN'S CIRCUS—NIGHT

The water in a porcelain basin turns pink with blood as Jenny rinses the waistcoat. Suddenly, Amsterdam is there, pushing her away and sending the basin crashing against the wall.

AMSTERDAM
(212) Is there anyone in the Five Points you haven't fucked?

JENNY
Yes! You!

He hits her, but she hits him back harder. He grabs her and freezes, suddenly. His eyes drop to her mouth.

JENNY (CONT'D)
Try it and I'll bite you.

Pause.

AMSTERDAM
If you were going to bite me, I don't think you'd warn me.

JENNY
Find out.

His face moves slowly toward hers, ready to recoil if necessary. The result is that he kisses her very, very slowly. She makes a sudden movement—he pulls back, afraid she's going to bite him. But she's not. Their faces are two inches apart. He suddenly seems quite vulnerable. This time, it is Jenny who moves in carefully, very slowly. They kiss again, tentatively at first, and then with a sudden eruption of pent-up passion that seems to have even more than just sex in it.

INT. UPSTAIRS—SATAN'S CIRCUS—SAME TIME

Johnny comes down the long darkened hall to a curtain in the doorway of the last room. Parting it slowly he watches something inside while we, instead, watch the pain in his face.

INT. ROOM & HALLWAY— SATAN'S CIRCUS—NIGHT

Bill stares at nothing in an opium haze. Surrounded by sleeping women, he disentangles himself from their limbs and slowly makes his way down a darkened hallway.

INT. UPSTAIRS ROOM / SATAN'S CIRCUS—NIGHT

Amsterdam wakes. Looks at Jenny sleeping. He looks worried. As he turns, he suddenly sees Bill staring at them, wrapped in a blanket. Amsterdam is startled, not sure how long he's been there.

BILL THE BUTCHER
I can't sleep.

AMSTERDAM
I hope you don't mind us laying out tonight here, sir.

BILL THE BUTCHER
Whatever takes your fancy, my young friend.

AMSTERDAM
Is it your shoulder, or—

BILL THE BUTCHER
No, I mean I can't sleep. Ever. I have to sleep with one eye open and I only have one eye. (*Pause*) How old are you, Amsterdam?

AMSTERDAM
I don't know.

BILL THE BUTCHER
Do you know what's kept me alive all these years? Monk does. Fear. The spectacle of fearsome acts. Someone steals from me, I cut off his hands. He offends me, I cut out his tongue. He rises against me, I cut off his head, and stick it on a pike. Hold it high in the streets so all can see. That's what preserves the order of things. That one tonight…Who was he? A nobody. A

coward. What a fitting end that would have been. I killed the last honorable man fifteen years ago. You've seen his portrait. Downstairs.

(*Pause*)

Answer me when I'm talkin' to you.

Amsterdam flushes angrily but speaks calmly.

AMSTERDAM
I've seen it.

BILL THE BUTCHER
(*Smiling*) Oh, you got a murderous rage in you and I like it. It's life boilin' up in you. It's good.

(*Pause*)

The Priest and me lived by the same principles. It was only faith that divided us. He give me this, you know: (The scar on his face) It was the finest beating I ever took. My face was pulp. My guts was pierced. My ribs was swimmin'. But when he come to kill me, I couldn't look him in the eye. He spared me, because he wanted me to live in shame. This was a great man. So I cut out the eye that looked away, and sent it to him, wrapped in blue paper. I would have cut them both out if I could have fought him blind. Then I rose back up with full heart and buried him in his own blood.

AMSTERDAM
Well done.

We see now that Jenny's eyes are open.

BILL THE BUTCHER
I'd trade all my so-called friends for that one enemy. He was the only man I ever killed who was worth remembering.

He stops. The next words come out with some difficulty.

BILL THE BUTCHER (*CONT'D*)
I never had a son.

(*Pause*)

Civilization is crumbling.

He stops abruptly. He seems uncomfortable—embarrassed, even. He gets up stiffly, smiling at his own abashment.

BILL THE BUTCHER (*CONT'D*)
God bless you.

He walks away. Amsterdam watches him go. He lies back down. He knows Jenny is awake, but he doesn't look at her, nor she at him.

AMSTERDAM
If you got anything to say, now's the time to say it.

She stares miserably at the wall.

AMSTERDAM (*CONT'D*)
Who is he to you, Jenny?

(*Pause*)

JENNY
When I was twelve years old, my mother was dead, I was livin' in a doorway. He took me in—took care of me, in his way. After they cut out the baby...Well, he doesn't fancy girls that's scarred up. But you might as well know in your own mind that he never laid a hand on me until I asked him to.

(*She looks at him*) Who are you?

(214)

AMSTERDAM
I'm the living son of Priest Vallon, sworn on the altar of God to avenge my father's death.

Jenny turns back to the wall.

JENNY
That's what I was afraid of.

INT./EXT. BACK ROOM, BARBERSHOP / ALLEY—DAWN

Monk stirs to a strange, muffled, rhythmic sequence of sounds: Footsteps, scrape, thunk, footsteps, scrape, thunk.

He gets up, looks out a window, sees Amsterdam at the end of an alley, taking fifteen paces, turning, hurling a knife into a fence rail, retrieving it, taking fifteen paces, turning, throwing it again.

The fence rail is only two inches wide. If Amsterdam misses, above or below, the knife will end up in the river beyond it. But he doesn't miss; he hits the same spot on the 2x4 every time.

EXT. STREET—NIGHT

Shots ring out as if from a machine gun. Chinese kids light another string of firecrackers and hurl it. Amid colored lanterns a posted handbill is revealed:

15th Commemoration of The Great Battle of 1844
A Celebration of the Stirring Native Victory

The venue of the celebration is familiar to us: Sparrow's Chinese Pagoda. Where a date should be, someone has slapped over it, **Sold Out**.

INT. UNDERGROUND CHAMBER—NIGHT

Amsterdam is sitting alone in the candlelight, sharpening his knife. He stops. His hands are shaking. He gets a hold of himself and resumes sharpening the knife.

AMSTERDAM
May God put the steel of the Holy Spirit in my spine and the love of the blessed Virgin in my heart...

INT. SPARROW'S CHINESE PAGODA—NIGHT

A Chinese acrobat cartwheels across a crowded room to cheers and sounds of gambling and Eastern music. Johnny comes past gamblers and gang members, politicians, whores, uptown thrill-seekers, journalists, cops, and even a few Chinese.

P.T. BARNUM (O.C.)
Gentlemen...Fine gentlemen, you are most welcome to this palace of wonder and enchantment. Where visions to rival the finest imaginings of Scheherezade and her tales of the perfumed nights of Arabia will greet your famished eyes...

The camera leaves him to find the source of the weird music—a stage on which musicians, dancers, and singers perform a mangled Five Points version of Chinese opera.

INT. UPSTAIRS ROOM, CHINESE PAGODA—NIGHT

Bill prepares for the celebration by donning his cutlery belt. He considers his image in a mirror.

P.T. BARNUM (O.S.)
And prepare for a munificent feast the like of which you have never experienced...

INT. SPARROW'S CHINESE PAGODA—CONTINUED—NIGHT

Johnny crosses past several men looking up. The camera follows their look and finds several women and children in gilded cages suspended from the ceiling. One of the "buyers" teeters on a table trying to grab a pretty girl through the bars of her cage. Kids yank on a rope to raise the frightened girl from the groper's hands.

P.T. BARNUM
What am I bid for this flaxen-haired Teutonic beauty? Feast your eyes on the magnificent plumage of these exotic creatures. Gentlemen, you've seen our caged birds—well...how'd you like to make 'em sing? Let me see the color of your money and they could be singing for you!

Johnny shouts something to a Native that can't be heard over all the noise. As he follows the Native's pointing finger to some stairs, the camera rakes across the fan-tan gamblers and money changing hands, then rises up with a basket on a rope to a railing where more gamblers collect their winnings.

EXT. PARADISE SQUARE—NIGHT

As Amsterdam crosses the almost-deserted square, it begins to snow.

INT. UPSTAIRS ROOM, CHINESE PAGODA— LATER—NIGHT

Two whores scuttle off in the dark. Johnny slams into frame against a wall where he's held firmly by the Butcher.

BILL THE BUTCHER
Carefully now. What did you say?

JOHNNY
He's not who he says he is. He's a traitor.

BILL THE BUTCHER
Let's say you've had a bit too much to drink. You don't know what you're saying. I'm going to let you leave this room. Count your blessings he considers you a friend.

JOHNNY
He considers only one thing every waking minute: How best to kill you.

Bill slams his knife into the door a fraction of an inch from Johnny's face.

BILL THE BUTCHER
What's he done to you that you come in here tellin' stories? You're nothing. You're a shadow— You're half a man.

You got a loose tongue in that head of yours. You want me to take it out for you? I'll bury it right up your fundament where it belongs. I can read right through you. You're empty!

(216)   JOHNNY
His name is Vallon!

Johnny waits for the death blow. But Bill steps back and stares, trying to make some sense of it, thinking back perhaps—wondering, is it possible?

INT. SPARROW'S CHINESE PAGODA—LATER—NIGHT

A beautiful Chinese girl—a child in traditional dress—sings like an angel on the stage.

TWEED (O.S.)
Curious people, these Celestials.

He's with a few Tammany brothers, gambling at a fan-tan table surrounded by Chinese. Killoran looks uneasy being elbow-to-elbow with so many of them. Tweed gestures to the dealer.

TWEED
Know why he wears short sleeves? So everybody sees he's got nothing stashed away. Let's hope it never becomes the fashion.

Johnny comes down the stairs and is hurrying past the bar to the door as Amsterdam comes in.

AMSTERDAM
Johnny—

Johnny ignores or doesn't hear him and disappears outside. Amsterdam watches after him, alarmed. He continues in, scanning the room. His eyes find and acknowledge the Chinese hoodlum.

P.T. BARNUM
Ladies and gentlemen, if I may have your kind attention. As some of you have surely noticed, our friend and benefactor, Mr. William Cutting, is wearing tonight a waistcoat of certain distinction.

The vest of the would-be assassin. The crowd cheers.

P.T. BARNUM (CONT'D)
Might we appeal to him on this evening, to favor us with another exciting exhibition of skill, courage, daring, and drama?

Bill stands to a great roar of approval. Amsterdam comes forward, towards a reserved table in "Native Territory" where Jenny is sitting. He sits down next to her and joins in the applause. Across the room, Bill hurls several knives at a female Chinese acrobat, who cartwheels across the stage to the accompaniment of Chinese opera music. The knives land inches from her hands and feet as she spins around. There are shouts of encore and specific requests: the Wheel of Death; William Tell; the Butterfly; the Butcher's Apprentice...Everyone is applauding. The Chinese in the room are watching coldly.

BILL THE BUTCHER
A command performance indeed!

JENNY
(*To Amsterdam*) Where have you been for six days?

AMSTERDAM
I want you to get out of here.

JENNY
I love you.

He looks at her.

AMSTERDAM
This ain't the ideal time to tell me that.

BILL THE BUTCHER
And now I beg the indulgence of my former assistant—the Butcher's original apprentice...! What do you say, Jen? One more time for the sweet souvenir? Come on!

Jenny is not expecting this, but she's got no choice. She gets up to great applause, and forces a convincing smile to Bill and a nod to the crowd. As she passes Amsterdam:

JENNY
Don't do it.

Amsterdam watches her make her way to the stage. Several kids, like busy ants, swarm onto a huge wooden chandelier, lighting its hundreds of candles.

Bill opens his coat, revealing all his cutlery as the cheering rises. Jenny takes her place against a scenery wall, perfectly still, a human target. She's done this many times before, but now she's afraid. A hush descends on the room as Bill weighs up several knives in his hand. Suddenly, without warning, he hurls two of them at Jenny. They fly through the air, and strike her above each shoulder, to gasps from the crowd.

BILL THE BUTCHER
You may be more comfortable without that garment, Miss Everdeane.

Jenny is actually relieved—this is the familiar old routine, after all. She steps away, leaving behind her shawl, which is now pinned on the wall.

JENNY
You'll have to filch me another, Bill.

Laughter all around. Except from Amsterdam. Bill picks up another blade as Jenny takes her place again.

BILL THE BUTCHER
Anything in your pockets tonight?

JENNY
I ain't started workin' yet.

BILL THE BUTCHER
(*Over more laughs*) What about the locket I gave you?

(217)

Jenny unclasps the locket awkwardly from around her neck, but before she can extend her arm fully to hold it out, Bill's knife suddenly flies through the air, almost passing through her fingers, startling her. The locket falls to the floor as the audience laughs.

BILL THE BUTCHER (*CONT'D*)
Apologies, my dear. Pick it up.

Warily Jenny stoops to retrieve it, another blade slams into the floor inches from her fingers.

BILL THE BUTCHER (*CONT'D*)
Whoopsie daisy! Now it's good and broke. I can't seem to do anything right tonight.

Jenny hesitates, then reaches for the locket tentatively. Another knife hammers into the wall behind her, exactly where her head was a moment ago. The crowd roars with laughter. Amsterdam is freaking out. Jenny is shaken.

BILL THE BUTCHER (*CONT'D*)
You got the sand to give them a grand finale?

JENNY
Maybe when you're aiming a little straighter.

She tries to smile and bow as she moves away from the stage. The knife suddenly flies out of Bill's hand, and slams into the wall by her neck. There's a sudden hush. A small trickle of blood runs down her white neck, but otherwise she's unharmed. The crowd bursts into applause, and cheers.

Amsterdam is on his feet, hand on his knife hilt. But Bill moves away from where he's standing and addresses the crowd.

BILL THE BUTCHER
(218) Enough of this Heathen music. This is a night for Americans!

American flags tumble down the walls, and the room bursts into spontaneous celebration. Amsterdam loses Bill for a moment in the crowd,

then sees him again, walking toward the bar. Amsterdam's eyes meet the Chinese hoodlum's now, whose nod to him says, Yes, this is it.

In the balcony, the second Chinese gangster gives firecrackers to the children.

A shot glass is set down in the foreground. A Chinese barman pours liquor into it. A candle is handed to Bill, who passes its flame over the glass, igniting it. The crowd quiets down now; Bill doesn't like to shout the invocation.

BILL THE BUTCHER (*CONT'D*)
We hold in our hearts the memory of our fallen brothers, whose blood stains the very streets we walk today. We also, on this day, pay tribute to the leader of our enemy, an honorable man, who crossed over bravely, fighting for what he believed in.

Bill holds the flaming glass. Amsterdam looks at the Chinese hoodlum. As if on cue, his accomplice is seized and bundled off by Bill's men.

In the balcony the second Chinese hoodlum starts lighting the wicks on the kids' firecrackers.

Bill continues on as if nothing has happened. He raises the glass. Amsterdam's fingers tighten around the hilt.

BILL THE BUTCHER (*CONT'D*)
To defeat my enemy, I extinguish his life, and consume him as I consume these flames. In honor of Priest Vallon—

Bill places one hand on the handle of his cleaver in his belt, and lifts the glass to his lips...

The kids throw their firecrackers—colored flashes and rat-a-rat-tats go off in the balcony. The entire audience turns to look up and to the right. Except Bill. He's looking right at Amsterdam.

AMSTERDAM
(*In Gaelic*) From the heart of Priest Vallon!

Amsterdam hurls his knife straight at Bill's heart. Bill's cleaver flashes up and, incredibly, he knocks the flying blade aside with a ringing clang. The knife embeds itself in a wall. Then Bill whips a knife out of his belt and into the air. Amsterdam gives a jolt and looks down. The knife is sticking out of his gut.

BILL THE BUTCHER
That's a wound.

Amsterdam falls to his knees. Bill strides forward.

BILL THE BUTCHER (*CONT'D*)
I'd like youse all to meet the son of Priest Vallon. I took him under my wing and see how I'm repaid. Saves my life in autumn so's he can murder me in winter. Like a sneak-thief, instead of fightin' like a man. A base defiler of a noble name.

Bill rips the knife out of Amsterdam's belly.

AMSTERDAM
Jesus Christ!

Amsterdam clutches at his stomach and collapses. There's a lot of blood and pain.

BILL THE BUTCHER
You got anything to say for yourself?

Amsterdam can barely speak. But he comes out with:

AMSTERDAM
Your time is nigh…And we'll be waitin' for you, Bill.

The Natives start to rush in—

BILL THE BUTCHER
Hang back, you dogs, I ain't through with him…!

In the corner, Jenny covers her eyes with one hand.

BILL THE BUTCHER (*CONT'D*)
This meat needs tenderizing.

AMSTERDAM
Forgive me—forgive me—

The first blow falls. As he beats the boy senseless, Shang and Jimmy Spoils slip away, terrified for themselves. The blows rain down. Finally Amsterdam stops struggling. Bill takes his cleaver and stands over his prostrate body, flipping it over and over in his hand.

BILL THE BUTCHER
What'll it be then? Loin or shank? Rib or chop?

Everyone is yelling The liver! The kidneys! The heart! The heart!

BILL THE BUTCHER (*CONT'D*)
The heart? This boy has no heart.

They start yelling Kill him! Kill him! Bill picks up a glowing poker from the hearth.

BILL THE BUTCHER (*CONT'D*)
No. He ain't earned a death at my hands. He shall walk among you cloaked in his dishonor, forever marked with shame. A freak worthy of Barnum's Museum of Wonders: God's only man, spared by the Butcher!

And with that the poker comes through the frame to Amsterdam's neck. There's a blood-curdling scream as the scene suddenly drops into **BLACKNESS**, the revelry echoing into **SILENCE**—

(219)

INT. CATACOMBS

Echoing footsteps on dirt and rock. A man we've never seen before moving through the tunnels in and out of the light from candles set into the rock walls. Reaching a crossroads, he hesitates, uncertain which way to turn.

He chooses a path and starts down it. Fewer and fewer candles light his way. Soon he finds himself in almost total darkness. He feels at the walls to keep from falling into some unseen abyss. He slows. Stops. Tentatively—

MAN
Hello?

Lost and uneasy, he peers into the darkness, hears a metallic sound behind him, turns around and sees: Jenny, pointing a cocked pistol at him.

JENNY
Here.

INT. UNDERGROUND CHAMBER

It isn't much lighter in here. A single candle burns on a grave in a corner of a dingy room where paving stones have been laid out like a cross. In faded paint on the rock wall is scrawled, "Elizabeth Everdeane."

The man removes from his coat various medicinal powders and medieval-looking surgical instruments. Jenny watches as he carefully lays them out.

MAN
I need the money before.

She takes out some money from inside her coat

and hands it to him. He counts it twice before pocketing it.

MAN (CONT'D)
Light another candle.

She touches one against the burning wick of the candle on the grave, and we notice for the first time a figure lying motionless under a blanket, turned away to a wall.

She sets a candle next to the surgeon, who begins setting out scalpels and other instruments next to Amsterdam's St. Michael's medallion and broken chain lying on a rock slab.

INT. UNDERGROUND CHAMBER

No day or night. No sense of time. Only darkness and echoing sounds. Jenny's face comes into the light, briefly, looking over him. She withdraws from the light.

Jenny's hands scrape at the dirt of the grave and lift a plank revealing a dark cavity.

JENNY
I want you to look at something.

We look inside in a kind of delirium, at human bones intermingled with valuables, like a pirate's plunder. She reaches into the grave and gathers some yellowed newspaper advertisements and a book.

JENNY (CONT'D)
My mother's bones share this grave. I wish you would have known her. She was a farm girl in Ireland and then a factory girl in Worth Street. We came here when I was six, escapin' the famine. Five years later she was dead from lead

(220)

poisonin' at the factory. That's how I learnt the value of skilled labor.

Comes over with them, sits with Amsterdam. From what little we can see of him in the shadows, he's a pulpy mess. She shows him the advertisements and the book. It's unclear how well he can see them. One shows a drawing of clipper ship, *The Commodore*, "Small, Sharp, Fast!—Passage to San Francisco, $250"; another, an article, reads, "Inexhaustible Gold Mines." Another is a drawing of an unwieldy zephyr, "Best Route to California."

JENNY (*CONT'D*)
I've saved ten cents out of every dollar I ever earned since I was thirteen. That's two hundred and fifteen dollars, from bludgeting and whoring and the rest. This is where we're going—as soon as you're well. Listen: This is what I wanted to show you. This is where we're gonna go as soon as you get well. San Francisco...California...You can have anything you want out there. These men are pulling gold right out of the river with their own hands.

Tracing a sea route on the map.

JENNY (*CONT'D*)
We're here. We need to get there. You start here. Go down around here, up to San Francisco. Shortest way to go. Would you go with me?

She watches him look over the pictures and testimonials. His eyes move across an illustration of men with picks and handfuls of gold on the cover of a book: "An Account of California and the Wonderful Gold Regions."

JENNY (*V.O.*)
"From the beginning of the Christian era, the Creator has implanted in the hearts of men that same disposition which compelled Columbus to turn the prow of his small vessel toward the center of an unknown and illimitable sea..."

Amsterdam reaches for Jenny and pulls her down to him. She kisses him, laying the book down gently on the ground. We move in on its cover, and the picture of the men with axes and all the gold fills the frame.

JENNY (*V.O.*) (*CONT'D*)
"A frenzy seized my soul—"

SEVERAL QUICK, flickering shots of their lovemaking **INTERCUT** with palpitating shadows from the candlelight thrown against the rock wall, the grave and across the illustrations of wild-eyed gold seekers—

JENNY (*V.O.*) (*CONT'D*)
Castles of marble and piles of gold rose up before me—

INT. TUNNELS—SAME TIME

A huge figure moves through the tunnels using Jenny's muffled voice as his guide—

JENNY (*O.S.*)
The Rothchilds, Girards, and Astors appeared to be but poor people compared to those around me—"

INT. UNDERGROUND CHAMBER—SAME TIME

Jenny hesitates. Looks up from the book. Under a blanket with Amsterdam, she listens to the footsteps approach, then reaches over and grasps her pistol. The plank door eases open revealing Monk, who tries to appear harmless as he considers the two of them and the gun pointing at him.

MONK

No need to fire or even aim that, miss. An audience with your mangled friend is all I want.

INT. UNDERGROUND CHAMBER—LATER

Jenny is sitting across the chamber from them. Amsterdam is sitting up. Monk is seated on an outcropping of rock.

MONK

There's forty-four notches in my club, one for every man I've killed. Do you know what they're for?

AMSTERDAM

To remind you what you owe God when you die.

MONK

(*Surprised*) How'd you know that?

AMSTERDAM

I find at this moment there ain't much I don't know.

(Pause)

MONK

My father was killed in battle too. In Ireland, in the streets, fightin' those who would take as their privilege what could only be got and held by the decimation of the race. That war's a thousand years old. More.

We never expected it to follow us here. It didn't.

(222) FLASHES from the battle—Less knives and fists and more religious iconography. It's hard to tell the century.

MONK (*CONT'D*)

It was waitin' for us. Could it always be the same? Here? Back home? Back before Christ. Who will lord over who? Which tribe? Which gang? Which faith? Which race. (*Pause*) Your father tried to scratch out a corner in this country for his tribe. That was him, that was his Dead Rabbits. I often wondered if he'd lived a bit longer, would he have wanted a bit more?

AMSTERDAM

Why'd you rifle his pockets, then?

Monk reaches into his pocket and takes something out.

MONK

For safekeeping. I thought someday it would mean something to you. Maybe you could use it.

He gives Amsterdam a worn velvet pouch. Amsterdam takes out his father's jagged razor, his blood still on it. Amsterdam slowly turns the razor in his hands. Something stirs in his memory. Finally:

AMSTERDAM

The blood stays on the blade.

Jenny watches them.

INT. THE CAVE—LATER

Jenny and Amsterdam lie together under the blanket. They are both awake. Jenny is holding her California book. From behind the walls we hear the scuffling and squeaking of rats.

AMSTERDAM

Listen to 'em, will you?

JENNY

I been listenin'.

AMSTERDAM

When I was in Hellgate, we used to nail our bread to the ceiling at night so the rats couldn't take it. You had to, 'cause if you kept it in your pockets when you was sleepin', them rats would chew right through 'em. It was this one kid's idea. We funned him when he first done it, but then you shoulda heard them little bastards jumpin' up and down all night tryin' to get that bread. I been thinkin'... suppose that kid never came to Hellgate, how long would the rest of us eedjits gone hungry?

JENNY

I don't know...

AMSTERDAM

How long would the rest of us eedjits have gone hungry all week—same dumb kids doin' the same dumb thing, year after year?

JENNY

I don't know and I don't care.

AMSTERDAM

Jenny, listen to me. I got the idea now. I ain't worked it all out yet, but...

JENNY

I don't care...! I want to get out of here! I don't care!

She holds on to him and cries bitterly.

EXT. THE FIVE POINTS—DAY

A moving point of view approaching some Shirt Tails idling in Murderers' Alley. One by one, they notice "us" and smirk.

We pass them and look at some Plug Uglies up ahead. As we approach them, they glance at "us" and grin derisively, but we move on without a word.

The square opens up. We "glance" from side to side at members of other gangs and groups of invalid soldiers, hold their looks, then return our attention to our destination up ahead—the flagpole in the middle of the square.

Amsterdam is carrying a burlap sack and limping badly. Reaching the flagpole, he stops, takes something from the sack, and moves out of frame.

In a few moments the frame is filled with Amsterdam's face. For the first time we clearly see the brand Bill burned into it. He stares down the people staring at him, and gradually the smirks become fewer and further between. Shang, Jimmy Spoils, and Johnny all watch, too fearful to join him perhaps, but, like the others, impressed by his courage. Jenny is less so. As Amsterdam walks away, the camera reveals on the ground, a rabbit pelt.

INT. SATAN'S CIRCUS—DAY

The rabbit pelt rests in the middle of Bill's card table like a sacrificial offering to "Saint" Vallon. Bill is flanked by his chief men. Happy Jack stands opposite.

BILL THE BUTCHER

That's a sad-looking pelt...And it's been so nice and quiet for the last three months...But it do call back old days, don't it? (*Pause*) Does this charge sit uneasy with you, Happy Jack?

HAPPY JACK

No, not uneasy, Bill, I wouldn't say that...But my allegiance is to the Law. I'm paid to uphold the law.

Bill looks at the others, confused.

BILL THE BUTCHER

What's he talking about? (*To Jack*) You don't want to start believin' that, Jack. That way lies damnation.

HAPPY JACK

(*Uncomfortably*) Oh—I'm in no danger of damnation, Bill.

BILL THE BUTCHER

That's what you think. Now, I don't give a damn about your misgivings. I want you to go out there and punish the person responsible for murdering this poor rabbit.

HAPPY JACK

Right.

BILL THE BUTCHER

Help yourself to some decent meat on the way out.

HAPPY JACK

Right.

INT. CHURCH—DAY

Amsterdam sits alone under the scaffolding in the church, gazing at Priest Vallon's medal in his hand. Suddenly a gun moves into frame, pointed at his head.

HAPPY JACK

I'm sorry, son. Your father was a good man.

AMSTERDAM

(*Without looking at him*) I'm sorry too, Jack.

Before we see anything else, we cut to—

EXT. SATAN'S CIRCUS— LATER

A crowd has gathered around the lamppost Happy Jack used to drape his watch on. Now he's draped on it, the chain around his neck, the watch broken. Bill and Tweed look down at him. Bill is not happy.

TWEED

This is bad for everybody. What's next? Dead politicians?

BILL THE BUTCHER

I could spare a dozen of you easier than I can spare him.

He becomes aware of the crowd watching him. He raises his voice just a little.

BILL THE BUTCHER (*CONT'D*)

Still, I think it shows dash. Give the boy some time and we'll settle with a good dust-up.

There are some scattered laughs of appreciation from the crowd. Good old Bill.

INT. CATHOLIC CHURCH— DAY

Under a maze of scaffolding, Amsterdam helps the one-armed priest—from the 1844 battle—prepare for communion.

The front door opens, admitting light and a figure. Shang comes in with food and bedding. The door opens again. Jimmy Spoils comes in. It opens again. Johnny appears.

INT. CATHOLIC CHURCH— LATER

The boys and Jenny sit around the church floor, Amsterdam breaking bread with them. They hang on Amsterdam's every word and gesture. Johnny is a bit uneasy but hides it.

AMSTERDAM

There's more of us comin' off these ships every day. I heard fifteen thousand Irish a week. And we're afraid of the Natives? Get all of us together and we ain't got a gang, we got an army. Then all you need is a spark. Just one spark. Something to wake us all up.

Johnny is watching Amsterdam uncomfortably. Amsterdam meets his eye.

EXT. ALLEY—LATER

Amsterdam and Johnny face off in the shadows. Johnny can't find the right words. Finally:

AMSTERDAM

Well?

JOHNNY

It was me played you false.

(*Pause*) Amsterdam bows his head.

AMSTERDAM

I wish you wouldn't have done that, Johnny.

JOHNNY

So do I.

(*Pause*) I never squeaked on a fellow in my life. If it wasn't—

AMSTERDAM

(*On "if"*) I ain't been much of a friend to you, Johnny, but why'd you do it?

JOHNNY

I'd take it back if I could—

AMSTERDAM

Take it back? Johnny, I gotta kill you.

JOHNNY

Well, then go ahead, settle me! I got no heart for it. Just settle me right now if you've a mind to. I won't fight you.

(*Pause*)

AMSTERDAM

Get out of the Points and don't come back.

JOHNNY

Where am I supposed to go?

AMSTERDAM

I don't know. Only don't let me see your face again. We're split out.

(*Pause*)

JOHNNY

I'm sorry.

Johnny walks away. Amsterdam watches him go.

EXT. FIVE POINTS— EVENING

The noise of the surrounding streets echoes through. Johnny seems lost in himself. Suddenly he bumps into someone. He looks up and sees a grinning McGloin.

McGLOIN

Where you going, boyo?

INT. SATAN'S CIRCUS— EVENING

Two drunken couples dancing. A musician playing strange music. The plaintive ring of a distant church bell follows

In the rat pit is Johnny, very scared, flanked by McGloin and some other natives. Bill steps out of the shadows. Behind him on the wall is a large old American flag.

BILL THE BUTCHER
Still hiding out with your friends?

JOHNNY
No Bill, I'm with you . . . I'm with the Natives, Bill.

Bill smiles at his men, then looks back at Johnny.

BILL THE BUTCHER
You always was a Native as far as I'm interested, John. Till you became a stag.

Johnny looks around. No way out.

JOHNNY
No—I'm your man. I told you what you needed to know.

BILL THE BUTCHER
That's true. But you're still a stag. Now if you were me—you're not me, but if you were me—would you trust a man like yourself?

Johnny has no answer.

BILL THE BUTCHER (CONT'D)
You've seen the flag in my room? That's my father's flag. Recovered from the Battle of Bridgewater, these many years ago. You want to know what a native is? He is a man what's willin' to give his life for his country, just like my father done. (Pauses) Are you willing to do that?

Bill lunges—

EXT. PARADISE SQUARE NIGHT

Johnny looks like he's leaning against the low spiked fence around the flag pole, but not leaning comfortably; more like a scarecrow on a post.

In the dead of night, Amsterdam crosses the otherwise deserted square to him. Though we don't see it, we gather Johnny is on the spikes. Amsterdam struggles with the idea of trying to move him. Takes hold of him as gently as he can, and pulls. Johnny cries out and Amsterdam stops.

JOHNNY
It hurts too much. Kill me.

Amsterdam takes his knife out. He steps forward to kill Johnny. He puts the knife to Johnny's chest, but finally falls back.

AMSTERDAM
I can't.

He feels a pistol as it touches his skin. Looks up. It's Jenny offering it. He takes it.

INT. SATAN'S CIRCUS— SAME TIME—NIGHT

Bill is behind his butcher's counter sharpening his knives when he hears the shot. He stops for a moment, as do some of his Natives—with their cards and drinks—and watch him.

EXT. PARADISE SQUARE— CONTINUED—NIGHT

Amsterdam is holding Johnny now and crying. He's dead. Jenny watches them, her face like stone. She's seen a lot of this kind of thing.

INT. CATACOMBS—LATER—NIGHT

Jenny stands over a fresh grave. Amsterdam kneels beside it, shaving at a brick with a knife and stirring water into the red dust on the ground.

Amsterdam has finished mixing the pigment and looks at the grave.

AMSTERDAM
Did you ever know his family name? When he was born? Or where?

She shakes her head no in answer to each question.

AMSTERDAM (CONT'D)
What year is it now?

JENNY
(Thinks a moment) 1863.

She sets the music box on the ground. Amsterdam dips his fingers into the pigment and scrawls onto the rock wall—John. d. 1863 A.D.

INT. CATHOLIC CHURCH—DAY

McGloin lights a votive candle, sets it next to others, and mumbles a prayer for his dead mother. As he lumbers to his feet and turns—

AMSTERDAM
What're you doing here, boyo?

Amsterdam stares at him in cold fury. McGloin seems surprised. He had no idea the group had taken this place for their hideout. He stares at the gang, and Jenny, all standing around under the scaffolding. His glance settles on Jimmy Spoils.

McGLOIN
(Defiantly) What's a nigger doing in here? This is my church!

Jimmy lays a brickbat across the side of McGloin's face. McGloin goes down. Amsterdam starts coming toward him. McGloin scrambles away.

McGLOIN (CONT'D)
Get that nigger out of my church!

AMSTERDAM
What's a Dead Rabbit doing with the Natives?

McGLOIN
There's no niggers among the Natives. Niggers and robbers is one thing, but a nigger in the church, that's something else.

AMSTERDAM
Run with the Natives, pray with the Natives.

McGLOIN
You're gonna wind up on a stake like your man did...!

Amsterdam bears down on him in rage. McGloin lurches to his feet to run away, when suddenly a voice calls out—

PRIEST (O.S.)
McGloin.

McGloin turns to see the one-armed priest behind him and regards him as the only sane person present.

McGLOIN
Father. Jesus. Did you know there's a nigger in your—

The priest swings a bat into McGloin's face—

EXT. PARADISE SQUARE—NIGHT

The biggest group of Natives we've seen since the first battle strides across the square with weapons and torches. Bill has his battle coat on, the cutlery gleaming. McGloin, alive but wearing a bloody rag tied around his head, limps behind the others, trying to keep up.

EXT. CATHOLIC CHURCH—NIGHT

A torch sails across the sky, heralding the Natives' arrival. A voice booms as if from the heavens—

BILL THE BUTCHER
WE are the People of the United States!

Rising up from the burning torch, the line of Natives, a hundred strong, comes around a corner and surges toward the church...then stops and stares:

Amsterdam, Jenny, some priests, Hell-Cat Maggie and the Rabbits, standing shoulder to shoulder in front of the church doors, form an inadequate defense. But they're not alone.

Armed and outnumbering the Natives are the plasterers and parishioners, encircling the church and manning the walls and tower. It looks like some fortified medieval citadel.

AMSTERDAM (V.O.)
The earth turns, but we don't feel it move. Then one day you look around, and everything has changed.

Then the rest of the Irish Catholic army appears— on the rooftops—completely surrounding the Natives like numberless birds of prey poised to strike with brickbats.

SHANG
(To Amsterdam excitedly) Look at this mob.

AMSTERDAM
We was a mob. Now we're a gang.

Amsterdam comes down the steps and stands over the burning torch. The heat from the flames makes him look like a mirage.

Bill looks from Jenny to Amsterdam, and considers him. His frustration grows into something deeper and more complicated. He sees his destiny before him, bathed in the light of the flames. He begins to smile.

BILL THE BUTCHER
A touching spectacle. We'll come back when you're ready for us.

The fire slowly sputters out, leaving only rising smoke.

AMSTERDAM (V.O.)
The past is the torch that lights our way. Where our fathers have shown us the path, we shall follow. Our faith, the weapon most feared by our enemies, for thereby shall we lift our people up against those who would destroy us.

EXT. CATHOLIC CHURCH—NIGHT

The one-armed priest administers Communion to the gang now calling itself the Dead Rabbits. As he intones in Latin the bloody crucifix above him begins to glow in flames superimposed over it.

AMSTERDAM (*V.O.*)

…Our name is called the Dead Rabbits to remind all of our suffering, and as a call to those who suffer still to join our ranks, however so far they may have strayed from our common home across the sea. For with great numbers must come great strength and the salvation of our people.

Amsterdam returns the chalice to the priest. As Christ disappears completely into the flames—

INSERT:

An illustration of the church blockade in the *Tribune*. A headline: ARCHBISHOP HUGHES PROMISES RETALIATION IF CHURCHES ATTACKED.

EXT. FIVE POINTS—DAY

Tweed folds the newspaper under his arm as he exits his coach with Killoran. In the background parishioners and Rabbits man barricades protecting the church.

Tweed is distracted by a commotion across the street. Outside a building, a draft registrar backed by police confronts an unruly man. A small crowd looks on.

REGISTRAR

…and I require the names of every man in this house, sir. I require every name in this house.

UNRULY MAN

I don't know who you are or where you're from.

REGISTRAR

I am from the Provost-Marshal's office to register eligible young men for the draft.

UNRULY MAN

I don't know nothing about that. We don't want your business.

REGISTRAR

Who else lives in this house? You've all got to register!

UNRULY MAN

You can't force me to join the Army!

REGISTRAR

You got three hundred dollars?

UNRULY MAN

Of course I ain't. Who the hell's got three hundred dollars?

REGISTRAR

If you're drafted, release from military service can be secured for three hundred dollars according to the Conscription Act. Otherwise you must serve.

UNRULY MAN

Three hundred dollars! Who the hell's got three hundred dollars?

The unruly man grabs the Registrar's papers, tears them up, and a fight breaks out.

As the man scuffles with the police, the crowd jeers and joins in. Tweed and Killoran walk toward the church.

KILLORAN

Backing this draft is going to hurt us. Especially in the sixth Ward. The poor can't buy their way out of this war.

TWEED

I don't care much for warfare or niggers, but Lincoln's always treated us with sufferance; we

(229)

must extend the same regard to him or brook the consequences.

He yells across to the fighting man.

TWEED (*CONT'D*)
Boys! The Union is in distress! We are bound by honor and love of country to fight in this time of crisis—

MAN IN THE CROWD
Go back to where you came from, you bastard!

REGISTRAR
I was born in this country, sir, you emigrated here, you will fight for this country, sir...

A pile of horse dung sails by him, just missing his head.

TWEED
Sweet Jesus, war does terrible things to men.

They reach the barricade. Tweed approaches a fierce-looking Rabbit. He unfolds the newspaper and stabs his finger at the illustration of Amsterdam.

TWEED (*CONT'D*)
I request an audience with this gentleman—Vallon.

An Irishman responds in Gaelic.

TWEED (*CONT'D*)
Doesn't anyone speak English in New York anymore?

IRISHMAN
I don't understand.

TWEED
Oh, you do speak English. I request an audience with this man.

INT. CATHOLIC CHURCH— LATER

Amsterdam sits with Tweed in the quiet of the church. The rest of the gang stands or sits nearby in shadow. Jenny has a repeating rifle aimed at Tweed. Tweed is still holding the newspaper with Amsterdam's headline and picture on the cover.

TWEED
Er—would Miss Everdeane be so kind as to angle her rifle in some other direction?

AMSTERDAM
Don't worry about her, Mr. Tweed, she ain't much of a shot.

Jenny looks at Amsterdam reproachfully. Amsterdam shrugs back at her and turns his attention to Tweed. Tweed taps his newspaper.

TWEED
I wonder, Mr. Vallon, if you understand the true value of this sort of publicity. Archbishop Hughes himself shoulder to shoulder with half the Irish in the Five Points. I'm native to this land, son. Of Scotch-Irish stock and God-fearing Protestantism. A bred-in-the-bone Democrat and the last in a long and distinguished line of chairmakers. Learned at age eleven from my father, who learned from his father. It was good, honest work and I never made a nickel. I gave it up and went into politics. And do you know what I discovered?

AMSTERDAM
That you love to talk.

TWEED
(*Promptly*) No, I already knew that. What I discovered, young man, was that there is a great

deal more money to be had from the selling of chairs than from the making of them.

Amsterdam looks around the room.

AMSTERDAM
Well, it's a beautiful story, Mr. Tweed, but I don't see what it's got to do with us.

TWEED
I'm offering, my boy, to form an alliance with you against Bill Cutting and his slate of Nativist candidates. I'll negotiate a handsome fee for every Irish vote you send Tammany's way in the coming elections and ever after. I need a new friend in the Five Points, son. I'd like that friend to be you.

AMSTERDAM
Well now, just a moment, Mr. Tweed...Suppose we vivificate that notion? Suppose...you back an Irish candidate, of my choosin', and I'll deliver all the Irish vote?

TWEED
Mr. Vallon, that will only happen in the reign of Queen Dick.

AMSTERDAM
Beg pardon?

TWEED
It'll never happen. Now, I might be persuaded to back an Irish candidate for say, alderman...

JENNY
We already got Irish aldermen.

TWEED
So we have. That's why—

AMSTERDAM
(To Jenny) What's bigger than alderman?

JENNY
Well, dear, there's the sheriff.

AMSTERDAM
All right, Mr. Tweed. You back an Irishman for sheriff and we'll get him elected—Why not?

TWEED
(On "You") I love the Irish, son, but higher than alderman you shall never climb—

TWEED (CONT'D)
For one thing, no man living can consolidate the Irish vote—

AMSTERDAM
I can.

TWEED
—and for another—and I mean no effrontery—no one's ever found an Irish candidate for sheriff worth voting for.

AMSTERDAM
I will.

Tweed studies Amsterdam while absently touching the edge of the chair he's sitting in, then glances down at it.

TWEED
This is a good chair.

INT. DON WHISKERANDO'S BARBERSHOP— DAY

(231)

Amsterdam watches Monk as Don Whiskerando gives him a shave. Jenny sits nearby. Monk's eyes are closed.

AMSTERDAM
Monk?

MONK
I'm awake. I'm just tryin' to remember what the sheriff does.

AMSTERDAM
Look, I ain't sure either—but if it gets the Irish together, then it's a step up.

MONK
Wouldn't I have to go down there and orate on the issues?

AMSTERDAM
Only 'til you win. Then you could come back up here, recline in your throne there, and look down on your kingdom. Here.

Amsterdam gives Monk a handbill Tammany has already printed with an idealized drawing of Monk's face on it.

MONK
Sweet Mary Mother, they got me looking as sober as my own grandfather.

AMSTERDAM
Another great man, I'm sure.

MONK
A thorough drunken bastard.

(Pause) Could I say anything I like?

AMSTERDAM
That's why I wanted you.

EXT. PARADISE SQUARE— DAY

The Nativist Know-Nothing incumbent alderman orates at one end of the square to a group of people—

NATIVIST CANDIDATE
This is a free country but not free for the taking. I stand shoulder to shoulder with community leaders like Bill Cutting against any and all inroads into our fine democracy—

The camera whips to the other end of the square where Monk speechifies to a larger group—

MONK
Our elected representatives is a gang of thieves who swear to better our lot while dipping their hand deep in our pockets—

Back to the Know-Nothing, whose platform is flanked by Bill and some Natives.

NATIVIST CANDIDATE
I stand against any and all who would surrender our spirit and livelihood to invading hordes of Hibernians—

And back to Monk's pulpit, surrounded by Dead Rabbits.

MONK
…I'll see to it that no one takes away what you've earned by pluck and application…

NATIVIST CANDIDATE
…against the potato-eaters, like them over there, thieving our jobs…

MONK
…You go to the polls, put your mark next to the name Walter McGinn. Why should so many Irish die down South when the first war to win isn't down in Dixie, it's right here in these streets!

And who's the grandest street fighter in the Five Points?

The crowd shouts "Monk!" drowning out the Nativist candidate.

MONK (*CONT'D*)
(*Taps his ear*) It's this bum ear of mine…(*they shout louder, "Monk!"*) That's right. Let the whole damn city hear it!

He swaggers down from the pulpit to lusty cheers and wades into the crowd, grabbing and shaking hands.

MONK (*CONT'D*)
And you'll get all those fingers back, too, which is five more than you'll get after a handclasp from William Tweed.

Tweed is watching from nearby, next to Amsterdam and beaming.

TWEED
That man was right born for this.

AMSTERDAM
He's killed forty-four and laid low a couple hundred more.

TWEED
Is that right? If I'd known the exact tally, I'd've run him for mayor.

INT. SPARROW'S CHINESE PAGODA—DAY

Bill the Butcher and his boys crash into the place.

BILL THE BUTCHER
All right, line up like soldiers! It's election day!

The Chinese gamblers stare at him, then scatter en masse. It's pandemonium as the Natives chase them down, grabbing at limbs and pigtails—some of them vanishing behind panels in the walls, under trapdoors—

EXT. ALLEYS—DAY

Other Rabbits gather up beggars and drunks. Jimmy Spoils scuffles with a crippled veteran.

JIMMY SPOILS
Come on, you bastard, we need your vote.

CRIPPLED VETERAN
Bastard? I fought for you, nigger. I lost an arm for you—!

JIMMY SPOILS
Well, it ain't much, but it's a start. (*Brandishes his knife*) Now scratch this ballot, you bastard, and do it quick.

INT. SPARROW'S CHINESE PAGODA—DAY

The Natives corral non-Chinese barflies and opium smokers out of the Pagoda and hustle them toward the door.

EXT. POLLS—DAY

We pass long lines of everyone whose been gathered up, spilling out of the polling place, some slumped in wheelbarrows. The other Rabbits have dozens of voters in tow. Shang is seen paying off an Irish cop, who walks off. As one voter staggers out, he's collared by Amsterdam.

AMSTERDAM
Where are you goin'?

DRUNKEN REPEATER
I already voted today. Cast for Monk and Tammany, by God. Twice.

AMSTERDAM
Twice? Only twice? Come here and do your civic duty. Again.

INT. DON WHISKERANDO'S BARBERSHOP—DAY

Amsterdam is shoving the Drunken Repeater into a barber's chair. Don Whiskerando, two other barbers, and Jenny cut hair, prune beards, shave some off entirely.

JENNY
Less art and more haste, Don.

Amsterdam walks to the door to watch other Rabbits arriving with more repeat voters in need of some disguising. The line extends down the hill and into the street.

EXT. POLLS—DAY

We race past long lines of everyone we've seen gathered up, spilling out of the polling place, some slumped unconscious in wheelbarrows. Reaching the front, Amsterdam still has his hand on the drunk's collar, but now he's beardless. The other Rabbits have dozens more repeaters in tow. An Irish cop tries to block their way.

IRISH COP
Not this lot.

AMSTERDAM
They got a right to vote.

IRISH COP
Not four times they don't. There'll be no damned repeaters here.

AMSTERDAM
(*Indignant*) They're repeatin' for Monk, aren't they, God damn it—

IRISH COP
I said none of your damned repeaters!

AMSTERDAM
—whose side are you on, brother?

IRISH COP
All right, in you go.

As Amsterdam and his charges rush past the Irish cop:

AMSTERDAM
(*Sotto voce to Shang*) Give him a fiver.

INT. TAMMANY—CONTINUED

IN JUMP CUTS: Fingers tapping at a telegraph machine…Sparks issuing from the wire atop a pole…The clacking telegraph machine at Tammany. Killoran appears with updated results. Tweed, speaking to reporters, is pulled away by Killoran—

KILLORAN
Monk's already won by ten thousand more votes than there are voters.

TWEED
Only ten? Make it twenty. Thirty. We don't need a victory, we need a Roman triumph!

KILLORAN
But we don't have enough ballots!

TWEED
Remember, the ballots don't make the results, the counters make the results. The counters...

Tweed turns back to the reporters.

TWEED (CONT'D)
Gentlemen, what our great city needs—nay demands—is a new courthouse. I would propose a modest, economical structure—but a gracious building of which our great metropolis can be proud.

EXT. PARADISE—SQUARE DAY

Amsterdam, Jenny, and the Rabbits move amongst the crowds of celebrating Irishmen, shaking hands, taking plaudits. For once there's a feeling of hope in these pale, drawn faces. The dawning of a new era.

INT. SATAN'S CIRCUS—DAY

Bill is alone at his table, a single candle burning before him. Behind him on the wall is the Nativist flag. Bill leans forward and blows out the candle.

INT./EXT. DON WHISKERAN-DO'S BARBERSHOP— EVENING

A Spanish dwarf polishes at Monk's war club, careful to work the oily rag into the forty-four notches, then returns it to its place of honor on the wall.

MONK (V.O.)
Scrape close, Don. They're expecting me to appear civilized.

Monk is seated on his throne, his barber's chair, with a hot towel over his face. Whiskerando, stands with a **LOCAL MAN** at the door, takes a tray atop of which is a severed pig's head. There's a note stuck in it.

LOCAL MAN
It's from Bill.

Whiskerendo brings the bloody head over to Monk.

WHISKERANDO
Monk.

MONK pulls down his towel, and detaches the note. It reads: "TODAY—B"

EXT./INT. DON WHISKERANDO'S BARBERSHOP—SAME TIME

Bill approaches the barbershop and hesitates. A few citizens are standing around. Monk is standing up on the big rock, addressing them, notched war club in hand.

MONK
Citizens of the Five Points! Mr. Bill Cutting is attempting to draw me into a quarrel that will no doubt end in bloodshed and the compromising of my office. Shall I adhere to my promise to be your chosen voice? Or should I engage and silence this relic of a dying world, or shall I be your chosen voice in the new testament, in the new world?

The citizens look around nervously, at Monk, at Bill, not sure what's going on.

(235)

MONK (CONT'D)
There now, Bill. The people have spoken. The very notion of violent reprisal benumbs them. Come on up, and let's resolve our grievances the democratic way.

He turns to go into the barbershop. Bill whips out his cleaver and hurls it through the air and deep into Monk's back. Monk goes crashing halfway through the door of the barbershop.

BILL THE BUTCHER
That, Monk, is the minority vote.

Monk tries to stagger into the barbershop, his hands trying to pull the cleaver from his back. Bill climbs the steps and picks up Monk's war club.

With his free hand he grabs Monk by the collar or the hair and drags him onto the rock. Monk sprawls out on the rock, trying to crawl away.

A series of shots as thieves and pickpockets and whores and Hot Corn girls stop in mid-action, noticing the fallen warrior and the Butcher standing over him.

BILL THE BUTCHER (CONT'D)
Now you've tasted my mutton. How do you like it?

Bill takes a knife from his belt and cuts a fresh notch in the club. He holds it down for Monk to see.

BILL THE BUTCHER (CONT'D)
This is you. Right here. Notch forty-five, you Irish bog bastard.

(236) Bill raises the war club high into the air. As it comes plummeting down at Monk's head—

INT. TAMMANY HALL—NIGHT

A roar of applause accompanies a tight shot of a ring held between two fat fingers—

TWEED
"Fortune Favors the Bold." What do you think, Your Honor? A fit motto for our fair city?

The crowd applauds. Tweed and several other sachems, in full regalia, are up on the stage of the packed Great Hall, along with Amsterdam, Archbishop Hughes, and the just-elected Tammany mayor.

SOMEONE IN CROWD
City's already got a motto!

TWEED
It does? What is it? (No one in the crowd knows) Well, by cracky, let's have one we can all remember! Fortune Favors the Bold!

The crowd cheers again. Tweed slips the ring onto the new mayor's finger. Amsterdam, flushed and excited, barely takes note as Killoran crosses the stage, whispers something to Tweed, and gives him a small package wrapped in brown butcher's paper.

Tweed unwraps the package. Inside is Monk's war club, bloodied.

INT. TAMMANY KITCHEN (EXISTING)—NIGHT

Terrified chefs look on in silence as Bill the Butcher slices at a shank of raw beef with a gleaming knife. Tweed stands in front of Bill. Killoran stands back at a safer distance.

TWEED
You killed an elected official?

BILL THE BUTCHER
Who elected him?

TWEED
You don't know what you've done to your-self—

He sticks his knife into the butcher block. Tweed takes an involuntary half-step back.

BILL THE BUTCHER
You think lightning strikes when you talk, Mr. Tweed. But I can't hardly hear you.

Bill comes out from behind the table.

BILL THE BUTCHER (CONT'D)
"I know your works. You are neither cold nor hot. So because you are lukewarm, and are nei-ther cold nor hot, I will spew you out of my mouth." You can build your filthy world without me. I took the father. Now I'll take the son. You tell young Vallon I'm goin' to paint Paradise Square with his blood. Two coats. I'll festoon my bedchamber with his guts. As for you, Mr. Tammany fucking Hall, come down to the Points again and you'll be dispatched by mine own hand. Now go back to your celebration and let me eat in peace. I've paid you fair.

INT. CATHOLIC CHURCH— DAY

Tight on Amsterdam and Shang.

SHANG
What do we do now?

Amsterdam speaks with trembling control.

AMSTERDAM
We run another candidate. And that's the all of it.

Shang and the boys nod. Pulling back we see that they are pallbearers, waiting to pick up Monk's casket—Amsterdam and Shang in the middle, then Jimmy, Tweed, the mayor, and Hughes.

On Hughes's signal they hoist the casket and carry it slowly along the scaffold-less aisle. They move past faces of Dead Rabbits, past workmen and poor Irish families. As they near the church doors, Jenny pulls them open, and light crashes in exactly like the day Monk kicked open the Old Brewery doors fifteen years before.

EXT. CATHOLIC CHURCH— CONTINUOUS

A huge crowd has gathered outside and watches in solemn silence as the coffin is carried down the church steps and carefully set upon a coach covered in flowers.

EXT. PARADISE SQUARE— DAY

No one is working. No one is thieving. It seems pos-sible the entire citizenry of the Points is part of the cortege as it crosses Paradise Square. Bill is standing with his Natives and the Nativist candidate, outside Satan's Circus, watching the procession. Amsterdam sees them. They stare as Amsterdam stays in step. They pass in silence, until:

BILL THE BUTCHER
Why don't you try burning him, and see if his ashes don't turn green?

Amsterdam tries to control himself for three sec-onds. Then he launches himself toward Bill. The coffin lurches and almost falls. The crowd holds Amsterdam back, everyone shouting at once.

AMSTERDAM
See what we do with your ashes, you red-mounted son of a bitch!

ONE-ARMED PRIEST
This ain't the place for it!

BILL THE BUTCHER
Let him come ahead! Come on ahead!

Bill and the Natives shout for him to come on. The whole crowd surges on the edge of total riot. We find Jenny, looking at the raging Amsterdam. She backs away, through the crowd.

EXT. BROADWAY— AFTERNOON

Silence. A man unfurls a long banner-newspaper. As he steps away, a headline announcing commencement of the first draft in American history is revealed.

Another man unfurls another long sheet of paper and posts it against a wall. As he steps away, a printed name fills the screen, then the one above it, and another, name after name, most Irish, until we reach the top and a week's date and the words, **Dead or Missing**.

The list is covered like sod thrown on a grave as people crowd around to find out if their relatives' names are on it. A woman's loud mournful wail is clipped short as—

(238) ### INT. SPARROW'S PAGODA— SAME TIME

Men from various gangs come in off the street, two or three representatives from each: Shirt Tails, Plug Uglies, Daybreak Boys, Chichesters, American Guards, Roach Guards, Little Forty Thieves, Kerryonians, True Blue Americans....

Half settle on one side of the room, where Amsterdam sits with Shang and Jimmy Spoils. The other half assembles across from them, where Bill and a couple of Natives sit.

INT./EXT. DRAFT OFFICE— SAME TIME

A spinning wooden lottery wheel slows and stops. A man pulls from a cavity a handful of slips of paper, carries them to the front door, and announces in a firm voice to an anxious crowd gathered outside the names of the first men in American history to be drafted into service to fight on a battlefield:

DRAFT OFFICIAL
James Mooney, Thomas O'Neill, Andrew Lewis, Jack McAuley, Sean O'Connell—

INT. SPARROW'S PAGODA

The camera moves from gang leader to gang leader as each calls out the name of the gang he represents—

IRISH GANG LEADERS
The O'Connell Guards—the Forty Thieves—the Kerryonians—the Chichesters—

NATIVIST GANG LEADERS
The American Guards—the Atlantic Guards—the Slaughter Housers—

BILL THE BUTCHER
The Native Americans—

AMSTERDAM
—the Dead Rabbits.

INT./EXT. DRAFT OFFICE

The spinning lottery wheel again. The slips of paper taken out. The draft official announcing more names to the crowd outside—which has grown in number.

INT. SPARROW'S PAGODA

The representative of the Forty Thieves, the oldest man in the room, addresses the others—

FORTY THIEVES LEADER
This council last met fifteen years ago. As many of you remember, it parted without a peaceful result. On which agenda are we gathered now: to negotiate or challenge? Mr. Vallon—

AMSTERDAM
Challenge.

BILL THE BUTCHER
Accepted.

AMSTERDAM
When?

INT. TWEED'S OFFICE / TAMMANY HALL

Tweed moves from birdcage to birdcage, replenishing his canaries' birdseed, then drapes a cape over his shoulders like an aristocrat and strides out past portraits of sachems and a bust of himself, his footsteps echoing.

BILL THE BUTCHER (*V.O.*)
Whenever you like.

AMSTERDAM (*V.O.*)
Daybreak tomorrow.

INT. DRAFT OFFICE

The draft wheel slows and stops again. The official grasps the slips of paper and heads toward the door. This time though, before he reaches it, both windows on either side suddenly implode from a storm of rocks—

BILL THE BUTCHER (*V.O.*)
Where.

INT. DRAFT OFFICE

The crowd, which can now be termed a mob, surges in brandishing bats and crowbars and sawn-off table legs. Some Black Joke firemen set about smashing the draft wheel with axes as others tear apart the rest of the place—

AMSTERDAM (*V.O.*)
Paradise Square.

EXT. DRAFT OFFICE / TAMMANY HALL

Tweed, standing next to his coach, stares at the mob in and outside the draft office. A bloodied draft official stumbles out. Furniture hurtles out behind him. Tweed's horse shies. Some men carry cans of turpentine into the draft office and Tweed hurries aboard his coach.

TWEED
Uptown, Coachman.

BILL THE BUTCHER (*V.O.*)
Weapons.

AMSTERDAM (*V.O.*)
That I leave to you.

INT./EXT. DRAFT OFFICE

Torches are thrown and the floor and walls erupt in flames. The mob surges back outside and is confronted by a regiment of arriving police.

BILL THE BUTCHER (*V.O.*)
Bricks, bats, axes, knives, and fists. No pistols.

A pistol shot is fired into the sky—

INT. SPARROW'S PAGODA—
CONTINUED

But it's only a distant echo down here in the Points as Amsterdam and Bill face each other.

AMSTERDAM
The terms are resolved. The council is concluded.

Amsterdam gets up. His gang gets up with him. As they start to leave...

BILL THE BUTCHER
That wasn't much of a council. You ain't got your father's flair.

AMSTERDAM
Maybe. But come tomorrow, if you look me in the eye or not, I'm goin' to put you to bed with a shovel.

Bill smiles broadly. The gangs split up. As Amsterdam and his boys reach the door they are confronted by the Forty Thieves and the O'Connell Guards, by young faces and old.

(240)

FORTY THIEVES LEADER
We're all with you, Mr. Vallon. But if we're to be an Irish army, that one'll have to stand down.

He gestures at Jimmy.

AMSTERDAM
Jimmy's a Dead Rabbit and a good fighter. There ain't no need for that.

JIMMY SPOILS
I'll kill Natives good as any man here.

FORTY THIEVES LEADER
Stand down or be strung up.

SHANG
You got no call talkin' like that, Forty Thieves—

There's a brief scuffle. Amsterdam gets between Shang and the Forty Thieves Leader—

AMSTERDAM
That's sufficient!

Amsterdam looks at the dozens of gang members threatening Jimmy.

AMSTERDAM (*CONT'D*)
Stand down, Jimmy.

Pause. Jimmy looks at Amsterdam, then shoulders his way through the crowd.

EXT. SPARROW'S PAGODA—
EVENING

They emerge from the Pagoda and move off in separate directions, down different darkening streets leading to their home turfs. In the quiet of the approaching night, smoke can be glimpsed in the distance, drifting up above the rooftops.

EXT. DRAFT OFFICE—
EVENING

Flames pour out of the broken windows as the fire guts the building. The mob scatters from the large showing of police. As the last of the rioters disappear down side streets, it's suddenly, strangely, quiet.

INT. DRAFT OFFICE— EVENING (2ND UNIT)

And the draft wheel, down on the floor but still slowly, eerily, spinning, burns black as the slips of paper printed with the conscripted men's names float up to the ceiling, lifted by the fire that consumes them.

INT. SCHERMERHORN MANSION—NIGHT

The Schermerhorns are entertaining. Tweed is there, the mayor, Horace Greeley, and several other politicos in the billiards room. The ice cubes in the mayor's drink are rattling.

SCHERMERHORN
For the nonce the rats have returned to their holes...

SCHERMERHORN (CONT'D)
...but it could have been much worse—No, I don't think so, Mr. Mayor. A brief burst of anger over Mr. Lincoln's draft and—

MAYOR
The better to arm themselves, perhaps—

SCHERMERHORN (CONT'D)
Well, there are two sides to that question, Mr. Greeley, as you are in a better position to appreciate than any of us—

In any case—

In any case, Mr. Greeley—

GREELEY
Entirely justifiable, in my view—

There are several sides to the question, in fact, Mr Schermerhorn, but only one right side, as with any question involving the abuse of executive power—

SCHERMERHORN (CONT'D)
—I think we can all be thankful it wasn't any worse.

GREELEY
Indeed we can, Mr. Schermerhorn—

SCHERMERHORN
And as Mr. Tweed is fond of saying—

TWEED
It may be worse yet, sir. I saw them. And I don't know what to think.

SCHERMERHORN
But what's that you're so fond of saying, Mr. Tweed?—Mr. Greeley won't like this—but what was it...?

TWEED
I don't remember.

SCHERMERHORN
..."You can always hire one half of the poor to kill the other half."

GREELEY
—I have heard they are going from door to door in the Five Points asking those who wish to see further rioting to put a lighted candle in the window. Irish, Poles, Germans—

SCHERMERHORN
Ah, Mr. Greeley. The city is not mad. And I will prophesy a very dark night.

He fires off the shot.

EXT. FIVE POINTS—NIGHT

A dark window…then the slightest flicker as someone emerges from another room and approaches with a candle in hand. The figure sets it down on the sill and we—

Drop back to a wide shot showing the entire Five Points: Almost every window in every building is glowing.

INT. UNDERGROUND CHAMBER—MORNING

A single candle glows in the underground room from the prologue. The only sound we can hear is the scraping of a blade against skin.

Tight on Priest Vallon's razor in Amsterdam's hand as it slides across his face. He stands in the same spot his father used to shave, bathed in the flickering candlelight.

He realizes he's not alone. Jenny is standing at the chamber entrance, dressed in her traveling clothes.

JENNY
I come to say goodbye. I've booked passage to California.

AMSTERDAM
Wait one more day, Jenny, and I'll go with you.

JENNY
You'll be dead by then.

AMSTERDAM
Jenny—what would you have me do?

JENNY
I don't know.

(*Pause*)

AMSTERDAM
It'll all be finished tomorrow.

JENNY
No it won't.

EXT. FIVE POINTS (FROM ROOFTOPS)—MORNING

Schermerhorn's "rats" emerge from their holes—from tenements and saloons—many of them armed with bricks and bats. They look like gangs but wear no "colors." They are, in fact, ordinary citizens of the underclass. We see Jenny skirting the square, avoiding them as she goes.

MAN
Nobody goes to work today! They shut the factories down.

AMSTERDAM (*V.O.*)
From all over the city they came. Ironworkers, factory boys, day laborers, schoolteachers, street cleaners…American, Irish, Polish, German, anyone who never cared about slavery or the Union—whole or sundered.

MAN IN MOB
The hell with your damned draft!

AMSTERDAM (*V.O.*)
The Earth was shaking now, but we was the only ones who didn't know it.

INT. SATAN'S CIRCUS— MORNING

Upstairs in a dank room, Bill the Butcher prepares for a battle of another kind, methodically sharpening his knives and setting each, when honed to his satisfaction, next to his leather cutlery belt.

INT. UNDERGROUND CHAMBER—MORNING

Amsterdam places the razor in its pouch and pockets it, then grasps his dagger and slides it into its leather sheath.

INT. STOREFRONT— MORNING (2ND UNIT)

A brick crashes through a window, showering glass onto shovels, picks, sledge-hammers and broadaxes. Rough hands reach into frame and grab the tools. Others break up tables to use the legs as clubs. Others grab furniture-making tools to use as weapons. In the B.G. Jenny passes, hurrying.

MAN IN MOB
Take these lads! We'll split their heads and crack some Fifth Avenue skulls!

INT. SATAN'S CIRCUS—MORNING

Bill's cutlery, now in his belt, rattles as he kneels and quietly begins intoning a prayer—

BILL THE BUTCHER
Lord Almighty, you are my dagger—

INT. UNDERGROUND CHAMBER—MORNING

Amsterdam is kneeling, too, before a Celtic cross painted on the rock wall, intoning a prayer—

AMSTERDAM
Guide my hand on this day of vengeance—

INT. SCHERMERHORN MANSION—MORNING

Black servants stand ready to serve breakfast as Schermerhorn says grace at the family table—

SCHERMERHORN
We give thanks to the Lord for He is good—

INTERCUT THE THREE PRAYERS:

BILL THE BUTCHER
With you, the swift cannot flee, nor the strong escape. With you, the roaring of my enemies will be silenced—

AMSTERDAM
Let my sword devour till it is satisfied—

SCHERMERHORN
He satisfies the thirsty and fills the hungry with good things—

AMSTERDAM
Until its thirst is quenched with blood and my enemies sleep forever—

BILL THE BUTCHER
For the Lord is God of Retribution—

SCHERMERHORN
For the Lord is merciful and His Love endures forever—

AMSTERDAM
For the Lord crushes the wicked. Amen.

BILL THE BUTCHER
Amen.

SCHERMERHORN
Amen.

INT. SCHERMERHORN MANSION—CONTINUED

The Schermerhorns' heads rise back up. Servants set out plates of food. Suddenly a window implodes, raining glass everywhere. An ax cleaves through the door—

EXT. SCHERMERHORN MANSION (2ND UNIT)

Black Joke firemen hack at the front door with fire axes—

INT. SCHERMERHORN MANSION—CONTINUED

Schermerhorn, armed with a brace of pistols, hurries the terrified family up the stairs.

SCHERMERHORN
Upstairs, be quick!

MISS SCHERMERHORN
Father! Father!

The front door rips from its hinges. The firemen and rioters pour in with picks and axes and hack up the furniture. Schermerhorn stands his ground and gets off a couple of shots before he is overwhelmed by the flood of rioters.

Hands grab vases, silverware, clocks. The maids and servants escape out a service door.

(244)

RIOTER
Let's smash the bastards to hell!

Rioters splinter the billiard table, shatter the gun case, and take the rifles.

TELEGRAPH VOICE #1
From Eighteenth Precinct, the mob have attacked the armory. Second Avenue, Twenty-first Street—There is danger of firing the building.

Someone hurls a Louis XIV chair at a window. It crashes through. The instant before it strikes a rag-clad girl, the daughter of a rioter, we cut to—

INT. UNDERGROUND CHAMBER/TUNNEL

Amsterdam emerges from his underground chamber. He has a sheathed sword with an iron Celtic cross hilt.

He joins the short line of his boys—Shang and the other Dead Rabbits—getting communion from the one-armed priest. The one-armed priest blesses the sacrament. His Latin prayer carries over:

EXT. SCHERMERHORN MANSION (2ND UNIT)

White Ghost firemen by their cart use torches to light more held in hands like spokes of a wheel. They're thrown and arc across the sky like burning arrows in a medieval battle.

INT. TUNNELS

Amsterdam passes in and out of candlelight as he strides down the tunnel. We hear the boys and the one-armed priest close behind O.C., and see their shadows play on the wall and on Amsterdam. Except for the echoing footsteps as they walk along the long tunnel, it's silent. The blessing continues over:

EXT. PRECINCT HOUSE

Jenny flattens into a doorway. Across the street a regiment of police emerges from a station house, but are unable to get down the steps before being met with a hail of brickbats hurled by crowds in the street and on the rooftops.

TELEGRAPH VOICE #1
From Sixteenth Precinct, all the stores are closing on Eighth Avenue from fear of the mob on Seventeenth Street.

TELEGRAPH VOICE #2
From Fourth, the rioters are attacking colored boardinghouses, robbing them and setting them on fire.

TELEGRAPH VOICE #1
From Twenty-first, the mob have just broken open gun store on Third Avenue and are arming.

INT. COMMAND POST (TAMMANY SET)

The camera rushes past armed police to a telegraph machine and operator receiving a message, at once writing it down and translating:

TELEGRAPH OPERATOR
Lexington, Forty-first, Second, and Third streets, sacked and fired—large mob outside Eighteenth Precinct House—will you allow us use of muskets?

POLICE COMMISSIONER
I'm not going to have good policemen turned into inferior soldiers. Tell him no, and call in all non-commissioned officers and volunteers. The police are overwhelmed. We need federal troops now!

MAN
There are fifty more Negroes outside that need help. The blacks are being attacked all over the city. Officers should give up their rooms for those who need refuge.

Outside the window a rioter with a pair of shears attempts to cut the telegraph lines, and is immediately electrocuted, falling back ensnared in the spider web of wires.

TELEGRAPH OPERATOR
The line is dead! They're trying to cut all the wires.

INT. MANSION (2ND UNIT)

Flames devour artifacts of the wealthy: manuscripts and books, smoking jackets and summer bonnets hanging in closets, lecterns and writing desks and linen stationery, pianos, music stands, and opera glasses, oil paintings, cut flowers, a butterfly collection, a framed map of New Amsterdam.

TELEGRAPH VOICE #1
From Twentieth: Send one hundred men to disperse mob assailing Mayor Opdyke's house.

TELEGRAPH VOICE #2
(overlapping)…building corner Thirty-third Street, Second Avenue: set on fire by the mob.

INT. TUNNELS

Coming down the quiet tunnel, Amsterdam is joined by more Dead Rabbits and new Irish recruits; Hell-Cat Maggie appears, her nails like talons.

EXT. BROADWAY

Jenny hurries past the outside of Barnum's museum. Barnum is out front, calling for help in front of burning murals depicting various oddities and talents of freaks and animals. Behind him his men are pulling a tiger cage out of the building.

TELEGRAPH VOICE #1
(*Overlapping*)... From Twentieth. The mob are sacking houses Twenty-seventh Street and Seventh Avenue: We have no force to send.

TELEGRAPH VOICE #2
Barnum's Museum on fire! Escaped animals running wild!

A well-dressed young man running for his life trips in front of him. As he drags himself up we recognize him as the one who bought his way out of the draft. A roving band of workmen armed with clubs swarms over him.

MAN IN THE CROWD
Hey! There's a three-hundred-dollar man! Get him!

MAN IN THE CROWD (*CONT'D*)
Did your daddy buy you out of the Army? Can he buy us out of the Army too?

TELEGRAPH VOICE #2
There is danger of mob attacking armory corner Twenty-first Street, Second Avenue. There is about five hundred stand of arms in it.

INT. TUNNELS

Groups of O'Connell Guards and Kerryonians emerge from underground rooms and fall in behind the Dead Rabbits.

INT. TAMMANY HALL

Tweed's canaries panic. He loads a shotgun. As he moves to a window, we look down on rioters surging past below.

MAN IN MOB
Tear Tammany down!

TELEGRAPH VOICE #1
Marshal's Office on Third Avenue is burning down. The police is of no avail. Two colored men brought in almost dead.

EXT. TAMMANY HALL

Tweed in his office window, ready with the shotgun if need be. Every other facing window, too, is occupied by an armed Tammany man.

INT. TUNNELS

Shirt Tails and Plug Uglies fall in behind Amsterdam and the Dead Rabbits gang.

EXT./INT. TRIBUNE PRINT ROOM (2ND UNIT)

TELEGRAPH VOICE #2
From Twentieth Precinct: A very large mob now going down Fifth Avenue to attack *Tribune* office.

TELEGRAPH VOICE #1
The mob is very wild.

TELEGRAPH VOICE #2

All three hundred police wounded or unaccounted for!

A Molotov cocktail hits a gold *Tribune* plaque. Flames ignite and consume printing presses and newspapers with illustrations of Abraham Lincoln and Frederick Douglass and the headline: **THUGS DESIST; DRAFT TO RESUME TODAY**.

INT. RESTAURANT

TELEGRAPH VOICE #1

The mob is about forty-five hundred strong! They're going to burn down Harlem Bridge. Harlem Bridge is to be torched!

Waiters are trying to barricade the door. We pick up Greeley outside in the street, running toward the restaurant away from the mob. His horrified face appears in the oval of glass set in it.

GREELEY

For God's sake, it's me! Let me in!

The waiters pull away the furniture and Greeley bursts in just ahead of a brickbat that shatters the glass behind him.

WAITER

Quickly, Mr. Greeley, under here!

GREELEY

The rats have taken over the city!

The waiter helps Greeley hide under a table.

INT. TUNNELS

All the Irish gangs now, two hundred strong and armed with their primitive weapons, move through the tunnels. The blessing carries over:

EXT. PARADISE SQUARE

The Dead Rabbits emerge from the underground catacombs. They hear a growl and immediately step back, alarmed. A Bengal tiger, escaped from Barnum's Museum of Wonders, prowls the streets in front of them. Behind the tiger is an apocalyptic tableau: Smoke and ash hide the sun.

EXT. BROADWAY—NIGHT

As a black man is lynched—

WOMAN IN CROWD

Come on, lads! Kill the nigger bastards! String them up!

TELEGRAPH VOICE #1

From Twenty-first: There is an attack on the colored people on Second Avenue between Twenty-eighth and Twenty-ninth Streets.

TELEGRAPH VOICE #2

(*Overlapping*) There's a mob headed for the Colored Orphan's Asylum. Send troops to protect the children!

TELEGRAPH VOICE #1

…Twenty-ninth. The rioters now on Seventh Avenue, Twenty-eighth Street. They have just killed a Negro.

Jimmy Spoils comes around a corner and stops short. A mob is gathered around the corner. Tilting up we see a black man hanging from the lamppost. Three or four more hang from other lampposts on the street. A white man hands a burning torch to a white woman. She reaches up to set the hanged man alight…

Jimmy turns to run before the crowd sees him. But a smaller crowd surges up the street behind him and he's trapped, cut off. As the crowd is upon him we cut away—

EXT. BROADWAY

A pair of Army boots caked with mud splashes through puddles of blood on cobblestones. A row of bayonets cuts through the air. Infantrymen are marching down Broadway.

TELEGRAPH VOICE
The major-general wants to know what he's to do with any prisoners captured.

INT. COMMAND POST

GENERAL WOOL
Prisoners? Don't take any! The mob isn't taking prisoners! Put the mob down! Don't bring a prisoner in until the mob is put down!

EXT. STREET AND ALLEYS

From a rooftop, the mob runs from the infantrymen down an alley only to find it blocked by more soldiers.

MAN IN THE CROWD
Firm, lads! They won't shoot.

MAN IN THE CROWD (CONT'D)
Lads, stick together...

TELEGRAPH VOICE
From Sixteenth—mob is coming down to station house. We have no men! I must leave. The mob is here with guns!

TELEGRAPH VOICE #2
Soldiers now on Thirty-eighth Street. The mob will not disperse. What are your orders? (more urgently) What are your orders?!

A commander barks an order and the first rank drops to one knee

SOLDIER
I order you to disperse!

[The crowd does not move]

SOLDIER (CONT'D)
FIRE!

Rioters fall. The second rank drops—the second volley carries into—

EXT. DOCKS

Jenny is trying to get through the crowd to the docks but the street is swarming with rioters, breaking windows, setting stores alight, looting the ships in the harbor.

TELEGRAPH VOICE #1
From First: Riot at Pier Four, North River. They have killed Negroes there. A crowd is here and is going to destroy this station.

Suddenly she is yanked out of the street by a SCRUFFY MAN who pulls her into the shadows where his WOMAN ACCOMPLICE is waiting.

SCRUFFY MAN
Get her bag! Get her bag!

He grabs at Jenny's bag. She goes wild fighting him. The woman yanks the bag out of Jenny's hands and rips it open with a knife.

TELEGRAPH VOICE #1
From Twentieth: Mob tearing up track on Eleventh Avenue. I have not force enough to prevent it.

As the woman finds Jenny's money, the man holds Jenny back.

SCRUFFY MAN
Let go that bag, my bene mort!

JENNY
Give me that bag!

WOMAN ACCOMPLICE
Hush the shickster!

Jenny pulls out her pistol and shoots the woman in the chest, point blank. The woman falls back dead.

SCRUFFY MAN
Jesus God!

The man grapples with her for the gun—yanking it out of her hand. He throws her down on the ground—she tries to grab at her money but the mob is upon them, scooping up the money and shoving her aside.

TELEGRAPH VOICE #2
From Admiral Paulding: Brooklyn Navy Yard. Have dispatched eight gunboats, now lying off the tip of Wall Street. They are ready to open fire.

Running and crawling she gets away, nearly trampled. She falls into a dark recessed doorway with some steps down as the mob surges by. She can still see the harbor, but there's no way to get to it.

EXT. PARADISE SQUARE

Facing the Dead Rabbits—assembled in almost-military fashion—are the Allied-Nativist gangs, equal in number, about two hundred, with Bill standing in the center.

BILL THE BUTCHER
By the ancient laws of combat, we offer our bodies to the ghosts of the warriors that have gone before us.

AMSTERDAM
And we'll send many more across the river today.

Bill parts his coat and selects a knife from his belt. Amsterdam unsheathes a cutlass with a hilt forged in the shape of a Celtic cross, and the rest take firm grasp of their own favored primeval weapons.

BILL THE BUTCHER
On your order, Vallon.

As Amsterdam raises his sword to give the signal—

MATCH CUT TO:

A sword in the hand of a Navy commander aboard a war ship moored in New York Harbor comes down and the mortars boom—

**EXT. PARADISE SQUARE—
CONTINUED**

Amsterdam's cutlass stays suspended as he and the others listen to a strange, completely foreign sound: a whistling that seems to be coming down upon them from the heavens.

The mortars suddenly hit all around them. Gang members hurtle into the air as the ground erupts. The Old Brewery explodes, hurtling bricks like missiles, mortar like shrapnel.

Fueling the pandemonium, rioters, retreating from the infantrymen, pour across the square seeking refuge in their closed saloons and hovels, only to have them explode in another round of mortar fire. The war has come home.

SOLDIER (O.C.)
Disperse or you will be shot...! Fire over their heads...! Drive them into the square!

The Rabbits and Natives can no longer be differentiated from anyone else as they all try to drag their dead and wounded to safety. Thick smoke veils the entire square.

Shots bark, find indiscriminate targets. Shang is hit, falls, McGloin goes down. Swamp Angels and Daybreak Boys slam up against walls, their different "colors" ripping open, but the blood spewing out all the same crimson.

Amsterdam can be glimpsed finally, lying injured on the street under a cloak of smoke. His eyes open and witness in a delirious haze the chaos all around him:

Men in Army uniforms battling in close combat with rioters and gang members; smoke and fire erupting from rifle muzzles; men and women falling; the one-armed priest administering last rites to a dying Hell-Cat Maggie is trampled—all to an eerie medley of cries and screams and rattling musketry.

(250)   As a rush of people clears, Amsterdam sees Bill the Butcher—like he first saw him upon his return, backlit by the flames of a burning building.

BILL THE BUTCHER
The world has ended. Prepare to meet the Lord.

He rushes forward through the smoke, covered in ash and blood, like a demonic ghost. Amsterdam slashes with his cutlass once wildly at the apparition as it swoops past.

He gets to his knees, to his feet, turns and peers at the walls of smoke all around him. Suddenly, Bill is bursting through again. Amsterdam slashes, misses, is caught in the shoulder by Bill's dagger, then in the thigh, sending him down to his knees.

He struggles back up.

Bill charges at Amsterdam. Amsterdam lashes out and catches Bill as he passes. Bill cries out and clutches his arm and side.

We see there is a very large spreading stain on Bill's left side.

A huge explosion knocks Bill and Amsterdam to the ground.

They stagger to their feet again. Bill and Amsterdam look around. Everywhere they look it's devastation and destruction. McGloin is shot to death by the soldiers. Shang attacks the soldiers and is beaten to death. The cart explodes and crushes Hell-Cat Maggie. The Points is wrapped in smoke and littered with bodies and rubble. Amsterdam turns to Bill.

AMSTERDAM
Bill...Bill...

BILL THE BUTCHER
(Shakes his head) I knew who you was. You think I didn't know who you was? You ain't got your father's sand.

(Pause)

AMSTERDAM
Nor do you.

Amsterdam lashes out at Bill with everything he has. He beats Bill back, hard and furious. Bill tries to fight back but Amsterdam just keeps smashing him back.

Amsterdam stops. Bill stands before him unsteadily. They are both breathing very hard.

BILL THE BUTCHER
That all the sand you got, Vallon?

AMSTERDAM
No!

Amsterdam lurches at Bill hitting him again even harder. Bill staggers back—Another explosion hits and they are knocked apart.

When the smoke clears they are lying on the ground covered with dust like a pair of fossils. They painfully rise until they are facing each other on their knees, clutching their knives.

Amsterdam, holding the knife, is looking at Bill. Bill is looking around at the demolished Five Points. Finally he looks at Amsterdam.

BILL THE BUTCHER
Thank God...I die a true American.

Bill nods to Amsterdam. Amsterdam plunges the knife in—the coup de grace.

He pulls out the knife and Bill's blood sprays him in the face. Bill collapses, clutching Amsterdam's hand. His body convulses—his hand still gripping Amsterdam's.

The lid of Bill's glass eye closes over the etched

American eagle like a curtain coming down. He's gone.

Amsterdam drops the sword and collapses, exhausted, breathing hard, spattered by the Butcher's blood.

Time seems to stop. We hear a single pair of footsteps echoing through the silence.

Jenny comes out of the mist and kneels down where Amsterdam is lying. Amsterdam opens his eyes.

We pan up and as the smoke begins to clear we see the entire square, littered with bodies. Amsterdam is a dot on the far end of the bloody field.

EXT. PARADISE SQUARE— NIGHT

Flames slowly rise from the bottom of the black frame as we descend from the night sky and consider the entire city, lit only by the fires still burning and smoldering in buildings in the distance.

As we come down lower, flames from Satan's Circus fill the frame.

A Tammany wagon travels across the square, police and soldiers heaving the bodies of dead rioters and gangs and blacks upon it.

The Old Brewery/Mission walls have fallen. The building looks like an ancient Roman ruin. A deep, craterlike pit resembling an archaeological excavation has been dug in the middle of it, caving in the network of tunnels underneath and exposing long-buried human bones and skulls.

It is here, in this common grave, that hundreds of bodies are now being dumped and covered with lye. Tweed, Killoran, the mayor, and the police commissioner stand watching the work with handkerchiefs held to their faces.

TWEED

Get a priest, say a mass, cover them up.

KILLORAN

Some aren't Catholic. That one certainly isn't.

The black tap-dancer spills off a wheelbarrow and rolls down to the bottom of the pit, coming to rest against the sleeveless arm of the priest.

TWEED

Then they'd better have made peace with God on their own.

Shang's body is down there among the others, and McGloin's, both covered in lye.

TWEED (CONT'D)

Tomorrow morning, get our people down to the docks. I want every man and woman coming off the boats given hot soup and bread. We're burying a lot of votes down here tonight.

Killoran looks at Tweed. Tweed is unflinching.

EXT. BROADWAY—NIGHT

The body of the child struck in the head by the chair, the first fatality of the riot, lies on the cobblestones clutching a lit candle in her gray hands.

(252)

Amsterdam and Jenny come past her, and the corpse next to her in the same pose, and the next, looking at the faces. We see Jimmy Spoils, Jenny's girls, other familiar faces. The camera rises as they continue on, revealing a thousand bodies illuminated by the candles held in their

hands, lying side by side and stretching off into the night uptown.

AMSTERDAM (V.O.)

It was four days and nights before the worst of the mob was finally put down...

A wind gusts across Broadway then, and all the candles are extinguished at once, throwing them and the street and their city into total darkness.

EXT. POTTERS FIELD—DAWN

A neglected cemetery atop a hill.

Ashes fall from the sky like snow onto a grave marker: **PRIEST VALLON, 1812-1846, DUBLIN**. Next to it stands a newer headstone. **WILLIAM CUTTING, 1815-1863, NEW YORK CITY**.

Amsterdam digs a shallow hole in the earth with his hands between the graves, sets the razor in, covers it with dirt, and kisses the St. Michael medal hanging from a strand of leather around his neck.

AMSTERDAM (V.O.)

...How many New Yorkers died that week we never knew. We thought there wouldn't be no country left by the end of it. And that no matter how much blood they spilt to build the city up again, and keep on building, for the rest of time, it would again be like no one even knew that we was ever here.

As they walk away from the graves, the camera pulls back, and the future skyline of New York takes shape, towers of steel and concrete rising out of the smoke and ashes.

FADE OUT

Director: .... Martin Scorsese
Story by: .... Jay Cocks
Screenplay by: .... Jay Cocks
.... Steve Zaillian
.... Kenneth Lonergan
Producer: .... Alberto Grimaldi
....................................Harvey Weinstein
Executive Producers: ....Michael Ovitz
....Bob Weinstein
.... Rick Yorn
.... Michael Hausman
.... Maurizio Grimaldi
Co-Executive Producers: ....Graham King
....Rick Schwartz
....Colin Vaines
Director of Photography: ....
.... Michael Ballhaus, A.S.C.
Production Designer: ....
.... Dante Ferretti
Editor: ....
.... Thelma Schoonmaker, A.C.E.
Costume Designer: .... Sandy Powell
Co-Producers: .... Joseph Reidy
.... Laura Fattori
Casting: .... Ellen Lewis

(254)

CAST

Amsterdam: .... Leonardo DiCaprio
Bill the Butcher: .... Daniel Day-Lewis
Jenny: .... Cameron Diaz

Boss Tweed: .... Jim Broadbent
Vallon: .... Liam Neeson
Monk McGinn: .... Brendan Gleeson
Happy Jack: .... John C. Reilly
McGloin: .... Gary Lewis
Johnny: .... Henry Thomas
Jimmy Spoils: .... Larry Gilliard, Jr.
Shang: .... Stephen Graham
Young Amsterdam: .... Cian McCormack
Reverend Raleigh: .... Alec McCowen
Horace Greeley: .... Michael Byrne
Mr. Schermerhorn: ....
.... David Hemmings
Mrs. Schermerhorn: .... Barbara Bouchet
Miss Schermerhorn: .... Lucy Davenport
Killoran: .... Eddie Marsan
One Armed Priest: .... Peter Hugo Daly
Hell-Cat Maggie: .... Cara Seymour
P.T. Barnum: .... Roger Ashton-Griffiths
Young Johnny: .... Andrew Gallagher
Native American Gang Member: ....
.... Liam Carney
Native American Gang Member: ....
.... Gary McCormack
Native American Gang Member: ....
.... David McBlain
Dead Rabbit Member #1: ....
.... Nevan Finnegan
Dead Rabbit Member #2: ....
.... Dominique Vandenberg

NOTE: Final Film Credits were incomplete at the time this book went to press.

CREW

Production Manager:........... Riccardo Neri

1st Assistant Director: .... Joesph Reidy

2nd Assistant Director: .... Chris Surgent

Set Decorator:...............................
.... Francesca Lo Schiavo

Supervising Art Director:...........................
.... Stefano Ortolani

Technical Art Director: ....
.... Robert Guerra

Supervising Props: .... Dennis Parrish

Gaffer: .... Jim Tynes

Key Grip: .... J. Patrick Daily

Second Unit Director for Fight Scenes: ....
.... Vic Armstrong

Director of Photography: ....
.... Florian Ballhaus

Stunt Coordinator:............. George Aguilar

Fight Coordinator: ....
.... Dominique Vandenberg

Special Effects Supervisor:...........................
.... Bruce Steinheimer

ILM Visual Effects Supervisor: ....
.... Michael Owens

Key Makeup Artist & SFX Makeup: ....
.... Manlio Rocchetti

Makeup Artist for Mr. DiCaprio:.................
.... Sian Grigg

Makeup Artist for Ms. Diaz: ....
.... Noriko Watanabe

Hair Designer: .... Aldo Signoretti

Hair Designed for Ms. Diaz by: ....
.... Anne Morgan

Consultant: .... David Parfitt

Dialect Coach: .... Tim Monich

Script Supervisor:............. Rachel Griffiths

1st Assistant Film Editors: ....
.... Scott Brock
.... Tom Foligno
.... Jeff Werner

Post Production Supervisors:........................
.... Michael Jackman
.... Gerry Byrne

Supervising Sound Editor:...........................
.... Phil Stockton

Re-recording Mixers: ....
.... Tom Fleischman
.... Eugene Gearty

Special Visual Effects By: ....
.... Industrial Light & Magic
A Division of Lucas Digital LTD.
Marin County, California

Insert Photography: . . . .
. . . . Phil Marco Productions

Historical Advisor: . . . . Luc Sante

Researchers: . . . . Marianne Bower
. . . . Deanna Avery

Publicist: . . . . Larry Kaplan

Stills Photographer: . . . . Mario Tursi

Titles Designed By: . . . . Dan Perri

Behind-the-Scenes photographs by
BRIGITTE LACOMBE

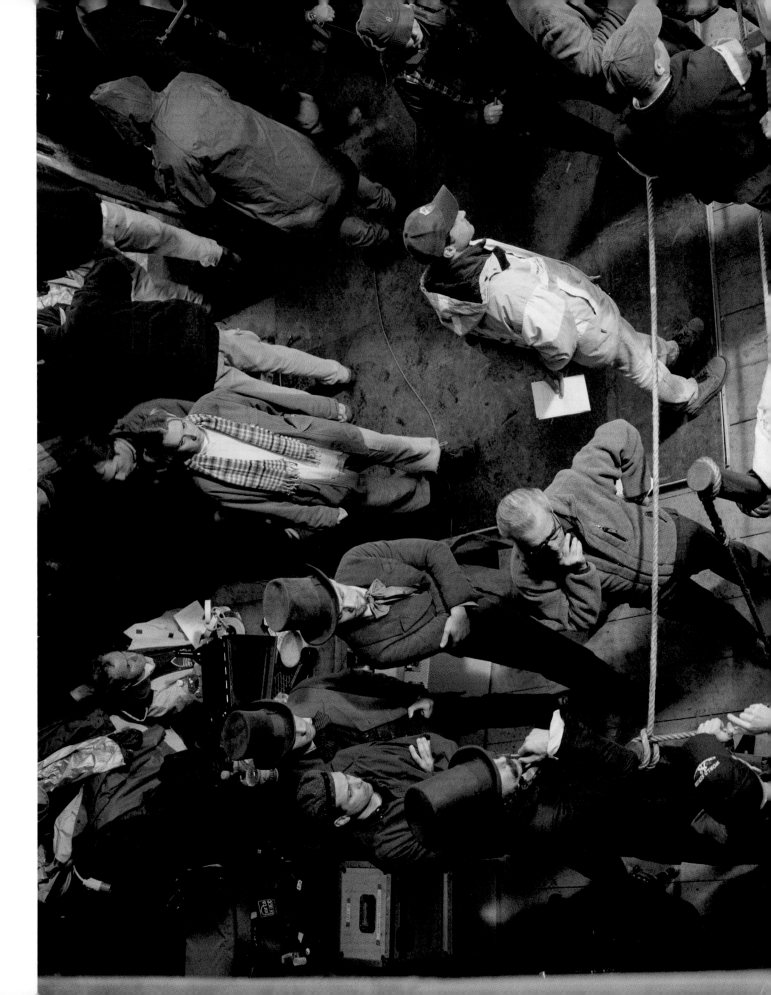

"New York City, 1844."

GREAT, I THOUGHT, AS I glanced at the opening of the script—another period costume drama. Don't get me wrong—my brother Bob and I have enjoyed great success with films like *Shakespeare in Love*, *Wings of the Dove*, *Emma*, and other "arthouse" movies. But it was the fall of 1999, and I was itching to tackle something edgier, meatier, riskier... As a courtesy, I looked at the cover page for the attached director's name. Martin Scorsese. Hmm, I had a feeling this movie might have some edge after all.

And so began the journey of *Gangs of New York*. Of course that was only *my* beginning—for Marty it started over thirty years earlier when he first read Herbert Asbury's 1927 book about street gangs in mid-nineteenth century New York. By the time the script inspired by this book arrived on my desk, every other studio in Hollywood had passed. As I continued reading, I couldn't help thinking: three decades of persistence—this is a guy whose passion matched my own.

When I finished, I knew I'd realize one of my dreams—one of those playing-shortstop-for-the-Yankees-only-in-New York kind of dreams: I was going to make a movie with Martin Scorsese.

Of course, no good movie is made without some tribulations and turmoil, and this one was certainly no exception. Right from the start, there were issues and obstacles to overcome. Being native New Yorkers, we wanted to shoot at the old Brooklyn Navy Dockyard; when that quickly turned into a political battle of its own, we ended up re-creating 1860s New York at the legendary Cinecittà Studios in Rome. With good food, better wine, great crews, and the specters of Fellini, DeSica, and other celebrated directors hovering in our midst, it ended up being a pretty good place to make the movie.

As Leo, Cameron, and a host of other wonderful actors came on board, we needed our centerpiece bad guy, Bill the Butcher. Both Marty and I wanted Daniel Day-Lewis to play this great character—but how? Here's a guy so uninterested in the bullshit of the film business that he'd been living in Italy making shoes for the last four years (very good shoes, I might add). Fortunately for us, Daniel—like most actors—loves Marty, so getting him interested wasn't as tough as we'd feared. To help clinch the deal, we took him to a famous restaurant in Harlem and pleaded our case. Surrounded by what looked like the cast of one of Marty's movies, Daniel understood this was an offer best not refused.

Once we started shooting, I was downright giddy. It's impossible to describe the excitement of sitting by the side of such a master director; you want to share the experience with everyone. One time Marty was setting up a spectacular tracking shot, a signature sequence reminiscent of the famous one at the Copa in *GoodFellas*. Though neither Leo nor Cameron were in the scene, I called and told them to run over from their dressing rooms just to watch the action. Marty brilliantly maneuvered the camera, weaving in and out of groups of actors, panning across a wide array of action and characters past Daniel sitting at a table playing cards ending up in a sporting area in the basement. When Marty finally called, "Cut," everyone on the set burst into applause. If you've ever been on a film set—especially one with a seasoned international crew—you know how rare it is to witness that kind of spontaneous, genuine enthusiasm.

Much like my own, Marty's passion manifests itself in varied and interesting ways (I'm putting that gently for both our sakes). There was the day when some young children were unable to perform exactly as he wanted. To Marty's increasing frustration, numerous takes yielded no results. When we heard him yell "Kill the kids!" everyone knew he was kidding. Everyone, of course, but the terrified kids.

Another day he got so mad with one of my production executives that he stormed into his office and threw the offender's desk—complete with computer, fax machine, and family photos—clear across the room. It turned out to be the wrong person's desk—and then, of course, Marty started to laugh.

Along with the fire in his belly, Marty's got a whole lot of savvy, and has made enough pictures to know how to best manage the director-producer relationship. Tom Cruise came to visit us in Rome one day, and our genius production designer, Dante Ferretti, gave him a walking tour of the incredible set. Marty and I had been at loggerheads over the increasingly massive set, trying to figure out where and when to stop building. Gazing up at the exterior of a half-built church, Marty turned to Tom and said, "What a shame we don't have the money to finish the church." As Tom turned to me and said—"Um, you know you gotta do this for Marty"—I knew two things for sure: the rest of the church would be built and it was time for Tom to go home. We named the church St. Thomas in his honor.

Marty liked to put me on the spot from time to time during the shoot. Once, when Daniel and Leo were bruised and battered after days of shooting their final fight scene, Marty decided his best solution would be to complete the action using stunt doubles. He told me that, as the producer, I should go and tell these two consummate actors, neither of whom ever wants to have a double, his brilliant plan. Though their response to my suggestion isn't anatomically possible, I certainly enjoyed the total lack of respect these two fine actors showed their producer. And I know Marty really enjoyed it.

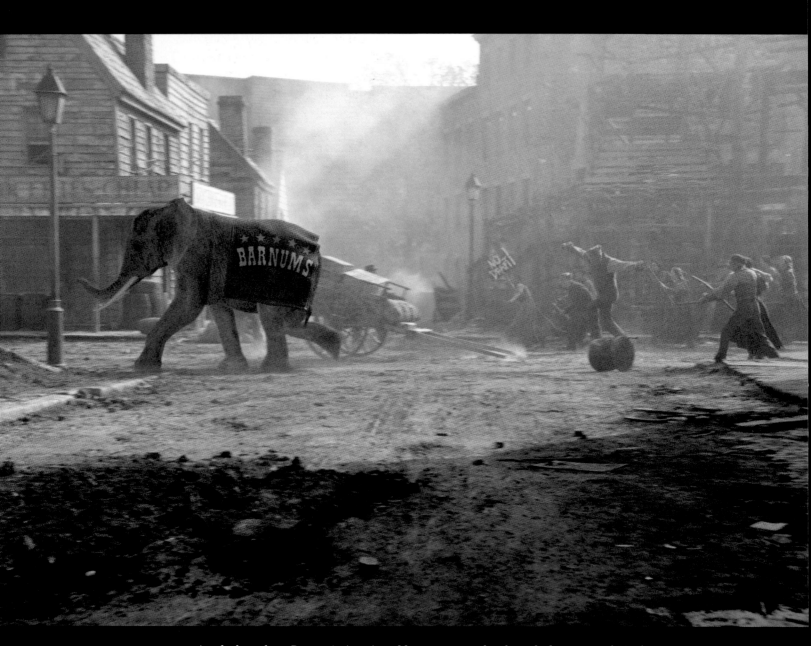

ABOVE: *An elephant from Barnum's American Museum stampedes through the streets of Manhattan*

Then there was the rampaging elephant. Marty insisted on having an elephant from Barnum's museum blasting through the Five Points at the end of the movie. While he waxed eloquent on the merits of the pachyderm, my thoughts were those of any sane producer. We were already behind schedule, it was going to be difficult to shoot, we'd need elephant wranglers and all the crap that comes with filming animals, and on top of everything, hoof and mouth disease was rampant in Europe, making it virtually impossible to do. It ended up being one of the few occasions I had to put my foot down and say—Marty, I love you, I love animals, let's go to the Bronx Zoo together—but I'm sorry, I can't give you this. In the end, of course, Marty had the last word.

A quick phone call to his good friend George Lucas and the wizards at ILM, and Marty has his New York elephant. And I'll be damned if it isn't a great moment in the film.

Frankly, losing battles is ultimately fun when you get to participate in the war—which is what making a movie with Marty is all about. And this was a great war. If I talk about the problems, I also have to talk about the sheer fun we had—the light and laughter Cameron brought to the set every day, the incredible pleasure of watching masterful actors like her and Leo and Daniel working with an amazing crew.

One of the true joys of my collaboration with Marty happened in an unexpected arena, neither on a set nor a soundstage nor an editing room—but rather, in screening rooms.

I'm sure everyone remembers a book called *Tuesdays with Morrie*, which changed a lot of people's lives with its story of a guy learning the meaning of life from his old professor.

I gave up trying to figure out the meaning of life a long time ago, but making *Gangs of New York*, I had my own life-changing experience called *Saturdays with Marty*.

Actually, it could just as well have been called *Mondays with Marty*, or *Wednesdays with Marty*—the day of the week didn't matter, it was just whenever he decided to send over a film for me to see, or when he invited the entire crew to share a screening. And afterwards, we'd discuss them.

During the three years it took to prep, shoot, and edit *Gangs*, I must have watched over eighty films at Marty's recommendation—from classics like Charles Laughton's *The Night of the Hunter* and David Lean's *Oliver Twist*, to lesser-known gems like Raoul Walsh's *The Bowery* and Luchino Visconti's *Senso*. His knowledge of film history is legendary, but for this jaded producer, it felt like I was a freshman at NYU Film School. Discussing these movies with him was like sitting at the feet of the world's greatest film professor, or learning the secrets of a Jedi master. And with each screening, I remembered all over again why I wanted to make movies in the first place. For a movie fan, it simply doesn't get any better.

Which is ultimately how I feel about *Gangs of New York*. In the end, for me, *Gangs* is about pride. I'm proud that I agreed to make this movie when no one else would. I'm proud that, through sheer will and determination, I was able to help a brilliant artist realize his vision. Most of all, though, I'm proud to have worked with one of the world's greatest directors—and a man I am thrilled to call my friend—Martin Scorsese.

Now if only the Yankees would call about that shortstop position...

Harvey Weinstein
Co-Chairman, Miramax Films
July 2002

(285)

GEORGE AGUILAR (Stunt Coordinator) worked with Martin Scorsese on *Bringing Out the Dead*. Some of his other recent film credits include *Pollack, The Peacemaker, Out of Sight,* and *Donnie Brasco*.

HOSSEIN AMINI (Screenwriter)is the author of the screenplay for *Jude,* and *Wings of the Dove* (which was nominated for the Oscar, BAFTA, and Writers' Guild awards for Best Adapted Screenplay). A graduate of Oxford, he also wrote the British TV film *The Dying of the Light,* and is the co-writer of the upcoming epic film *The Four Feathers*.

VIC ARMSTRONG (Action Unit Director) has worked as a stuntman, stunt coordinator, and director on more than 250 movies and, in 2001 received an Academy Award for Technical Achievement. He did stunt work for many of the James Bond films, doubled for Christopher Reeve in two of the Superman movies, and for Harrison Ford on all three Indiana Jones pictures. As action unit director and stunt coordinator he has worked on films by such directors as David Lean, Ridley Scott, Steven Spielberg, Richard Attenborough, and Paul Verhoven.

MICHAEL BALLHAUS (Director of Photography) marks his sixth collaboration with Martin Scorsese on *Gangs of New York*. (Their earlier films were *After Hours, The Color of Money, The Last Temptation of Christ, GoodFellas,* and *The Age of Innocence*.) Ballhaus's numerous other credits include fifteen films with Rainer Werner Fassbinder in Germany, and such American movies as *Broadcast News, Working Girl, The Fabulous Baker Boys, Francis Ford Coppola's Dracula, Quiz Show, Air Force One, Primary Colors,* and *The Legend of Bagger Vance*.

JIM BROADBENT (William Tweed) won the 2001 Academy Award as Best Supporting Actor for his performance in *Iris*. The same year he co-starred in *Bridget Jones's Diary* and *Moulin Rouge*. His many films include *The Rise and Fall of Little Voice, The Avengers, Bullets Over Broadway, The Crying Game, Life Is Sweet,* and *Dogs of War*. Broadbent has performed extensively in the theater and on television, appearing on stage in *Habeas Corpus* at the Donmar Warehouse, *A Flea In Her Ear* at London's Old Vic, and in several Royal Shakespeare Company productions.

JAY COCKS (Screenwriter) collaborated with Martin Scorsese on the screenplay of Scorsese's film adaptation of Edith Wharton's *The Age of Innocence,* for which he received an Academy Award nomination. His other screenwriting credits include *Strange Days* and *Made In Milan*. Cocks is a former film critic for *Time* magazine.

DANIEL DAY-LEWIS (Bill Cutting) won an Academy Award as Best Actor for his performance in *My Left Foot*. He also starred in *My Beautiful Laundrette, The Unbearable Lightness of Being, The Last of the Mohicans, In the Name of the Father, The Age Of Innocence, The Crucible,* and *The Boxer*. Day-Lewis trained at England's Bristol Old Vic and devoted over a decade in the 1970s and early 1980s to theater, appearing with the Bristol Old Vic, the Royal Shakespeare Company and the Royal National Theater.

CAMERON DIAZ (Jenny Everdeane) made her feature film debut at 21 as the femme fatale in *The Mask*. She appeared in *She's The One, Feeling Minnesota,* and *My Best Friend's Wedding*. She was named Best Actress by the New York Film Critics for her role in the Farrelly brothers' hit comedy *There's Something About Mary*; and was nominated for a Golden Globe Award and a British Film Academy Award for her performance in *Being John Malkovich*. Her recent films include *Any Given Sunday, Charlie's Angels,* and *Vanilla Sky*.

LEONARDO DiCAPRIO (Amsterdam Vallon) was nominated for an Academy Award as Best Supporting Actor for his performance in *What's Eating Gilbert Grape?* He has starred in such films as *The Basketball Diaries, Total Eclipse, William Shakespeare's Romeo and Juliet, Marvin's Room, Titanic,* and *The Beach,* and co-stars with Tom Hanks in the upcoming *Catch Me If You Can*. DiCaprio began his acting career at age 14 on a television revival of *Lassie*. His passion for environmental awareness led to his being invited to chair Earth Day 2000.

DANTE FERRETTI (Production Designer), a five-time Academy Award nominee, has created designs for Martin Scorsese's *The Age of Innocence, Casino, Kundun,* and *Bringing Out the Dead*. Among his many credits for cinema are five films for Pier Paolo Pasolini (*Salo, Arabian Nights, Canterbury Tales,*

Decameron, and *Medea*), and five for Federico Fellini (*La Voce Della Luna, Ginger and Fred, And the Ship Sails On, City of Women*, and *Orchestra Rehearsal*) in Italy, as well as such international productions as *Baron Munchausen, Interview with the Vampire, Meet Joe Black*, and *Titus*. He also has designed operas for such houses as La Scala in Milan, the Bastille Opera in Paris, and the Teatro Colon in Buenos Aires.

BRENDAN GLEESON (Monk McGinn) attracted international attention with his starring in John Boorman's *The General*, for which he won numerous honors including Best Actor Awards from the London Film Critics and the Boston Society of Film Critics. He has also appeared in *Far and Away, Braveheart, Michael Collins, The Tailor of Panama*, and *A.I.: Artificial Intelligence*. Gleeson began acting full time at age 34, and has acted on stage with Dublin's Abbey Theater. His next role is in Anthony Mingella's film *Cold Mountain*.

MICHAEL HAUSMAN (Executive Producer) has worked with director Milos Forman on seven films, three films for director Robert Benton, three films for David Mamet, as well as on several other productions. *Gangs of New York* is the first picture that he has produced for Martin Scorsese. Mr. Hausman is a member of the Board of Directors of Du-Art Laboratories, and he teaches at the Graduate Film School at Columbia University.

BRIGITTE LACOMBE (Photographer) French photographer Brigitte Lacombe lives in New York. Her first book, a retrospective entitled *Lacombe cinema/theatre* was published in 2001 by Schirmer/Mosel, with an introduction by David Mamet and an essay by Adam Gopnik. Brigitte's passions are portraits and travel. She works for publications such as *The New York Times Magazine, Vanity Fair*, and *Conde Nast Traveler*. Brigitte is at work on her second book, *Travel*.

ELLEN LEWIS (Casting Director) has worked with Martin Scorsese since *New York Stories* in 1989, and has cast all his subsequent films (*GoodFellas, Cape Fear, The Age of Innocence, Casino, Kundun*, and *Bringing Out the Dead*). Among her other credits are *Wit, What Lies Beneath, Forrest Gump, Big Night*, and *Dead Man*.

GARY LEWIS (McGloin) was born in Glasgow. He received international attention for for his role as a British miner whose son wants to study ballet in

Billy Elliot, and has appeared in *Gregory's Two Girls, The Good Son, My Name Is Joe, Carla's Song*, and *Shallow Grave*. Lewis has also appeared on television throughout the United Kingdom, starring in *The Princess Stallion, Life Support, California Sunshine, Hope and Glory*, and *Dr. Finlay*.

KENNETH LONERGAN (Screenwriter) wrote and directed the film *You Can Count On Me*, for which he received many honors, including awards from the New York Film Critics, the L. A. Film Critics and the National Board of Review for Best Screenplay. He was also nominated for an Academy Award for best original screenplay. Lonergan's plays include *Lobby Hero, The Waverly Gallery*, and *This Is Our Youth*.

FRANCESCA LO SCHIAVO (Set Decorator) has collaborated with Dante Ferretti for many years. Among her credits are Franco Zeffirelli's *Hamlet*, Terry Gilliam's *Baron Munchausen*, and Federico Fellini's *And the Ship Sails On*.

LIAM NEESON (Priest Vallon) played the title role in *Schindler's List*, earning an Academy Award nomination as Best Actor. He has also starred in *Rob Roy, Michael Collins, Les Miserables, The Haunting*, and *Star Wars: Episode I—The Phantom Menace*. Recently, he co-starred with Harrison Ford in *K-19: The Widowmaker*. Neeson is a former member of Dublin's Abbey Theater. On Broadway, he appeared in Eugene O'Neill's *Anna Christie*, as Oscar Wilde in David Hare's *The Judas Kiss*, and in Arthur Miller's *The Crucible*.

TIM MONICH (Dialect Coach) studied with Edith Skinner and for twelve years taught at the Juilliard Theater Center. He worked previously with Martin Scorsese on *Kundun* and *The Age of Innocence*. Among his eighty feature film credits are *Ali, The Talented Mr. Ripley, Dead Man Walking, JFK, Thelma and Louise*, and *Schindler's List*.

SANDY POWELL (Costume Designer) won an Academy Award for *Shakespeare In Love*, and was nominated for an Oscar the same year for her work on *Velvet Goldmine*. Among the many films for which she created the clothes are: *The End of the Affair, Hilary and Jackie, Michael Collins, The Crying Game, Orlando*, and *Wings of the Dove*—the latter two received Oscar nominations. She has designed costumes for the films of Derek Jarman, for the London Festival Ballet, the English National Opera, and the Royal Shakespeare Company.

JOE REIDY (First Assistant Director) began working with Martin Scorsese on *The Color of Money*, (1986) and served on all of the director's subsequent films, with the exception of *Kundun*. He has also worked as first assistant director for Oliver Stone (*JFK, The Doors, Born on the Fourth of July*), and Robert Redford (*Quiz Show, The Horse Whisperer*, and *The Legend of Bagger Vance*), among others.

JOHN C. REILLY (Happy Jack Mulraney) won the hearts of filmgoers and critics in two films by Paul Thomas Anderson, *Boogie Nights* and *Magnolia*. He has also appeared in *Anderson's Hard Eight, What's Eating Gilbert Grape, Dolores Claiborne, State of Grace, Hoffa, For the Love of the Game*, and *The Perfect Storm*. As a member of Chicago's Steppenwolf Theater, Reilly starred in *A Streetcar Named Desire* and a stage version of *The Grapes of Wrath*. On Broadway, he played opposite Philip Seymour Hoffman in Sam Shepard's *True West*.

LUC SANTE (Technical Advisor) teaches creative writing and the history of photography at Bard College. His books include *Low Life: Lures and Snares of Old New York, Evidence*, and *The Factory of Facts*. He has received a Whiting Award, a Guggenheim Fellowship, an Award in Literature from the American Academy of Arts and Letters, and a Grammy for album notes.

THELMA SCHOONMAKER (Editor) won both an Academy Award and a British Film Academy Award in 1980 for editing *Raging Bull*. Subsequently she has worked on all of Martin Scorsese's feature films (including *GoodFellas, The Age of Innocence, Casino, Kundun*) and documentaries (most recently *Il Mio Viaggio In Italia*). In addition to film editing, Schoonmaker works tirelessly to promote work of her late husband, director Michael Powell.

MARTIN SCORSESE (Director) has directed 17 feature films (among them *Mean Streets, Taxi Driver, Raging Bull, Goodfellas, The Age of Innocence*) and several documentaries, most recently *Il Mio Viaggio In Italia*. He has also produced several films (*The Grifters, Clockers*) and has acted (in Kurosawa's *Dreams* and Robert Redford's *Quiz Show*); and has received numerous honors and awards for his work. In 1990 he founded the Film Foundation with several other prominent directors to foster film restoration and preservation; and he fights tirelessly for artists' rights.

HENRY THOMAS (Johnny) had his first starring role at age ten playing Elliot in *E. T.: the Extra Terrestrial*. He has since co-starred in *Legends of the Fall, Curse of the Starving Class, Valmont, Suicide Kings, Niagara, Niagara*, and *All the Pretty Horses*, as well as such independent films as *The Quickie, SS, Briar Patch*, and *Dead In the Water*.

MARIO TURSI (Still Photographer) worked on two previous Martin Scorsese films: *The Last Temptation of Christ* and *Kundun*. He was the photographer on many of the great italian films directed by Fellini, Visconti, and Passolini.

HARVEY WEINSTEIN (Producer) Harvey Weinstein founded Miramax Films in 1979 with his brother Bob. Miramax Films has released some of the most critically acclaimed independent feature films, including eleven consecutive Best Picture nominations: *In the Bedroom, The Cider House Rules, Shakespeare In Love, Life Is Beautiful* (*La Vita É Bella*), *Good Will Hunting, The English Patient, Pulp Fiction, The Piano*, and *The Crying Game*.

STEVEN ZAILLIAN (Screenwriter) won an Academy Award for his screenplay for *Schindler's List*. His other screenwriting credits are *The Falcon and the Snowman, Awakenings, Jack the Bear, Clear and Present Danger, Hannibal*, and *Black Hawk Down*. Zaillian has directed his own screenplays in *Searching for Bobby Fisher* and *A Civil Action*.

(288)

ACKNOWLEDGMENTS

We're indebted to Larry Kaplan and Helen Morris; to Jonathan Burnham and especially Kristin Powers at Miramax Books; to Jon Glick for his elegant design: to photo editor Holly Landon at Miramax Films; and to Thelma Schoonmaker and Marianne Bower at Cappa Productions for their help on this book.

And most especially we thank Michael Ovitz, Rick Yorn, Harvey and Bob Weinstein, Graham King, Colin Vaines, Rick Schwartz, and Lois Smith for their perseverance in making *Gangs of New York* the movie a reality.

—The director, cast and crew of *Gangs of New York*, August 2002

'It took twenty-five years to bring **Gangs of New York** to the screen. Finally in the late 1990s everything came together and in September 2000, I passed through the gates of Cinecittà Studios. I walked into the New York of the 1860s and began shooting the movie I had imagined all these years about the city I love and how it recreated itself. This film is my impression of that extraordinary time.' **Martin Scorsese**

GANGS OF NEW YORK tells the story of Amsterdam Vallon (Leonardo DiCaprio), a young Irish-American who has returned to New York after fifteen years in a house of reform to seek revenge against Bill the Butcher (Daniel Day-Lewis), the nativist gang leader who killed his father. The movie follows Amsterdam as he infiltrates Bill's inner circle, falls in love with Jenny Everdeane (Cameron Diaz), a beguiling pickpocket, and fights for the honour of his family and people.

THIS LAVISHLY ILLUSTRATED BOOK includes interviews with the principal people involved with the making of the film including all the leading actors and Scorsese himself, a historical introduction to the period, sketches for costumes and sets, exclusive photographs and the complete screenplay of the film.

Front cover photographs © Brigitte Lacombe
Back cover photographs © Mario Tursi

headline
Non-fiction/Film tie-in

UK £16.99
ISBN 0-7553-1210-4